ACKNOWLEDGMENTS

W hen I first visited the United States in 2000 and 2001 and sought political asylum here in 2002, I was fortunate to find a community of Americans who were knowledgeable about Chechnya and sympathetic to my situation. Without the support of American friends and American non-governmental institutions this book would not have been possible.

The American Committee for Peace in Chechnya, which was chaired at the time by the former National Security Advisor, Zbigniew Brzezinski, the late General Alexander Haig, former senior State Department official Ambassador Max Kampelman, did a great deal to help me promote peace. The committee arranged meetings with government officials, Senators, and Congressmen, and enabled me to continue to advocate for negotiations, hold confidential meetings with Russian parliamentarians, and promote the peace plan that I developed. Dr. Brzezinski with whom I discussed Chechnya frequently became an enthusiastic supporter of this project.

I recall fondly my first public presentation in Washington D.C., which was at Johns Hopkins University, Central Asia and Caucasus Institute, where I first met its chairman, Fred Starr, whose cheerfulness and optimism proved invaluable during many complications and setbacks while writing this book.

The work began during my Reagan-Fascell Fellowship at the National Endowment for Democracy where Miriam Lanskoy and I began to draft the first two chapters. I am particularly grateful for the personal warmth and moral support of NED President Carl Gershman and Deputy to the President for Policy and Strategy Barbara Haig who had faith in me at a very difficult time, when Chechens were nearly universally feared and ostracized.

I owe the biggest debt of gratitude to Edward Kline and Nicholas and Ruth Daniloff for their thoughtfulness, kindness, and generosity, which sustained me over several years while writing this book. I am grateful for Edward's and Nicholas's detailed reading of the manuscript and their many insightful edits, comments, and suggestions.

ILYAS AKHMADOV

★ ★ ★

This journey began for me in the fateful winter of 1994, when the war was starting in Chechnya while I was embarking on my graduate studies at Boston University and my father put in my hands his tattered copy of Tolstoy's *Haji Murat*. Thanks to my father, Alexander Lanskoy I grew up with an appreciation of Russian literature, the moral example of Soviet-era dissent, and was captivated by Russia's post-Soviet transition. In graduate school, I benefited enormously from the mentorship of Professor Uri Ra'anan who taught me about the importance of immersing myself in my subject, the historian's demand for precision and detail, and the value of oral history.

When I set out to write a dissertation about Chechnya I found that my best sources would be the Russian scholars, journalists, and human rights activists. It was with their help, and thanks to their research, and advice, that I wrote my dissertation: "The War of the Russian Succession: Russia and Chechnya between the Wars," which analyzed Chechen effort at state-building and Russia's Chechnya policy during President Boris Yeltsin's second term, 1996–99. Ever since then, I have viewed my work as a partnership with the activists.

When I met Ilyas Akhmadov and was presented with an opportunity to work with the Foreign Minister of Chechnya to write a history of their struggle, this appealed to me not only because of his many fascinating insights but also because the act of writing one's own history—for a nation under foreign domination, war torn and scattered into exile—is to become the subject of history. Most books about Chechnya are written by foreign journalists or scholars, and hardly any are written by the Chechens themselves.

THE CHECHEN STRUGGLE

THE CHECHEN STRUGGLE

INDEPENDENCE WON AND LOST

Ilyas Akhmadov and Miriam Lanskoy

Foreword by
Zbigniew Brzezinski

First published in 2010 by
PALGRAVE MACMILLAN®
in the United States—a division of St. Martin's Press LLC,
175 Fifth Avenue, New York, NY 10010.

Where this book is distributed in the UK, Europe and the rest of the world,
this is by Palgrave Macmillan, a division of Macmillan Publishers Limited,
registered in England, company number 785998, of Houndmills, Basingstoke,
Hampshire RG21 6XS.

Palgrave Macmillan is the global academic imprint of the above companies
and has companies and representatives throughout the world.

Palgrave® and Macmillan® are registered trademarks in the United States,
the United Kingdom, Europe and other countries.

ISBN: 978–0–230–10534–8

Library of Congress Cataloging-in-Publication Data

Lanskoy, Miriam.
      The Chechen struggle : independence won and lost / Miriam Lanskoy
and Ilyas Akhmadov ; with a foreword by Zbigniew Brzezinski.
        p. cm.
      Includes index.
      ISBN 978–0–230–10534–8
      1. Chechnia (Russia)—History—Autonomy and independence
movements. 2. Chechnia (Russia)—History—Civil War, 1994–
3. Government, Resistance to—Russia (Federation)—Chechnia—History.
4. Chechnia (Russia)—Foreign relations—Russia (Federation) 5. Russia
(Federation)—Foreign relations—Russia (Federation)—Chechnia.
6. Akhmadov, Ilyas, 1960– 7. Foreign ministers—Russia (Federation)—
Chechnia—Biography. 8. Maskhadov, Aslan Alievich, 1951–2005.
9. Presidents—Russia (Federation)—Chechnia—Biography.
I. Akhmadov, Ilyas, 1960– II. Title.

DK511.C2L36 2010
947.086—dc22   2010013319

A catalogue record of the book is available from the British Library.

Design by Newgen Imaging Systems (P) Ltd., Chennai, India.

First edition: December 2010

10 9 8 7 6 5 4 3 2 1

Printed in the United States of America.

CONTENTS

For a nation, particularly one that has endured such turmoil, the record, analysis, and debate of recent history are needed for the maintenance of the national idea.

I am very grateful to my colleagues at the National Endowment for Democracy, and especially Carl Gershman, Barbara Haig, Nadia Diuk, Marc Plattner, and Sally Blair for encouragement and good advice; Zbigniew Brzezinski, and Edward Kline, who read and commented on drafts of the manuscript and our editor, Luba Ostashevsky, for her patience and professionalism. We owe the biggest debt of gratitude to Nicholass Daniloff who read early versions of the manuscript and suggested numerous revisions and clarifications, particularly during a two-day editing session in October 2009. My mother, Anna Lanskoy, and my friends Catherine Osgood, Irakly Areshidze, and Ruth Daniloff provided tremendous encouragement and moral support.

MIRIAM LANSKOY

FOREWORD

Ilyas Akhmadov's story is simultaneously a personal account of the turmoil and confusion of the national rebirth of Chechnya, and the tale of a young intellectual-turned-fighter, eventually Chechnya's Foreign Minister, who sought peace for a state that the international community preferred to ignore.

This small nation—in a poor, mountainous, landlocked territory—after two hundred years of Russian domination attempted to realize a centuries old dream: to fashion their own nation state on the basis of its national customs and culture, relying on the inspiration of the heroic warrior tradition with which Chechens resisted Russian conquest in the nineteenth and twentieth centuries. Among its most serious internal obstacles were the acute post-Soviet ideological confusion among the Chechens, and the challenges from radical Islamic religious ideas.

In this book, a remarkable person, with a graduate degree in political science, recently discharged from the Soviet army, joins the Chechen resistance and becomes a witness to the trials of establishing statehood. He provides the first authoritative, inside account of the problems they encountered, the splintering of the resistance, and its eventual fragmentation and radicalization.

Fighters of Akhmadov's generation modeled themselves on the *murids* of mid-nineteenth century when Imam Shamil sought to unite the Caucasus nations against the Russian annexation. Tsar Alexander II eventually defeated Shamil and took him prisoner. The Chechens, a fierce warrior people, gained the reputation through Tolstoy, Pushkin, and Lermontov's literary works of being fearsome enemies and cutthroats. That reputation has lived on and successive Russian governments have exploited it to marginalize or terrorize the Chechens into submission. In the 1890s, the Russian government expelled significant numbers to Turkey and Jordan. In 1944, Stalin deported almost the whole Chechen nation, more than 500,000 persons, to Central Asia, while falsely accusing it of collaboration with the invading Nazis. This deportation, recognized by the European parliament as genocide, resulted in the deaths of a third of the Chechen population during their transportation and the first year of their resettlement.

Ilyas Akhmadov's balanced, honest, and courageous voice stands in sharp contrast to extremist Chechens and Russians alike and makes it glaringly obvious that the authorities in Moscow and Washington and European capitals missed an opportunity to engage with moderate Chechen leaders in an attempt to avert the twin catastrophes that unfolded over the course of the two Chechen wars: the mass slaughter of the Chechens and Russia's slide into dictatorship. Far from establishing peace or stability, western silence as Russia destroyed the Chechen moderates only encouraged and buttressed the radical elements in both Russia and Chechnya.

President Boris Yeltsin attempted to remove the Chechen President Dzhokhar Dudayev, who had declared independence in 1991, by sending in troops three years later "to restore constitutional order." However, his ground forces were woefully unprepared and Marshal Pavel Grachev, Chief of the General Staff, seriously miscalculated. He declared that a regiment of assault paratroopers could conquer the Chechens within forty-eight hours without assessing the Chechen potential for armed resistance.

Within two years, no more than 10,000 Chechen fighters had brought the Russian invasion force, made up largely of poorly trained recruits, to a standstill and Moscow was forced to negotiate a cease-fire at Khasavurt in 1996 and a peace treaty in Moscow in 1997. The agreements called for the removal of Russian armed forces from Chechen territory, and for both sides to respect each other; to desist from using force; to develop their relations in accordance with generally recognized principles and norms of international law; and to conclude an agreement by 2001 on Chechnya's final and definitive political status. Elections were organized for January 1997, during which Aslan Maskhadov, Dudayev's top military officer, defeated several opposing candidates in balloting that was recognized by Chechens and the Organization for Security and Cooperation in Europe (OSCE) as "free and fair." For the first time in its history, Chechnya had acquired a legitimately elected President through a democratic process.

In Moscow, however, Maskhadov's election was viewed with hostility. Chechnya was said to be "a bandit state." Moscow's hardliners and military men itched to reverse the Khasavyurt agreement. In the fall of 1999, Prime Minister Vladimir Putin, was determined to use force again to "correct" the situation on Russia's southern flank. A dramatic *causus belli* was needed. His administration blamed a series of apartment bombings in Moscow during 1999 on Chechen terrorists, and Putin declared that the Chechens were "international terrorists" backed by outside interests. Moscow would go all out to crush them. His famous words were, "We will pursue the terrorists everywhere. In the airport…in the airport…it means, and you will excuse me, if we catch them in the toilet, we will drown them in the shithouse! That's it! The matter is closed." Putin's admirers cheered.

The Russian military used intensive shelling of rebel groups, towns, mosques, hospitals, and cemeteries employing bunker-busting bombs, cluster bombs, and vacuum bombs. It seeded thousands of mines on Chechen territory, including mines cynically disguised as toys that unwary children would pick up, blowing off arms and legs. The army set up "filtration camps" ostensibly to weed out the innocent from those guilty of mutiny but which actually became torture and execution centers for most of those who were arrested.

The tragedy of Chechnya stands as a failure of the U.S. policy of indifference and neglect. Throughout this conflict, under successive Democratic and Republican administrations, the United States essentially stood aside, asserting that the Chechen problem was a Russian internal matter. At one point the Clinton White House even compared the conflict to the U.S. civil war and President Lincoln's determination to preserve the Union. U.S. officials, responding to Moscow pressure, declined to meet in any official capacity with representatives of the Chechen resistance. The Chechens who viewed the United States as a beacon of light and democracy were deeply disappointed that the State Department declined to denounce forcefully the seemingly endless human rights abuses. Indeed, after 9/11, the Bush administration officials adopted the Russian view that the Chechen resistance was really part of an international terrorist movement, alleging (falsely as it turned out) that Chechen fighters were battling alongside Al-Qaeda in Afghanistan and in Iraq. The global indifference gave the Russians a free hand in Chechnya.

This inside view of Chechnya's latest struggle for independence was written by an intellectual, who had served earlier in his life with the Soviet strategic rocket forces. Like many of his peers, Ilyas Akhmadov was attracted to the struggle for independence and became a fighter for Chechnya's freedom.

His candid and courageous memoir highlights the challenges facing Muslim moderates as they tried to form a democratic society from a pool of politically inexperienced followers driven by sometimes primitive tribal traditions. It describes the hopelessness of a diplomat sent abroad on a multi-year assignment with no diplomatic immunity, no foreign visas, no money, and no established contacts to obtain U.S. and European support for democracy. And it portrays in vivid detail the difficulties of an isolated Chechen President trying to appease opposing political factions, conceding too much to one group or another as his opponents became increasingly radicalized.

In the end, the tragedy of Chechnya is not just the story of the blood and cruelty of modern warfare, but also of the fact that the moderate voices of President Maskhadov and his Foreign Minister Akhmadov were overwhelmed by radical opponents and a lack of interest and attention in the West.

Akhmadov benefited in his work from the support of organizations like the American Committee for Peace in Chechnya (co-chaired by the late General Alexander Haig, former senior State Department official Ambassador Max Kampelman, and myself), which supported Akhmadov when, even in exile and separated from his family, he sought avenues to promote peace. In 2004, despite numerous Russian efforts to obtain his extradition, the U.S. government granted Akhmadov political asylum. In the difficult period of separation and a two-year asylum case, Akhmadov relied on the support of his new American friends—chief among them Miriam Lanskoy, Nicholas and Ruth Daniloff, and Edward Kline—who thought that his voice and views could be an important contribution to preserving an accurate record of this period in Chechnya's history. And, let us hope, it will inspire a future generation of Chechens and of Russians to fashion an alternative and a better tomorrow.

ZBIGNIEW BRZEZINSKI

Chechnya

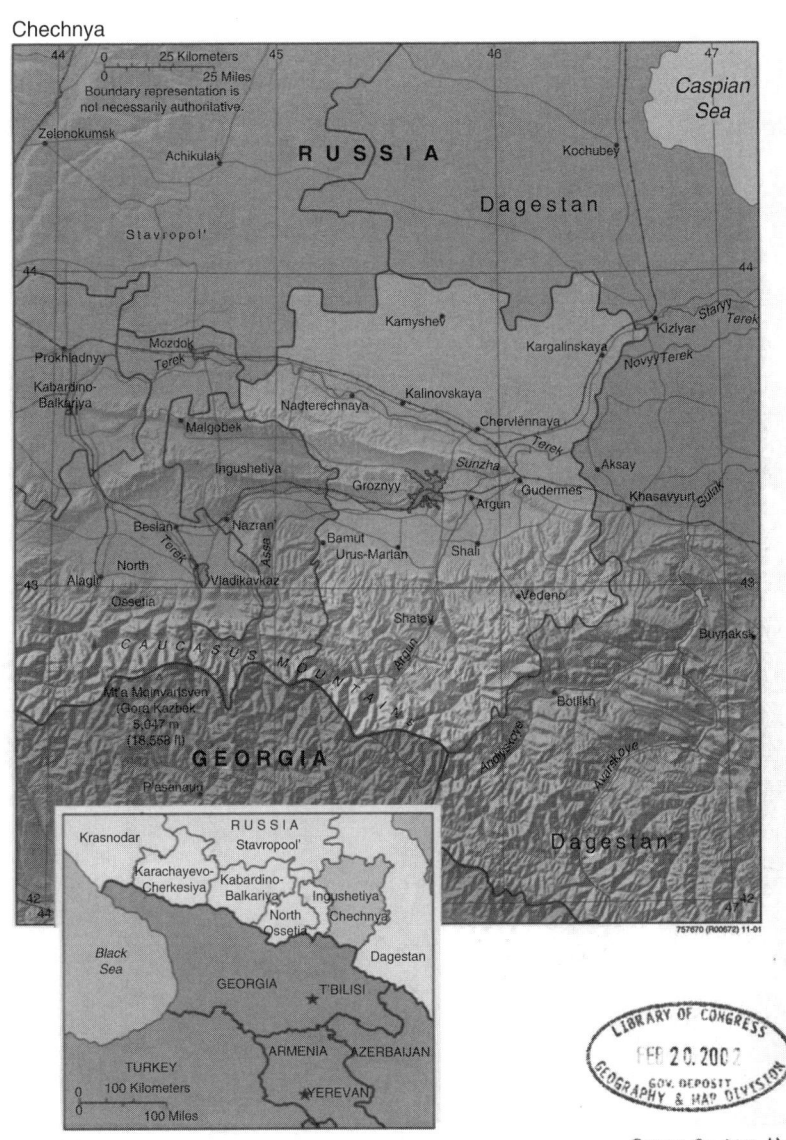

Map of Chechnya

CHAPTER 1

THE WAR BEGINS

Prior to the summer of 1994, I considered myself an ordinary person. I was not involved in politics, and I had the equivalent of a master of arts in political science from Rostov State University in Rostov on the Don. I had served in the Soviet Strategic Rocket Forces for almost five years when I was demobilized in 1985. I held a minor clerical job in the Chechen Foreign Ministry for about six months in 1992 under Foreign Minister Shamil Beno.

When I realized that war with Russia was imminent, I joined up with Shamil Basayev, a famous Chechen commander with whom I had formed a friendship and had later served under Aslan Maskhadov, the Chechen Army Chief of Staff. During the first war (1994–96), I had frequent and close contact with these two men, who were brilliant military commanders and dominant figures in Chechen politics. Their relationship, sometimes cooperative and other times competitive, determined the course of the nation's history in the ensuing decade. Joining up with Shamil in August 1994 gave me a unique vantage point from which to view and analyze Chechen politics.

Politically, I was a nationalist who favored independence and supported General Dzhokhar Dudayev. As the head of the National Congress of the Chechen People Dudayev proclaimed Chechnya's independence in November 1991, just as the Soviet Union was collapsing. Dudayev's pro-independence government had domestic legitimacy and was enthusiastically accepted by most of the population. After 1991, Chechnya did not participate in the referendum on the Russian constitution, had no representation in the Russian parliament and Dudayev did not take policy directions from the Russian government. Chechnya maintained its own economic and foreign policies and did not participate in Russian national elections.

In the Soviet period Checheno-Ingushetia was an autonomous republic within the Russian union republic. When the Soviet Union dissolved, the Ingush and the Chechens separated; the Ingush preferred to remain in the Russian Federation while the Chechens wanted independence. However, though the international community recognized union republics as independent states, it did not extend the same recognition to autonomous republics like Chechnya. Nonetheless, even without de jure recognition, Chechnya began functioning as an independent state in 1991. The dissolution of the Soviet Union presented a historic opportunity for Chechnya to finally achieve the independence it had sought for centuries. Many Chechens believed that if Chechnya could function as an independent state, it would eventually receive official recognition from other states and the United Nations.

My support for Dudayev and Chechen independence did not mean that I approved of everything that was happening. There were different political factions that challenged Dudayev's leadership, and these internal disputes were not resolved transparently. People with little experience in politics were exercising their freedoms of speech and assembly for the first time, and the absence of established political institutions led to a variety of conflicts. The political environment suffered from an unstable mix of Soviet-era structures, such as a strong executive system, new efforts to import Western institutions—a new parliament and electoral system—and attempts to introduce national institutions such as the *Mekh Khell* (a traditional council of elders) which should have been purely consultative. Dudayev used the *Mekh Khell* to legitimate his decisions when the parliament would not. He eventually disbanded parliament in 1993 and appointed a new one. I felt a strong distaste for such power struggles and for the constant rallies that took place in the center of Grozny where, in the presence of armed men, orators gave inflammatory speeches. The summer of 1994 brought new and unwelcome changes to city life, including the appearance of armored personnel carriers in the streets and occasional gunfire at night.

Those who were not involved in politics managed to ignore these scenes and go on with their daily lives. Politics involved only a small sliver of the population of one million; most people did not understand why a particular shoot-out had occurred or why the supporters of one politician or another were rallying in front of the presidential palace—like others, we too thought it was palace intrigue that did not concern us. But everything changed a few months later when the first war dragged all Chechens into a battle for survival.

Before the first war, there were many fiery speeches from Dudayev and his supporters proclaiming the imminent threat of war with Russia. I did not believe it would ever go that far. Dudayev's style of rule was very secretive; knowledge of the inner workings of his administration did not spill out beyond a very small circle of insiders, and decisions were made behind closed doors. I concluded that the rallies and shoot-outs between the government and the opposition had to do with internal power struggles. Many people assumed that Dudayev had exaggerated the Russian threat and falsely cast his political rivals as traitors, so most of us ignored his exhortations.

On August 2, 1994, the Russian media reported that a telegram had been sent from Umar Avtorkhanov, one of the politicians who opposed Dudayev, to Boris Yeltsin, the president of the Russian Federation. This telegram sent from the Provisional Council which represented Chechen politicians who opposed Dudayev invited Moscow to intervene militarily, creating the pretense that Chechens sought Russian military intervention. For me this was a revelation. I finally understood that Dudayev was telling the truth: the opposition to Dudayev was being supported by Russia, and the Kremlin was planning an intervention.

A few days later I attended my first rally at the parliament building and ran into Shamil Basayev. I had first met Shamil in 1992 when he had just returned from one of his tours in Abkhazia. He was of average height and build and did not particularly stand out either in his appearance or behavior. He had thin facial features and long, thin fingers which he waved around during discussions. He was already famous for hijacking a plane bound for Turkey in 1991, and for victorious battles in Abkhazia. I was working for the Chechen Foreign Ministry and we met to compare notes about the Chechen fighters in Nagorno Karabakh, a disputed territory between Armenia and Azerbaijan. Shamil himself did not fight in Nagorno Karabakh but several of his people were embedded in Azeri units, and when those units were surrounded by Armenians, he had gone there to get his men out.

At the time, Dudayev wanted all Chechens who were combatants in post-Soviet disputes to return to Chechnya, and it was my job to make it happen. Shamil's so-called Abkhaz Battalion had gained considerable notoriety while fighting in Georgia in support of the Abkhaz separatists from 1992 to 1993. In the Soviet Union, Abkhazia was an autonomous republic within Georgia and, like Chechnya, Abkhazia declared independence during the dissolution of the Soviet Union. Shamil went to Abkhazia to demonstrate his solidarity. The Abkhaz are ethnically and linguistically distinct from Georgians and are viewed as one of the many small nations of the Caucasus, which brought many such solidarity-minded volunteers to the conflict, including Chechens, Kabardins, Ossets, Karachai, Cherkess, and even Cossacks. They volunteered on their own or through an organization called the Confederation of the Mountain Peoples of the Caucasus. The Confederation sought to unite these nations and eventually form a new confederation modeled on the Mountain Republic, which had included all these nations and had established a fleeting existence as an independent entity in 1917–18 during the tumult of the Russian civil war. Upon their arrival, volunteers were assembled under the leadership of Vladislav Ardzinba, leader of the Abkhaz, who was supported by the Russian military intelligence, Glavnoye Razvedovatelnoye Upravaleniye (GRU). (While their involvement was coordinated and directed by this agency, this is not the same as being agents of the GRU, as has been so frequently asserted.) Shamil told me that during the storming of Sukhumi, Georgian President Eduard Shevardnadze was within his reach, and he could have captured him on the airport's landing strip. Shamil claimed that GRU and Ardzinba's administration instructed him to stop his attack. Standing on the airport runway, Shevardnadze announced that Georgia would join the Commonwealth of Independent States (CIS), an alliance of the former Soviet states, which Russia uses to control the foreign and defense policies of its members. When the Russians had achieved their goal of undermining Georgia's independence, they stopped the Abkhaz offensive.

By the summer of 1994 Shamil was back in Chechnya, supporting Dudayev against the pro-Russian opposition. When I ran into him at the rally, I asked Shamil if he would take me into his Abkhaz Battalion; he dismissed my request saying, "With your higher education you should find a better occupation than running around with a Kalashnikov submachine gun." Soon Shamil was summoned to meet with Dudayev's administration. "Don't take it personally, wait for the next opportunity," he said. And he was gone.

I had no intention of waiting and the next day set out for Shamil's base, which was located on the outskirts of town. For the first time since the end of my Soviet army career I saw a clear and meaningful path to follow. My military experience could serve an honorable and patriotic purpose. I had something valuable to contribute to a cause that I believed in deeply. The realization that Dudayev's opposition was conspiring with the Russians, and that full-fledged war with Russia was imminent, dissipated all my doubts. I knew what I had to do; I had to join in the war preparations. I persuaded Shamil's Chief of Staff, a dapper young man named Ella, nicknamed "Lambada," to take me with him. The base was located on the grounds of an old Soviet army encampment. I was horrified by the conditions; it looked like an abandoned construction site, and only a single artillery piece suggested that we were on a military base. Lambada had picked up two grenade launchers and a store of munitions from the arsenal of the National Guard; he was very pleased with himself, bragging to the others that he had managed to get more than the battalion was originally allotted.

When Shamil saw these grenade launchers he turned to Ella, "What is this?"

"That's a grenade launcher."

"No, this is a rusty sewer pipe!" Shamil retorted. "And the main problem isn't even that, but the fact they unloaded this stuff not on some new guy but on *you*, with all of your experience."

"They swore that this was all they had," Ella replied.

"Okay. You take this junk back and tell them where they can put it and I'll worry about what they have."

After this exchange, Shamil noticed me and said, "So you ignored my advice and came here anyway? Fine, we'll find work for you." He glanced at the disarray around us. "All of this was in much better condition before we went to Abkhazia. While we were gone, a different unit was here and they let everything crumble," he grumbled.

Shamil explained that he had long been trying to procure better supplies from Dudayev, but these materialized only in the summer of 1994 when Dudayev needed him to fight minor battles against different elements of the pro-Russian opposition. Over the preceding three years there had been several important disagreements between Dudayev and Shamil. In the past, Dudayev had insisted on including Shamil's Abkhaz Battalion, within the National Guard, which was under the overall command of Ilyas Arsanukayev. Shamil had no desire to take orders from Arsanukayev and suspected that he was being penalized for the events of 1993, when Shamil and other commanders had staged a protest against Dudayev. They had led their units into the street to stand outside the presidential palace, accusing Dudayev of taking on excessive powers by combining the presidency and the premiership. They had demanded that Dudayev appoint a Prime Minister. In response Dudayev invited a delegation of these commanders, including Shamil, to the presidential palace and persuaded them to end their protest. They withdrew their demands and vacated the public square.[1]

Prior to that, the two men had first clashed in 1991 over the disposal of the KGB's high-tech weapons arsenal, and (overriding Shamil's objections) Dudayev had made a tremendous error by entrusting that arsenal to Beslan Gantemirov, the mayor of Grozny. In 1994 Gantimorov turned against Dudayev, stole the weapons, and joined the pro-Russian opposition, turning the weapons against us.

Another point of mistrust and contention between Dudayev and Shamil was that Dudayev had never authorized Shamil's adventures in Abkhazia and considered them very dangerous for us. When I was briefly on the Foreign Ministry staff in 1992–93, I saw correspondence between Dudayev and President Vladislav Ardzinba of Abkhazia in which Dudayev refused to permit the Abkhaz to set up representation in Grozny. It is hard to imagine Dudayev taking sides in a post-Soviet conflict. He did not want Chechens to participate in foreign adventures; their freelancing hurt his plans and ambitions and undermined his authority. Furthermore, he also thought that the concept of a North Caucasus Confederation, for which Shamil, Ruslan Gelayev, and others from Chechnya were fighting in Georgia, was ill-conceived and would only sour our relations with the states of the Caucasus.

So it was only in July 1994, when pro-Russian Chechens started staging armed insurrections, that Shamil's unit—perhaps the most experienced and battle-ready of the Chechen forces—received supplies from Dudayev's government. I found this difficult to believe at the time, but the evidence was all around me. "Lots of my guys left," Shamil admitted, "I only have about forty men." Now that the battalion was considered an autonomous formation within the Defense Ministry he could expect supplies, but they were slow to arrive. "In short, we're regrouping," said Shamil. "I appointed Ella chief of staff only recently. He has plenty of battle experience but record keeping is not his strong suit. This could be a good starting place for you—the only documentation I have is a list of the men."

Shamil took me into a room that contained several boxes of bullets, cellophane-wrapped grenades, a light cannon, and a "pyramid" of brand new Kalashnikov submachine guns. Shamil explained that Dudayev had provided forty-five Kalashnikov submachine guns for the new draftees. Though Dudayev had instituted conscription, he had little ability to enforce it and in reality our forces were completely voluntary. The modestly grow-ing number of volunteers was causing real problems for Shamil. He did not have the means to train or equip the men, who, like me, could sense the change in the atmosphere and were starting to gather around different commanders.

In the same room there were two cots covered with blue wool military blankets. "Ella sleeps in one," Shamil said. "You take my cot, I'll be traveling now regardless." He gave me one of the Kalashnikovs and, pulling out a box from under the cot, held out pants and a jacket of local manufacture, which vaguely resembled fatigues. "I'm sorry, we don't have any army boots, this is a highly sought after item like weapons and ammunition, really hard to get," he explained. He went on,

> I had forty-five draftees, but as the situation is heating up, the parents of several took them home, so you can have one of the Kalashnikovs. The record of issuing weapons and ammunition can begin with you. You can also help to train some of the younger volunteers. You are empowered to issue ammunition only if neither I nor Ella is present and only if you have a written order from me and even then you will count out the bullets. If you disobey this, you will have very serious problems with me.

And that was the extent of my orientation.

I moved to the base and for the next several weeks I helped to train the new recruits while Shamil and the active part of the battalion were fighting against Ruslan Labazanov in Argun. I wanted to be with them, but Shamil rebuked me, "War is an ugly thing, and your turn will come. Don't be in a hurry; just do your job." He left me at the base to establish basic order and record keeping, and to train the new volunteers.

The opposition to Dudayev fell into three groups: the political opposition headed by Umar Avtorkhanov, the criminals around Ruslan Labazanov, and Dudayev's former associates around Beslan Gantemirov. The political opposition to Dudayev was composed of several parties including Daimokh ("Fatherland"), which was led by Lecha Umkhayev, and Marsho ("Freedom"), which was led by Umar Avtorkhanov. These two united with other, smaller parties to form the roundtable that refused to recognize the October 1991 parliamentary elections and appealed for new democratic elections. The roundtable was the wing within the Congress of the Chechen Nation in rivalry with Dudayev's wing. They staged rallies in Theater Square in Grozny and denounced Dudayev for taking on excessive presidential power.

Ruslan Labazanov, a famous criminal, represented another type of opposition. He had fled a prison in Krasnodar in 1991 after killing two Armenian "thieves-in-the-law" who were his fellow inmates. A "thief-in-the-law" is the Soviet equivalent of a don in the Sicilian mafia, and is considered untouchable in the criminal world, so to kill two of them is completely off the charts. Labazanov barricaded an area of five houses in the Microrayon section of Grozny that became a mini-fortress and his men practiced extortion and hostage taking. In 1991–93 Russia was gripped by mafia wars. Their epicenter was Moscow, where all the big money was concentrated, but the ripples reached into Chechnya. Labazanov was the person used by criminal bosses outside Chechnya to collect debts within Chechnya and for this he was paid handsomely. Dudayev, who until 1991, had not lived in Chechnya, did not immediately recognize the threat posed by Labazanov. He was born a few days before the deportation of 1944, spent his childhood in Central Asia and his entire career in the Soviet military; so he did not understand the implications of having dark characters like Labazanov so close to the throne.

The third opposition camp was grouped around the mayor of Grozny, Beslan Gantemirov, who had turned against Dudayev. The first armed confrontation was between Dudayev's men and Gantemirov's police in the summer of 1994. It was an intense battle in the center of Grozny, but it was all over within forty minutes. Gantemirov's supporters were destroyed and he and a couple of his guards fled to Gekhi, a small town in the west of Chechnya. The mayor's office was not far from Theater Square where the roundtable opposition had been holding protests. Seeing what had happened to Gantemirov, they thought it prudent to cease the rallies and relocate to Tolstoy Yurt in the Nadterechnyi district of Chechnya. This was the area north of the Terek, traditionally a pro-Russian stronghold.

After decimating Gantemirov's forces, the next battle was against Labazanov, who was in open rebellion and even calling on people to kill the Melkhi, a *teip* whom he accused of usurping power in Chechnya. *Teips* are subdivisions of Chechen society that originally may have referred to geographic location but now are seen as large bloodlines. The Chechen nation is composed of nine major *teips* that are further subdivided into many smaller *teips*. Dudayev himself was from a different *teip*, the Yalkhoroi, but there were many Melkhi among his close supporters. Labazanov's fortress in the Microrayon was ambushed by a combination of the Melkhi, who were his *krovniki* people whom he had wronged and who had a blood feud against him, and members of the "Abkhaz Battalions," the units that had fought in Abkhazia under Shamil

Basayev, Umalt Dashayev, and Ruslan Gelayev. Labazanov fled to his hometown of Argun. As resistance scattered, there were three different areas of armed resistance to Dudayev by July 1994: Tolstoy Yurt, Gekhi, and Argun. In the context of these early battles against the armed opposition and growing fears of a Russian invasion, Dudayev started to provide support for Shamil's unit.

When I arrived in Shamil's camp the first order of business was Argun, where they fought a major battle against Labazanov on September 5, 1994. Apparently there were armed personnel carriers (APCs) making their way from the Nadterechnyi district to assist Labazanov; the different groups were starting to forge a common front, but this did not save him. Labazanov's men were criminals with many *krovniki* who made use of this opportunity to get their revenge; after the battle, hardly a man was left alive from his unit. Labazanov himself escaped like a bank robber in a 1930s film, alone on a locomotive.

The next major battle was near Gekhi against Gantemirov, and for the public in Chechnya it represented the debut of the two men whose personalities and relationship would shape the next ten years of Chechnya's history. It was a battle from which both Shamil Basayev and Aslan Maskhadov, recently named Chief of the General Staff, emerged as popular heroes. Of course, both men had extensive military experience, but their exploits had occurred abroad and were of marginal interest to most Chechens. It was this minor battle in Gekhi that catapulted both men to domestic fame and became a harbinger of their ensuing decade-long competition for power.

Gantemirov's men were staying on a base near Gekhi, and our column was moving along the main road to Gekhi when we were ambushed from an adjacent cemetery. Gantemirov's tactics struck all of us as highly unusual for Chechens. To us this was evidence that he already had Russian trainers. It is sacrilegious for Chechens to fire into a cemetery. The whole column, which was made up of different units, including our National Guard under Maskhadov's command and with our one precious tank at the head, stopped and stood still. They were being fired upon from the cemetery and had several casualties, but our men would not return fire into a cemetery. The column stopped and all the men lay down. Maskhadov alone stood up, brandishing his pistol, walked into their fire, and exhorted the others to keep moving along the road. It was the kind of personal courage that we had read about from World War II, and it made Maskhadov a hero overnight. But at that moment Shamil and his men arrived on the scene, and Shamil without any hesitation led his men straight into the cemetery. They defeated Gantemirov that day, and the two very different men, Shamil and Maskhadov, had to share the credit.

It became Shamil's hallmark to break taboos, and I remember a conversation several months later in Vedeno when Maskhadov said, "We can't do these things because history will judge us," and Shamil replied, "It's early yet to worry about history." This exchange characterizes the two men. Shamil was not a radical at this point, but already he had the attitude that he was not going to worry about how others would perceive him. The war changed many of us; it caused people to abandon values and traditions, but Shamil was the first to cross boundaries that were sacred for most. Shamil did not mind being the bad guy—in fact, he relished it.

Maskhadov's character was different; he was formed by decades of military service. He had been an Army Colonel until 1992 when, as the Soviet military was essentially collapsing, Dudayev invited all Chechen officers to serve in the new Chechen military. Maskhadov answered his call. When he returned to Chechnya, he was appointed head of civil defense. The Head of the General Staff was the first Chechen General, Viskhan Shakhabov, a Soviet-era Colonel who was awarded the rank of General by the Chechen parliament. At the same time the parliament awarded the rank of Lieutenant General to Dudayev, but he rejected this—he did not need this validation. Dudayev was the only Chechen to become a Major General in the Soviet military; he was used to this status and did not need further affirmation.

When the armed opposition first became active, Shakhabov showed signs of irresolution. He ignored several orders from Dudayev which had to do with confronting the opponents, and was removed from the General Staff for that reason. After the dismissal of Shakhabov, Maskhadov became the Head of the General Staff. Maskhadov was a good-looking, well-mannered and educated man, and he spoke Chechen beautifully. He was always calm, and had a way of speaking that, even when stern or tough, remained polite.

The Russian government did not accept Chechen independence and made unsuccessful attempts to take it back by force in 1991. In the Kremlin there were different groups with different strategies for bringing Chechnya back into the constitutional space of the Russian Federation. There were negotiations from March 1992 to January 1993 regarding a treaty between the center and the republic. There had been such treaties between the Kremlin and Tatarstan among others, but talks broke down with the Chechens. A plan developed by Deputy Prime Minister Sergei Shakhrai called for coercive diplomacy; that is, continuing negotiations in the context of applying increasing pressure short of large-scale war. Shakhrai's plan was premised on the notion that Dudayev could be persuaded to compromise on independence. At the same time, Russian Security Services had coordinated successful covert operations in the former Soviet space, most notably in Abkhazia; similarly they were supporting Dudayev's rivals, and now it looked to some in the Kremlin as though there was a viable Chechen armed resistance that could be used to remove Dudayev, and bring Chechnya back into Russia.

The Russians must have noted that following the battles at Argun and Gekhi, Labazanov and Gantemirov had made their way to the Nadterechny region and united around Umar Avtorkhanov to form the Provisional Council. So far, all the battles were minor, lasting no more than a couple of hours with only a few dozen killed. The Russians mistook our hesitation to kill fellow Chechens for a deficiency of battle readiness. What actually existed was an aversion to kindling the blood feuds that could result from killing fellow-Chechens. The long tradition of blood feud—which required immediate male relatives to avenge wrongs against a family member and could be carried on for up to seven generations—was a powerful penalty for crime and had actually helped maintain social harmony in the era before state institutions took over the monopoly on violence. In the 1990s, withering state institutions created a confusing gray-zone that permitted blood feuds to flourish. So although volunteers were gathering around both camps—the Dudayev government's and the opposition's—Chechen fighters were reluctant to engage for fear of triggering a blood feud in the course of battle. But the Russians acted on their incorrect interpretation of this misleading picture.

The Kremlin abandoned Shakhrai's coercive diplomacy, stopped negotiating, and sought to covertly overthrow Dudayev. That is what Avtorkhanov's telegram, dated August 2, 1994, to Yeltsin, signaled; this tactic was very familiar from a whole host of Cold War-era conflicts. Provisional Council, like many KGB-sponsored fronts before it, called on Russia to intervene to protect the nation from the Dudayev "regime." It could have been Hungary in 1954 or Czechoslovakia in 1968 or Afghanistan in 1979—the only innovation now was the new language about "restoration of constitutional order."

Back at our base we were trying to manage the growing influx of volunteers. I remember a very young man who sought to enlist with us because his brother had died fighting in Abkhazia and he sought revenge against the Russians.

Shamil corrected him, "First of all the Russians did not kill your brother, and since he died in battle, there is no blood feud. Second, today we're not fighting the Russians; we're fighting Chechens who have sold out to the Russians. Are you ready to shoot at Chechens?"

The young man looked down, "No, I'm not ready to shoot at a Chechen against whom I don't have a personal problem, even if he has sold out."

And then Shamil said very gently, "Go home, and come back to us when the Russians come, I don't think you will have long to wait." My blood ran cold hearing him say that—intellectually I knew they were coming, analytically I could read the signs, but I did not have Shamil's certainty and resolve.

At the end of September 1994 there were helicopters in the sky supporting the opposition in several battles, which indicated a new level of direct Russian involvement. There were also increasingly frequent statements from Yeltsin himself expressing concern about the worsening situation in Chechnya.

In October 1994, the Russians were ready to launch their covert operation. The Federal Counterintelligence Service (Federalnaya Sluzhba Kontrazvedki, FSK) recruited tank drivers from the elite Taman division and Kantemirov division, which are based near Moscow, and sent them to Mozdok, in the North Caucasus

Military District, where there were forty tanks waiting for them. The tanks, with Russian army tank crews, supported the forces of Avtorkhanov's Provisional Council, which on November 26 attempted an assault on Grozny. They were not just defeated— they were spectacularly defeated. The infantry was easily separated from the armor, the tanks were bombed and stopped, and the tank crews were taken prisoner.

Dudayev held a press conference in front of Russian television crews during which the Russian prisoners explained who they were, how they were organized by the FSK, and how they came to be driving tanks into Grozny. In Moscow, one minister after another—starting with Defense Minister Pavel Grachev—denied that these were their men or that there had been any operation. But on November 28 there appeared "The President's Appeal to the Participants of the Armed Conflict in the Chechen Republic," which contained an ultimatum that demanded the release of the prisoners, the disbandment of the illegal armed formations, and the laying down of weapons by all sides within forty-eight hours. On the following day there was a meeting of the Russian Security Council, and on November 30, Boris Yeltsin signed the Secret Order No. 2137, "On Measures for Restoring Constitutional Law and Order on the Territory of the Chechen Republic," which called for disarming the Chechen resistance and establishing a state of emergency.

Dudayev, who had served as a General in the Soviet Strategic Air Force during the Cold War, could read the signs: the security services had bungled a covert operation; they were humiliated; and they would call on the army to save the nation's honor in "a victorious little war." At this stage, Shakhrai's coercive diplomacy might actually have worked, had anyone in the Kremlin been interested. On December 6, Dudayev made very conciliatory statements, suggesting that Chechnya could have the same currency, army, and foreign and defense policy as Russia. However, the Kremlin was dominated by the hawks, who were on a course to remove Dudayev, not to negotiate with him. A delegation was formed under the General Prosecutor Usman Imayev, which held talks with the Russians from December 11–15, 1994. These meetings were essentially propagandistic. The military and security chiefs were in charge, but it allowed the Kremlin spin doctors to create a pretense for public consumption, while the war machinery moved into action. It was the same basic game plan as every Soviet intervention of the Cold War; a palatable pretext was being developed and a full invasion was not far behind.

During these events, I was in St. Petersburg recovering from a knee injury I sustained at our base. We had been worried that while the main part of our group was attacking Labazanov in Argun, others such as Gantermirov might attack our base; when I heard shots in the night, I ran out to investigate and accidentally stepped in a hole and injured myself. One of my university friends had a business in St. Petersburg and invited me there for treatment—it would take several months for my knee to heal. As the November and December events were unfolding, my friend did not want me to leave. He was being kind, but his concern was offensive to me. He kept saying, "What are you worried about? By the time you get down there, it will all be over." I finally convinced him to buy me a plane ticket to Rostov. There I met another friend and we drove back to Grozny through Nalchik and Malgobek, where we were stopped and had to pay bribes of 100 rubles to soldiers to let us through.

Starting in Nalchik, in Kabardino Balkaria, we saw enormous columns of armor moving along the main road. I could not believe what I was seeing; these were columns of Russian Interior Ministry troops, strapping soldiers six feet tall, well-equipped, and traveling in dozens of vehicles. We felt that we were rushing to get to Grozny before the whole thing ended. We knew very well that there was not much in Chechnya to oppose this force.

The threat of imminent invasion consolidated Chechen society around Dudayev and his government, and the opposition was reduced to only the top layer of its leadership. The statements coming from the Russian government were deeply offensive, calling us a nation of bandits, and clearly showed the government as being bent on war. For the first time, Dzhokhar Dudayev, who had not been popular with some segments of the population, emerged as the charismatic leader of the entire Chechen nation. The Russian columns encountered fierce resistance virtually everywhere and it took them from December 11 to December 30 to reach Grozny. The civilian population panicked. The advance of the columns was being broadcast on television and there was no way to evacuate people in an organized fashion. Each family did what it could. There were huge numbers of people migrating within Chechnya and to neighboring republics, creating gridlocks that hampered the Russian advance as well as Dudayev's efforts to organize lines of defense around the capital.

The Russian military and security ministers had persuaded Yeltsin that the problem of Chechnya's status was merely one of who would be its president. The expectation in Russia was that Dudayev could be easily removed, if not by a covert operation then by a small-scale war, followed by which, the Chechens would simply accept Russian rule. Russia did not expect the scale of resistance that the military encountered, and the Russian high command certainly did not expect this to turn into a full-blown war. The columns were ordered to go to the center of the Grozny, annihilate Dudayev's supporters (estimated at a few dozen men), and arrest Dudayev. When I read the memoirs of the operation's main military masterminds, Marshal Pavel Grachev, Generals Anatoly Kvashnin, and Gennady Troshev, what I concluded was that they expected an operation in three maneuvers that would last a couple of weeks. The army was instructed to collect all weapons from the population.

We arrived in the city late at night on December 30, 1994, coming from the southwest, through the neighborhood called Chernorechie. I thought I would find the city in worse shape with the damage from the air strikes. As it was, there was no electricity, there were few people around, and you could hear bombardments in the distance. The goal of the Russians was to move in from four directions and take over the presidential palace. These included the western direction under the command of Major General Valeri Petruk, the eastern direction under the command of Major General Nikokai Stas'kov, the northern direction under the command of Major General Konstantin Pulikovksy, and the northeastern direction under the command of Lieutenant General Lev Rokhlin. The columns met staunch resistance in Ingushetia and in Dagestan; only the column moving through Chechnya's northern district, Nadterechnyi, encountered no resistance. This was the most pro-Russian area. Russians said that the southern part of the city was being kept open to permit civilians to leave, but they must have understood that this was convenient for us because it was the most direct route to the mountains through the Argun Valley. I think they just did not have the opportunity to cut off all the exits at the same time.

When we arrived in Grozny on the night of December 30, the columns were surrounding the city on three sides in preparation for an attack. I came home to the Staropromyslovskii rayon and found my father and two brothers, but my mother and sisters had left the city for the village. My father was furious with me for returning; he was much happier thinking I was in St. Petersburg. I didn't know how to reconnect with Shamil, and in my house I had only a uniform and two grenades. I didn't have a submachine gun, and in my neighborhood there were few men who were going to fight. Those who were fighters had already left, though I did find one neighbor who, like me, was trying to figure out what to do next.

My neighborhood was between two heights, Sunzhenskii khrebet and Groznenskii khrebet. The main highway, Staropromyslovskoe Shosse, was where the tank columns were trying to break through. That night there was artillery bombardment in our area and, walking outside, we could see the columns along the heights. The Sunzhenskii khrebet was all lit up, endless columns of tanks and armor were visible, artillery was being set up, but the shelling was not systematic. Those columns were an awesome sight. I did not think that we could stop them, and it is still on many levels a real mystery to me that we did.

I experienced the battle of Grozny as total chaos. I pieced together the overall picture of what had happened in the city only later, having read news accounts and memoirs of the Russian military commanders. While I was in the midst of urban warfare, I couldn't understand what was happening on the next block, or sometimes, in the next building.

General Pulikovsky's column had divided up into smaller groups of four or five vehicles that were trying to break onto Staropromylsovkoe Shosse from several side streets. Commander Gelayev and his men were at a key intersection. At around five in the morning on December 31, there was a huge explosion, and I thought of joining Gelayev's group along with my neighbor who accompanied me. By the time we got there, we saw several armored vehicles and a tank burning. An artillery gun had been blown up, which had lots of explosives and made a very loud noise. We did not understand then that this was not the full column—it was one of Pulikovsky's subgroups of four or five vehicles and a few dozen men. It amazed me how easy it looked—it took only a few grenade launchers to take it out. We got there in time to see a Chechen fighter killing a Russian soldier who was wounded in the stomach and crawling on the ground. We asked, "What are you doing?" The fighter ignored us and Gelayev's men took a few Russians prisoner, but most of the Russians ran away. This was a typical scene that was repeated all day throughout the city. We had not realized our own strength, and we had had no idea how vulnerable such tank columns are within cities.

My neighborhood was within Gelayev's zone of responsibility, but this did not mean that all the men there were under his command. For the most part, Chechen fighters came voluntarily from villages, and they had no instructions. At best, they were told to "stay here and defend this intersection." Then they would hear an explosion, and someone passing by would announce, "The real action is over there, tanks are being destroyed, and you can get weapons there." Hearing that, these volunteers moved on to locations where they could pick up more "trophies" (weapons taken from the enemy). Units came in and out of position unexpectedly. As we started to move into the city center, we did not know who was firing or from where. We had to proceed very slowly, occasionally taking cues from other fighters or the few civilians on the scene. The situation was so dynamic that a position occupied one hour by Chechens could be held by Russians the next. Most of us had no radios and could not communicate with one another, so we had to proceed cautiously and grope our way forward like blind men.

At the Dom Kino movie theater, which is also known in Grozny as the bus stop Neftyanika-2 on Staropromyslovskii Shosse, we encountered another group of vehicles that had been destroyed. One of the vehicles was an Armored Personnel Carrier (APC) that could carry about a dozen people. The doors burst open and burned bodies fell out; the smell was overpowering. The bodies looked like mannequins with body parts intact but their skin was cracked. As they fell out of the APC, some of them twitching and others already dead, our side started firing on them. Civilians were gawking at this; there is a weird curiosity on the first day of war and most of us were seeing combat for the first time; the curious were also leaning out of windows and staring.

The New Year's offensive of December 31, 1994, to January 1, 1995, was composed of three major events: the encounter with Gelayev in my neighborhood, the fighting in the city center, and the battle in the south of the city. The column from the east, under the command of General Stas'kov, attacked Khankala, which was being defended by the battalion of Umalt Dashayev, one of our best units, which had fought in Abkhazia. That battle began on December 28, and only by the end of the day on December 30 did the Russians enter Grozny from the east. The price of that three-day delay was the destruction of our entire unit, including the commander, with only two or three men surviving that battle. During the New Year's Eve battle, the Russian's eastern group attempted to reach Minutka Square, but because of very heavy losses had to return to its initial position.

There are different explanations as to why we were able to hold out as long as we did. The persistent view of the Russian high command was that Dudayev was very well prepared with many men and weapons. For instance, General Troshev claims there were several divisions and 41,000 units of different types of assault rifles, grenade launchers, and other types of weapons. I have no idea how he come up with such figures. There may have been large arsenals of weapons in 1991 because Chechnya was one of the staging grounds for Soviet troops bound for combat in Afghanistan. But by December 1994 these arsenals were no longer under the control of our government; they had been sold on the black market. Some of these stores found their way to other conflicts in the Caucasus, such as South Osettia, North Osettia, and Nagorno Karabakh. Certainly weapons were not distributed among the fighters in an organized fashion, and this was a source of great bitterness for us. We were risking our lives to get our hands on weapons, when we all knew that there was an arms bazaar up the road where everything was on sale, and that is where those Soviet-era arsenals went.

We had essentially four battle-hardened units: three groups that fought in Abkhazia under Shamil, Gelayev, and Umalt Dashaev, and one called the "Afghan Battalion" that was composed of veterans of the war in Afghanistan. Umalt Dashaev's battalion was destroyed at Khankala prior to the New Year's Eve offensive, leaving only three groups of experienced fighters. For the most part the fighters in the city were volunteers from the villages; they came spontaneously in groups that were formed on the spot. They were not like an army combat group that is carefully equipped to be self-sufficient. A unit from a village might number ten people, with three rifles and two grenade launchers; the others had no guns at all and were hoping to find trophies in the field. How does one get a machine gun if one does not have one? You borrow a weapon, kill someone and take their weapon, or you take it from a vehicle that has been incapacitated. This is very tricky because there is no way to know in advance when a vehicle might explode—it might take a second or it could take half an hour. Lots of Chechen fighters died going into APCs in search of weapons. On the Russian side, there were at least 20,000 men and we counted 300 vehicles that we destroyed in the first few days. On our side there were only 1,000 to 1,500 experienced fighters; the rest were inexperienced, poorly armed, poorly equipped, and totally uncoordinated. Yet we held up the advance for a week, and held on to parts of Grozny for seven weeks.

How was this possible? For one reason only: we attacked. This was the spontaneous activity of amateur volunteers who ran into—not away from—explosions. I do not think this is something exclusively Chechen, although of course we were all reared on Chechen ideals of courage and subscribed to the Soviet cult of heroism from World War II. But I think there was something more fundamental involved. Numerous memoirs about the start of wars contain something similar, for instance the enthusiasm with which young men joined the American Civil War, or the romance of Europeans marching into World War I. I think these are universal human reactions. Young men are motivated by patriotism, romance, a desire to prove themselves, freedom, glory, and willingness to die for their country—but only very briefly, because soon the reality of war reveals itself as boring and ugly. But for the first few days there was exhilaration, enthusiasm, and euphoria among the men, particularly because it was our city, our territory that we were defending; there was nothing artificial or abstract about our goals and motives. But the feeling cannot last; the romance dissipates, war becomes work, and the most horrible work at that.

Russian sources speak of 15,000–20,000 Chechen fighters in Grozny. If Maskhadov had had this kind of force he would have stationed them around the perimeter of the city. He had at best 1,500–2,000 men, and to maximize their effectiveness he brought them into the center of the city. Grozny is an old city with narrow streets where vehicles, much less columns of vehicles, cannot turn around. This was a suicidal mission for the Russians. The men who did the best in the beginning and were able to get past Gelayev's brigade and enter the center of town experienced the worst of the fighting. Our fighters were using grenade launchers to take out tanks on narrow streets by firing from second-floor windows. On these streets all we had to do was stop the first tank, then the whole column was trapped and easily destroyed.

The first week, December 31 until January 7, saw total chaos in the city center. There was very little coordination or communication between Dudayev's army and the spontaneous volunteers. It is a miracle that Maskhadov, Gelayev, and other commanders were able to keep the general outlines of their strategies in place, which testifies to their personal discipline and drive. Shamil told me that he felt as if he were directing traffic; he was trying to assign certain units to specific areas, but they lacked any notion of discipline. They did not understand how the block they were asked to defend fitted into an overall plan. If they thought they would hit more tanks or get more trophies by moving, they would go to a completely different neighborhood. There was constant movement during that first week, with detachments of Russian columns dashing madly in all directions and chased by Chechen fighters.

Within the first couple of days the Russians started to learn certain basic lessons. They stopped carrying out their orders to attack and instead dug in and started using their armor to defend themselves. They had much more firepower than we did and we began to experience serious casualties. The Russian command regrouped, combining the remains of Pulikovsky's column with Rokhlin's, under the command of the latter, who was a more capable tactician. Rokhlin did not take his men into the thick of the fighting but waited outside the city center, by the canning factory; his forces also managed to capture our arsenal, which had mines, artillery shells, and bullets. This eased their situation because it made them less dependent on their own supply lines. By January 7 General Kvashnin was in charge of the United Group of Forces and General Rokhlin was in charge of the northern group, General Babichev the western, and General Stas'kov the eastern, and in the course of a few days they started to react very skillfully. They developed front lines and pushed particularly hard on the northern and western fronts, which maximized their advantage.

Chechen units were also learning; the volunteers started to accept the authority of our General Staff; with each new day the chaos was increasingly unbearable and people began to organize their activity. On January 7, 1995, there was the second—and more powerful—assault on the city. On that day I was trying to get to the city center. I was at Dom Pechati (Press House), an eight-storey building, substantially higher than other buildings in the area, which overlooked an important intersection. It was a transit point for fighters going in to the presidential palace and out to Staropromyslovskii rayon. About 100 of us were there at any one time. We formed little groups and waited for an opportunity to get deeper into the city center. I was with a group of seven or eight men, including my third cousin.

There was very heavy artillery fire. Within my gaze there were three explosions at any one time, followed by crossfire from machine guns, tracer fire, and when we finally thought we might cross the street, sniper fire. In the middle of all this, as we were dodging bullets, there were civilian women asking us for bread. I thought they were trapped there, but I learned later that they had come from the presidential palace and were supplying those inside. As we were trying to cross an alley, we were almost caught by sniper fire, which has a very distinctive sound even amid all the noise. We were on the ground, and on the top floors were men shooting madly at each other; we could not figure out which side was ours, or where we should go.

We made it a bit further until we ran into more pockets of very heavy fighting, which forced us to return to Dom Pechati. Under normal conditions, this distance takes five minutes to walk, but it took us hours. I decided to return to Staropromyslovskii rayon and a group of us made our way back late in the night. After I got home, I was laid up for a couple of days coughing blood, but did not suspect tuberculosis. It was not diagnosed until a few months later. I merely thought I had a cold from too much running around in a heavy uniform.

I made another attempt to join Shamil's unit in the city center on January 12, but by this time it was too late. General Rokhlin's and Babichev's groups joined forces, regrouped into one column, and blocked off my neighborhood. I left with the refugees through Nadterechnyi rayon and went back down through Achkoi-Martan and Gekhi.

According to Maskhadov, he made the decision to leave the presidential palace on January 19 after the building came under heavy bombardment; a rocket had destroyed a whole corner of the building. The palace sustained direct hits from bombs that reached all the way down to the basement where Dudayev, his associates, Russian parliamentarians, press, and prisoners were all quartered. A bomb had hit a makeshift hospital in the basement of the building. The Russians were holding buildings within a few meters of the presidential palace, and were closing in. However, the building was never stormed and those inside relocated south across the Sunzha River, through areas still controlled by Chechens.

Maskhadov's men regrouped on the other side of the river where a stable front line eventually emerged across which there were constant battles. The consequences for the city were disastrous. Corpses lay in the street and dogs were chewing on them and becoming wild. I saw bodies that had been partially eaten, bodies from which the heads had been gnawed off. Maskhadov called for a humanitarian cease-fire to bury the dead and shoot the wild dogs, which were becoming dangerous to people. Sergei Kovalev, who was briefly Yeltsin's human rights commissioner before being fired (largely for his presence in Grozny), also called for a humanitarian cease-fire. Kovalev told me later that when he asked Yeltsin personally to order a cease-fire, Yeltsin responded, "The time hasn't come yet."

Maskhadov, Shamil, and General Anatoli Kulikov did reach a cease-fire agreement when they met in Sleptskovskaya, but it lasted only three days, from February 16–19. At that meeting, Shamil recalled, Kulikov was behaving arrogantly toward him and Maskhadov. At one point, Shamil jumped up and yelled, "You want a bloodbath? You got it!" and stormed out the door. After that, Kulikov asked Maskhadov, "Please, don't bring this one with you anymore."

CHAPTER 2

JOINING MASKHADOV'S GENERAL STAFF

I saw Shamil Basayev once again in February 1995 in the eastern part of the city, near the dam and the Grozny reservoir, which the locals refer to as "The "Grozny Sea." I had said goodbye to the group I came with. We camped in abandoned factories above the Sunzhenskaya River and slipped in and out of the city center.

When I saw Shamil, he was yelling at a commander named Ruslan who had broken the cease-fire. I knew Ruslan from Nagorno Karabakh, where I had made several trips during 1992–93. On February 16, Ruslan had been in Chernorechie where he saw Russian paratroopers, who had weapons and uniforms that he wanted. He attacked them, disobeying the cease-fire. Ruslan's group killed several Russian soldiers and grabbed seven new sub-machine guns, two of which Ruslan was holding. He had gone up to Shamil to show off his trophies, but instead uncovered a real sore spot. Shamil saw me in the crowd and waved for me to come over. The first thing he said to me was, "And you? You also want to be a hero? Like this animal?" He screamed at Ruslan a little longer, then told me to follow him and we got into his car, a red Niva.

"I know you want to run around and shoot and be a fighter and that's all cool," he said, "but what do you think you will accomplish? You'll kill a couple of Russian soldiers, maybe you'll kill ten soldiers, and if you're really lucky you'll blow up a tank. But then, in a week or so, you will get whacked, and that will be the end."

"The Russians have plenty of tanks and a million soldiers," he went on, "and no matter how many we destroy, that will not end this. Maskhadov is forming the general staff and he needs people; he needs well-educated people who have experience in the military. There is nothing there yet; we don't have an analytical or information service. Why don't you go there?" Movladi Udugov was the Minister for Communications and Press and he was usually the one giving interviews to the media but he was traveling with Dudayev. Apart from Udugov's statements, there was no other organized effort on the part of the Chechen resistance to provide information, to counter Russian propaganda, or conduct analysis. Shamil wanted me to help Maskhadov to conduct this type of activity out of the general staff.

"Actually, I've been trying to find you. I want to stay with you. I don't even know Maskhadov," I replied.

"Stay with me? You'll stay with me and then what? What use is that? I'll drop you off and introduce you to Maskhadov."

The general staff had moved to Mesker-Yurt, the village beyond Argun along the road out of Grozny. The Russians had taken control of most of the city, when Generals Rokhlin and Babich combined their forces; this meant that the entire city, except for the Oktyabrskii district was in their hands. This was the southern end of the city, so we were still in control of the southeast and southwest sections. Shamil and I met at the southeastern exit and proceeded to the 56th district, where he had his base and his training camp. During the battle of Grozny, when new fighters arrived, Shamil would send them to this camp for our version of "basic training"; it was a three- or four-day course in how to shoot an automatic rifle, a submachine gun, and a grenade launcher.

In December 1994 as the columns pulled into Grozny, some split off and took up positions around Argun. When the cease-fire was broken, their artillery started firing near Argun. They said that the cease-fire applied only to Grozny and we said it applied to the entire front-line. During this time there were a couple of minor incidents in the city, which included the periodic shelling of Argun. Shamil gathered the small units that were coming out of Grozny into Chernorechie.

As more and more neighborhoods fell to the Russians and all the fighters were concentrated in smaller areas, Shamil realized how many women fighters there were. There were fifteen to twenty young women at Shamil's base, who had fought in the city center along with the men and were determined to keep going. But Shamil decided to send them away rather than keep them at the base.

At the same time, the Russians were starting to press against Argun. The general staff was behind Argun in a factory called *Krasnyi Molot*, which is a large, multi-storey building where the general staff occupied the basement and the first floor. This factory contained a sturdy bomb shelter.

I told Shamil that I wanted to see my mother and say goodbye and then would join Maskhadov's general staff. I had been at war in Chechnya for almost two months and had not seen my mother during that time. She had not heard from me since I returned from St. Petersburg, and did not know until a couple of weeks earlier that I was even in Chechnya. Shamil told me to go see her and then go to see Mashkhadov together with Abu Movsayev, the head of the security service for Shali.

My mother was staying with our relatives in Ghekhi-Chu, a village near Gekhi, which is near Urus Martan. This town was an oasis of tranquility—it was treated by all sides as neutral territory, where you might find Russian troops, pro-Russian Chechens, and the resistance. I went to my uncle's house and was told that my mother was in the neighboring village of Roshni-Chu. She was attending the funeral of a distant relative (a twenty-five-year-old man named Rizvan). He had served in one of the "Grad" units, an artillery system that uses 122-mm rockets with a range of forty kilometers. His unit had been resting in an apartment in Grozny when Russian soldiers saw them and fired into the window with a flamethrower and all the Chechens were incinerated.

When I arrived in Roshni-Chu, the mourning ceremony was easily spotted at the house with the open shutters and the silent, polite young people milling about outside, waiting to greet everyone and escort them to the relatives. One of these young men escorted me to the interior yard, where several old men were sitting under a wide awning in somber silence. Opposite them there were twenty younger men who were standing up. I stood in the center of the semicircle and greeted the elders who stood up to welcome me. I asked them to recite the "Do'ya," a short prayer said at funerals prior to expressing condolences. After the prayer,

I said, "May the Almighty accept his *gazavat!*[1] May He grant you patience!"

My mother was sitting with all the other women, who mourn separately from the men. I relayed through other women that I was outside, but she refused to leave the mourners, so I had to walk into the women's half, where they were wailing and crying. Usually, if a man needs to speak to the wife or mother of the deceased, he knocks on the door and someone calls for them—he never actually goes inside. There were about twenty women there, two were my cousins, the others I didn't know, and my mother was sitting next to Rizvan's mother.

I went up to her and very quietly whispered in her ear, "I did not have an opportunity to see you. I came to say goodbye and I don't know when I'll see you next." I did not mean that I might die; I meant that Chechnya was being divided and it might be a long time before I could come from Argun to Ghekhi-Chu.

"Go ahead," she said, "don't worry about anything. Everyone is going and you must too. And if you get killed, we will find your body and give it a proper burial like this one."

And that was it; I was relieved and immensely grateful to her. I understood that what my mother said was not primarily for me; it was not about me or about her; she meant to comfort the woman sitting next to her. I was grateful that I did not have to stay in that room any longer.

I went to the Shali Security Department to find Abu Movsayev, instead I found the mothers of Russian soldiers who were looking for their sons. Dudayev had announced that he would release prisoners to their mothers, and the mothers came from all over Russia. They would keep the prisoners company. The prisoners were allowed to sit outside the prison and spend the day with these mothers, and the women wrote down names and information about the prisoners and would circulate these lists.

Shali was had a market where villagers went for gasoline, fuel, or medicine. There were many people going back and forth and in Shali I ran into Shivrani Basayev, Shamil's younger brother. He told me that Shamil would arrive soon, in the meantime, he invited me to dinner in the cafeteria.

The cafeteria was a small room with a front door at one end and a service window at the other. In the middle of the room there was a table with seating for ten people. The meals were not bad; there was fresh meat and soup. We didn't have the facilities to set up separate kitchens so the prisoners were fed from the same kitchen as the fighters. Shirvani and his men stacked their weapons along the wall. All the Chechen fighters carried their weapons fully loaded—all you had to do was take the safety lever off and press. They even kept grenades in the launchers; all you had to do was click it in. This is not what they taught me in the army and it always made me very nervous. As we were eating, the door opened and a fourteen-year-old Chechen boy in uniform, carrying a rubber night-stick like a policeman, escorted two prisoners, draftees, carrying a big pot. The three of them passed behind us and waited for the women to fill the pot to take back to the prison. I was sitting there, with my eyes trying to make their way to the back of my head. I did not say anything to the others because they would think I was a coward. The Chechen fighters were eating and joking, unaware of the situation, an example of Chechen recklessness. The boy was standing in front, behind him the two draftees, and the back of my head, the only thing watching them.

When the boy and the prisoners finally left, I said to the others, "Do you understand how lucky we are that neither of those draftees was an actual soldier? A prisoner is supposed to use every opportunity to try to escape and inflict maximum damage to the opponent. All those prisoners had to do was to pick up one of the machine guns, which was within their reach, and in a closed space like this, we ten would be in heaven already." The response this provoked was laughter and, "Yeah, those Russians aren't real soldiers." I tried to explain to them that it wasn't some wise man that sat down and wrote the rules of the army, they were written from mistakes; stupid, needless, careless mistakes, which spilled soldiers' blood. In the beginning of the war we couldn't persuade Chechens to dig trenches—trenches were for cowards—who needed trenches? When the bombings got bad, they started digging. But we never did learn to exercise caution around prisoners. At the end of the war, when the peace talks had already started, there was a group of prisoners that did escape in this way. Their guards, six Chechens, dropped their weapons into a pile and kneeled down to pray. No one had put handcuffs on the prisoners, who picked up the machine gun and shot the guards. This was the first and only group escape. I don't know why it hadn't happened earlier in the war.

In the evening Movsayev finally arrived and a little later Shamil arrived as well. The three of us drove from Shali to the general staff in the huge factory building outside Argun. It was very close to the front, about three kilometers away. We went to the basement; it was enormous and built to withstand a war. This factory was part of the military industrial complex and was considered an enterprise of national significance. It was dimly lit and had concrete floors and walls. There were about fifty fully armed people in the room. This was the Presidential Guard that Dudayev said should be quartered with the General Staff.

After the others left, Shamil introduced me formally to Maskhadov. "This is an officer," he said, "and I know him well and I trust him completely. He wanted to be with me, but I thought you might use him here." Maskhadov was like a sphinx, very calm and not very talkative. "Very well," he replied, "my aide-de-camp will come in a minute and will explain everything to you." The two of them talked longer while I waited, then Shamil said goodbye to me and left.

Husein Iskhanov, Maskhadov's aide-de-camp, in time became a very good friend. He made his staff what it was and interestingly he was not a professional soldier. He had been a painter of posters; he painted Communist murals proclaiming various holidays and quoting our sage leaders. Husein did not have a particularly menacing appearance, but there was something in his manner that impressed even the most unruly types, who were coming in directly from the front. He gently and calmly impressed upon them that they were in the general staff and the head of the staff was their overall commander. Husein showed me the third floor, where our communications were. This was always an interesting place to be; the radios were on, and we could hear the Russians talking to each other. We had a Chechen with a Ukrainian accent. There were many Chechens who didn't have Caucasian accents, but this was a Chechen with a Ukrainian accent! He was very good at getting the Russians to bomb their own positions and then the radio would explode with anti-Ukrainian diatribes, "*khokhlyatskaya morda.*"

Husein escorted me to a room I would share with two other officers. One performed the same functions as a political officer in the Soviet army, the *zampolit*,[2] who was there to ensure that proper communist ethics were observed, although in our case he watched over our observance of religious norms and values. He had been educated in Syria and knew Arabic and had some sort of clerical title. He was supposed to make sure that we were living in accordance with proper Islamic morals and values. His goal was to throw the women fighters out of the general staff.

The issue of women fighting in the war was very painful and complicated for us. Chechen women had a history of fighting. They had fought in the nineteenth century wars against Russia. Blood feuds among Chechens are a wholly male endeavor and revenge can only be carried out by and upon a male older than fifteen years of age. However, in rare cases, if the last person in a family is a woman, she can take it upon herself to carry on the blood feud.

There were two women in the Presidential Guard who had gone through the entire battle in the city and the men regarded them as their comrades and did not want them to leave. There was a battle brewing between Akhmed, the Presidential Guard Commander, and the *zampolit*. There were many Chechen women fighting in Grozny, and they were just as brave and capable as the men. I had witnessed small, frail-looking women crawl into impossible places and pull men out. I don't know if it would be the same in a professional army abroad, but in their own territory, Chechen women were very good fighters. For the most part, the women in the war: fighters, nurses, and technical personnel, were saints. On rare occasions there were cases of loose morals, but that is a different story altogether. The overwhelming majority of women came to fight because they had lost family members and were seeking revenge. They knew that being at the front, they would constantly have to prove they deserved to be there, that they were brave enough, and tough enough. It was much harder for the women than it was for the men; no one questioned why we came there, but the women had to prove to us that they were braver.

The following morning Maskhadov called everyone into formation and started to talk about morality during war. It was very

difficult for him to say that these two women should leave, it
would have been an insult to them and their service and he clearly
did not want that. I think Maskhadov did this reluctantly and I
suspect that the *zampolit* had forced this whole situation.

"We have to remember all the time that we are at war,"
Maskhadov said, "and we may meet our maker in an hour and we
should be clean." Then he abruptly ended his remarks. Finally, he
addressed the Head of the Presidential Guard. "Akhmed," he said,
"thank them for their service and please within twenty-four hours
have them leave the premises so that I don't see them again."

Then Maskhadov took me out of the line-up and introduced
me to the others and said that I would be responsible for "seeing
to the political and moral education" of the staff. I was thinking to myself, "How on earth did I become the *zampolit*?" I was
dreadfully uncomfortable. I understood what the others were
thinking of me at that moment, that I would be some kind of
rat. Thankfully, as it turned out I did not have to do anything
of the sort.

After the Russians occupied Grozny they began to take control
of more territory, and our general staff had to continually relocate, moving eventually high into the mountains. In the third
week of March, due to the threat of the complete encirclement of
Argun, the general staff moved to Serzhen-Yurt, in the vicinity
of Shali. During the first half of April, we left Shali for Vedeno,
which is where Imam Shamil, the leader of the mountaineer resistance, retreated in the nineteenth century.

About a month passed before I was fully accepted by the general staff. When Maskhadov started relying on me, and asking
my opinion about political matters, such as the possibility of talks
with Russia, the coldness that I initially felt from his subordinates dissipated. Husein explained to me, after I was already being
tasked by Maskhadov constantly, that when Shamil first brought
me to the staff, they all thought that I was supposed to be Shamil's
eyes and ears in the general staff. I was shocked, I was no one's
spy, and Shamil had introduced me with his best intentions. I had
felt some tension between Shamil and Dudayev prior to the war,
but I did not expect this suspicion from Maskhadov's staff. It was
only when Husein shared that first impression that I started to
analyze the relationships among the leaders.

Maskhadov's first moment of fame was the battle at the cemetery, in the summer of 1994, where he had to share the glory with Shamil. The two were together again leading our forces in the battle of Grozny, after which Dudayev promoted Maskhadov to Division General and Shamil to Colonel. Maskhadov was Head of the General Staff, but Shamil was Head of the Grozny garrison.

Particularly among Chechens this is bound to lead to competition; but when does a healthy competition become a destructive rivalry? Dudayev's forceful character limited the competition between Shamil and Maskhadov; he was the Commander-in-Chief; and he was the General. He kept everyone at arm's length and while he was President, Shamil and Maskhadov were closer to each other than either were to Dudayev.

From what I saw at this stage, Maskhadov and Shamil were close and helped each other. We were not a regular army and the hardest part of it all for us was not the battles—battles are quick—but the logistics, the myriad organizational issues of housing and supply and discipline in our ranks. Although it is a small place, Chechnya has three distinct zones: Nadterechnyi, Vedeno-Nozhayurtovskii, and Shatoi-Itum-Kalinskii, and although all are Chechens they are different. What do you do when 300 men from a different part of Chechnya arrive suddenly and need to be quartered? All kinds of conflicts come up with the local population and having Shamil on his side was very advantageous for Aslan. Shamil did things unofficially that one could not do officially. He would, unofficially, wave a gun in someone's face and this was immensely useful to Aslan.

Relations with the civilian population were very painful. I experienced this myself when I was asked to carry out Dudayev's order to expropriate cars for the war effort. Taking cars away from private individuals was one of the worst things I had to do during the two years of the war. Dudayev ordered the population to turn over vehicles that had belonged to the government but were privatized in the early 1990s. These were usually buses or trucks. Special groups were formed to commandeer the vehicles and I had to participate in one such group on several occasions. I complained to Maskhadov about it and he simply told me that this was a decree and someone had to carry it out. Twenty of us, Presidential Guards and others, would close off a street, stop vehicles and take them forcibly away from the owners. Once we stopped a mini-bus and it turned out the driver had no papers. Our leader said, "We'll have to take this bus." If a group of Russian special forces jumped out of the bus I would not have been so scared, or at least it would be clear to me what I had to do, but this was a bus full of furious Chechen women.

The next vehicle we stopped was an old, beaten up hatchback with a family inside and all their possessions in the back. An ordinary middle-aged man was at the wheel. He got out of the car and explained to us that his house had been destroyed in a bombardment and this vehicle was all he had left in the world. He said he was taking his family to stay with relatives in Vedeno. I tried to intervene but to no avail. The brigade I was with had become utterly hardened to such cases. Shortly thereafter, a few cars carrying local men arrived. They were not part of the resistance but were well armed and we wound up in a standoff. In our group there was a particularly foolish man who could think of nothing better than to start firing from a machine gun over everyone's head. At this moment, a MiG interceptor plane flew over and came in so low and I could see the pilot's face. There were twenty of us at this intersection, with our weapons drawn, plus the locals and the women charging at us.

Suddenly, everyone started firing at the plane. I yelled to stop the firing because the pilot could come back and fire on us. We were totally exposed on this road with no cover. He did circle back and flew very low while the women screamed. But for some reason he did not fire on us. In the end, we forcibly confiscated the man's car, but let the women keep their bus because it would have been really dangerous to take it away from them. A bit later, we stopped and overtook a gasoline truck.

But why did that poor old man have to lose his car? All he wanted to do was get his family out of harm's way. I went to see Maskhadov over this. This was one of my first serious conversations him and I don't think he liked it. At first, he didn't say anything. He just listened to me patiently and finally replied that we were at war, that there was a decree, and there was no use crying about it. I saw the old man's car abandoned few days later. It was a limping old jalopy to begin with and our guys had driven it off the road and abandoned it.

There were profound gulfs between the civilians and the combatants. That small portion of the population that formed the armed resistance was terribly arrogant. We did not want to recognize the simple fact that many others would have joined in except for the lack of weapons. I ran around with two hand grenades during the first week of the battle of Grozny. But even this lack of weapons was not the biggest problem; we simply did not know how to relate to each other, and our roles were not well defined. The fighters were arrogant and the population did not recognize us as the authority. Yet no matter how you look at it, during war time, we simply had to take charge. This problem lasted for two years. From my point of view, this was the crisis of a barely formed state and a government that had trouble organizing the war effort.

Behavior in war time involved a different code of conduct and it pertained to much more than simply combat. There's a saying in Russian, "War permits everything." This is a temptation for the armed person: a feeling of superiority over the civilian, who after all is also a man. It was unfair. Our government did not organize a mobilization, it could not equip its forces, and it permitted stocks of weapons to be plundered. How many civilians died while trying to join up with one of our divisions? The longer the war lasted, the more you were likely to change, and maybe not in the best way.

One day while at the staff headquarters of the Presidential Guard, I saw four Russian prisoners—two young soldiers and two older men—sweeping the floor. They were dressed in civilian rags because their uniforms had been taken away. One of them turned out to be Lieutenant Colonel Vitali Seregin; he had given himself up in Khasavyurt on December 11, and he became infamous because this was early in the war and the event itself was reported on television. His convoy had not yet entered Chechnya as Khasavyurt is in neighboring Dagestan, close to the Chechen border with a large Chechen population called *akkintsy*. The Russian convoy was surrounded by local civilians who begged them to stop. Lieutenant Colonel Seregin and eleven soldiers complied and were disarmed by the *akkintsy* who managed to maneuver around the enormous convoy of armed cars to deliver the prisoners to the Presidential palace in Grozny and eventually take them out of the city with the general staff. Seregin and I pointed all this out to Akhmed and tried to explain that an officer should not be sweeping the floor. But I could not persuade him of this so I asked him to send Seregin upstairs to my desk to chat with me.

When he came up, I introduced myself, and I offered him a cigarette. I told him, "This is not an interrogation. You don't have to talk to me and if you refuse, I give you my word, this will not in any way affect your situation here."

Previously, I had spoken only to Russian soldiers. They were completely confused; they did not understand where they were or how they got here. They did not admit to themselves that they were at war and that they were prisoners. It had not completely dawned on them that they could be killed just as they were killing us. Some were scared, but more profound than their fear was their denial; they were in a kind of dream state. They were young conscripts and I wanted to talk to an adult, an officer, from the same army in which I had served.

I said to Seregin, "I just want to talk to you man to man. I want to know what you thought and felt when they told you that you were going here; and what you felt when you were taken prisoner, and how you feel now. But you don't have to talk to me."

"No, I don't mind talking to you," Seregin answered, and he recounted his odyssey. It's a paradox that the only Russian column that did not meet resistance on its way was the one that came through the northern part of Chechnya, the Nadterechnyi district. That district was controlled by the opposition and was generally pro-Russian. The population met the Russian tanks with flowers and speeches. The other two columns went through Ingushetia and Dagestan and both made very slow progress because of the resistance. In Ingushetia, in the town of Barsuki the locals put up barricades and threw Molotov cocktails at the column, setting several vehicles on fire. In Dagestan, in the town Khasavyurt, Seregin's column had surrounded by local civilians who pleaded with them to stop. That was when he surrendered.

"Were you maltreated?" I asked him.

"I thought that because of the way I behaved, they would simply let me go," Seregin explained. "At the same time, I was not particularly maltreated; there were no beatings, although there were a couple of times when I was hit. Some people were rude to me, some decent. Overall, I was not treated badly."

"What happened after you surrendered?" I asked.

"I was taken to the Presidential palace in Grozny, I was held with other prisoners in the basement of the palace. One time, when the building was shelled and a bomb hit the infirmary, in the commotion all our guards left and an old Chechen man opened the door to us and we went outside."

"Why didn't you escape?" I continued.

"There was nowhere to go. We did not know the city. It was night, there was shooting from all directions, it was total chaos. We would have simply gotten killed," he said.

I then said, "Let's pretend that you and I met by chance on a train. Can you tell me how you felt when you were told you would go to Chechnya?"

"It was an order, I had to obey the order that I was given."

"I heard this from soldiers," I commented, "and I have heard this from one First Lieutenant. The soldiers were eighteen, the First Lieutenant was twenty-three or twenty-four. They were children; I expected nothing from them, but you, you are an adult. Didn't you understand that you would be shooting women and children?"

"I didn't shoot anyone."

"Yes. I know you did not. But others did and it's still going on unabated. You see what is going on here?"

"It was an order."

"Stop it," I intervened. "I was in the army and I can quote you the military code of conduct that states that no military personnel are obligated to carry out any orders that constitute criminal acts or contravene the Geneva Conventions."

"I thought that given the way I had behaved, I would simply have been let go," he said.

"Do you see the chaos around you? It's the Warsaw ghetto. Who is keeping track of your particular case? The guys here are not drawing distinctions between who surrendered and under what circumstances. To them you showed up in their city and destroyed it. I agree that you should not have to be a prisoner. I will talk to Akhmed and I will try to explain to him that you should not have to sweep the floor and you should not have to endure humiliating treatment. What else is there that I can do for you? Sometimes journalists come through and if you like I can ask them to mail a letter from you to your relatives."

"No one has spoken to me this way," Seregin said, "during the three months that I have been a prisoner." He was apparently deeply touched by my remarks and tears welled up in his eyes and he began to cry. I tried to calm him down.

There is nothing more frightening than being a prisoner. What does it mean to treat prisoners decently? Don't beat them, don't humiliate them, give them food and water and let them sleep. Even if he's treated decently, his whole existence depends on factors outside his control, and he feels an incredible amount of stress. Seregin was terribly offended that his act of honor was not appreciated and I couldn't help but agree with him; I thought he deserved better. I spoke to Maskhadov about Seregin and told him, "The Presidential guards do not answer to me, I am not one of them, and they might misunderstand me. I served in the army for a long time. They just came out to fight against an enemy. I might have some things that I cling to, but even the Nazis held to the Geneva Conventions in their treatment of prisoners of war, although not in respect to Soviet prisoners because the Soviet Union had not signed the Geneva Conventions." Of course, Maskhadov agreed. He understood all of this perfectly well and the two officers were eventually traded.

I don't know if I would have behaved the same way during the second war with Russia. This was March 1995 and it was all very new. We still did not understand that what was going on was mass murder. I still thought it was some mistake, some misunderstanding and that the Kremlin did not have all the information about what was happening. I expected the war to end soon, and I was trying not to let myself become fully submerged into the environment that permits everything, that permits you do to anything to anyone. It was my illusion that it would end, but it all got progressively worse.

Our population was getting pulled into the conflict. The Russians introduced cleansing operations, *zachistky*, ostensibly to identify fighters, but they mostly killed and terrorized the population. Gradually, we were no longer one Soviet people, we were embroiled in an ethnic war, but I must say I think that on the

Chechen side this process evolved more slowly and was more a reaction to what was being done to us than a deliberate policy. During the entire first war (1994–96), Russian mothers went from one Chechen unit to another looking for their sons. Can anyone imagine Chechen mothers going to Russian units? Russians did not let their own women come near their divisions; imagine if our women had gone there?

Prisoners became a problem. In the spring there were mass desertions of Russian soldiers. They did not come to us, rather they went to the villages and the villagers helped them survive, but could not help them to go home. They simply didn't have the channels to accomplish that. Hence the deserters wound up with us and it became impossible to say who had been taken prisoner and who had deserted. There was a deserter, a warrant officer, who wound up in the hands of our military intelligence, our *osobyi otdel*. He could not persuade them that he was not a spy, and they shot him during the interrogation. After that incident I wrote Maskhadov's Decree 241 on the different categories of prisoners, their proper treatment, and criminal responsibility for violations. I want to think that this decree was honored and did help some people, but of course many problems persisted.

In Argun, we used the largest building but for some reason the Russians did not bomb us; or bombed us only intermittently. Maybe they were waiting for Dudayev to go there. Some of their artillery missed our factory and landed in the village, which of course displeased the villagers. There were episodes when locals threw grenades at us, trying to persuade us to leave. We suffered no casualties, however, and Maskhadov resolved the problem by talking to the elders. We expected fire from the Russians, but not from the villagers. Of course, we could have sent a few men down to the village to turn the place upside down, but we were not about to become the occupiers! About half of Argun was opposed to us, and as the Russians advanced into village after village, the divisions among the population deepened.

CHAPTER 3

RAID ON BUDENNOVSK: BASAYEV FORCES PEACE

In the spring of 1995 there was a pause in the fighting. Besides Grozny, the Russians had occupied the entire flatland of Chechnya including Shali and Gudermes, and we had withdrawn to the mountains. The Russians called for a moratorium on military action for ten days in May to celebrate the fiftieth anniversary of the end of World War II. The moratorium was in part to save world leaders the embarrassment of honoring the same military that was committing grave war crimes in Chechnya. The indiscriminate bombing of Grozny brought about considerable criticism in Europe and the United States. The Organization for Security Cooperation in Europe (OSCE), which includes the United States and all the European and Eurasian states, was seen as an appropriate institution to engage with Russia on these issues. A special assistance group was formed in March 1995 whose mandate was to facilitate humanitarian assistance, contribute to the search for a political resolution to the crisis, and to promote the functioning of democratic institutions.[1] The proclamation of the temporary moratorium on military activity permitted the assistance group of the OSCE to visit Chechnya and this gave us hope that conditions were being created in which it might be possible to commence talks. Until now, there had been only temporary and local cease-fires in order to clear away bodies, but there had been nothing resembling negotiations so far on the larger political issues.

This pause in military activity coincided with the arrival of the representatives of the newly formed OSCE Assistance group for Chechnya. Our headquarters had retreated from Argun to Shali, and then to Vedeno. Because Maskhadov was not available, Information Minister Movladi Udugov and I received the OSCE envoy, Sandor Meszaros, a Hungarian. Despite the moratorium on military activity, the OSCE delegation came under aerial bombardment on the way from Grozny to Vedeno and arrived rather distraught and shaken up. Minister Udugov was very guarded and almost unpleasant with Meszaros,. He pretended that he didn't understand the questions he was being asked, which I thought was inappropriate for an initial meeting whose purpose was merely to establish contact. Listening to Udugov's short responses, I felt certain that Maskhadov would have been far more gracious and forthright. Unfortunately, Meszaros, had to return to Grozny before nightfall and he left with what he must have considered an unsatisfactory encounter. Indeed, when Maskhadov returned he was very sorry to have missed the meeting and angry at the way Udugov had handled himself.

One evening, I got a call from Khamad Kurbanov, Dudayev's representative in Moscow, who wanted to speak to our president. I replied that this was Maskhadov's General Staff and that Dudayev was in a different part of Chechnya. He then asked to be connected to Maskhadov. They spoke briefly and Maskhadov relayed their conversation to me that evening. He said that Kurbanov was in contact with Yuri Baturin, then President Boris Yeltsin's Chief of the Presidential administration, and other intermediaries who were somehow related to the Vatican. Maskhadov and I understood how exotic this sounded but we had to explore any opportunity that presented itself.

Our satellite telephone was in my care and we were naively unconcerned about it being used to identify our location. This was presumably how the Russians pinpointed Dudayev the following year in April 1996 and ordered an aerial strike against him. But prior to Dudayev's death, we did not consider satellite conversations dangerous and I had the telephone on for hours. There were hours when we were available for calls from journalists and we received calls from all over the world.

One day Dudayev arrived unexpectedly, when there were very few of us at the headquarters. We were located in a school building and had just one sentry in front of the building. Dudayev had a particular style, and he was always making jokes. Sometimes it was barracks humor and not always tasteful. He was very vigorous and saw his role as keeping everyone's morale up. I knew that it was Dudayev arriving because I could hear the commotion outside. He had come up to the sentry and asked him, "Young man, how many tanks did you blow up?" The sentry very proudly answered, "One tank." Dudayev patted him gently on the cheek, "Oh you have barely fought at all!" You could see tears well up in the young man's eyes, but Dudayev was already on to the next man, who happened to be Maskhadov's adjutant. Dudayev picked him up off his feet in a bone-crunching bear hug, and spun him around.

After putting him back down, he found himself facing me. "How are things?" he asked. "Good," I responded. "No!" he corrected me, "Very good!" I understood I had to follow his example. "Very good!" I blurted. I remember Dudayev, who knew some Spanish, singing *Bessame Mucho* ("Kiss Me a Lot") over the telephone to an American professor whom he occasionally consulted. When she voiced fears about explosions that could she heard in the background, he dismissed her concerns and started singing that Mexican love song. This was Dudayev's style of interacting with people: to distract them from the gravity of a situation with any spontaneous, jovial gesture. He did not like it when people complained, and he always projected confidence.

Maskhadov summoned several others, including Shamil and Usman Imayev to confer with Dudayev after which Maskhadov asked me to phone Kurbanov. All of them were in the room when Kurbanov came on speaker phone. Dudayev spoke a little in the beginning but quickly transferred the receiver to Imayev who did most of the talking with Kurbanov. This was a rare opportunity for me to observe the relationships within this top circle. Imayev and Dudayev were very informal with each other; clearly there was a lot of trust there. At one point Imayev covered the receiver and whispered to Dudayev, "I don't trust this." Kurbanov was urging us to call a cease-fire along the entire line of contact as a way of proving our capacity to control our forces and exhibit our good will. Dudayev shot back, "Ask if this is agreed on with the Russians." Kurbanov responded merely that he was coordinating with Baturin. Kurbanov asked us to treat this conversation as top-secret information; that we should not let others know that there was an agreement. The Russian government was to transmit the order to halt all military activity to their forces and we were to do the same to ours without further explanation.

After we hung up the phone, Dudayev asked what the others thought. Maskhadov said, "We have to try, there is no choice but to try to pursue every possible opportunity, even something as strange as what we just heard." Shamil was skeptical and said, "I don't believe a word of that; I just can't take it seriously. If you do decide to try this, I will cooperate, but if the Russians attack in my area of the front, we will return fire." Dudayev listened to them and summed up, "I also do not believe everything that I heard, but let's demonstrate that we are making an effort." Dudayev asked Maskhadov to prepare orders for all our units. The order was to cease fire from May 31 to June 1 beginning at midnight. I wrote this order and showed it to Dudayev. He authorized it and soon after, left the headquarters. That was the last time I saw him alive.

That night, Maskhadov's guards were advising him not to sleep at headquarters because one of our buildings, where our security department was located, had been bombed. Maskhadov would spend the night elsewhere nearby. I, however, slept in the room with the telephone. I had a fold-out couch and Shamil sometimes stayed with me. He brought newspapers that journalists had given him and we solved crossword puzzles. That's what we were doing that night when we heard the rumble of planes; I think it was around half-past midnight. Shamil looked up from his newspaper and quipped, "Sounds like negotiation!" and with that he left to return to his unit. One commander after another called on my radio demanding an explanation; they had been ordered to hold their fire but now there was clearly a Russian offensive across the entire front line.

In the morning our building was bombed. I was saved by the arrival of two journalists, Aleksandr Yevtushenko of *Komsomol'skaya Pravda* and Andrei Babitsky of Radio Liberty who got me out of bed early in the morning, so I was no longer there when the bomb fell on Maskhadov's office. The Russians had excellent local intelligence and they hit Maskhadov's office directly. I managed to reach Kurbanov, who did not understand what was going on. He said he would contact Baturin and asked me to call him back. I never heard an explanation of this episode. The phone was destroyed in the bombardment and Kurbanov himself, was killed with Dudayev on April 21, 1996. How can this be explained? Was this possibly an attempt by someone affiliated with the Vatican to mediate? Did Kurbanov misread signals or try to force the situation? Was there a deliberate attempt by the Russians to deceive us as they were launching an offensive into the mountains? Was this a sincere attempt by some part of the Russian establishment that was thwarted by other factions? This remains a mystery to me. The only mention that I ever came across was on the pages of a tabloid newspaper, *Moskovskii Komsomolets*, which published an excerpt from a book by Aleksandr Khinshtein, *Yeltsin, Kremlin, the Medical History*, in which he wrote the following, citing General Anatoly Kulikov as his source:

> In May 1995 the Federal Forces had surrounded a large group of our opponents in the mountains. And at the moment when it was necessary to strike a decisive aerial strike, the Kremlin suddenly gave an order to desist.
>
> General Anatoly Kulikov, the Head Commander of the Interior Troops at the time, kept the treasonous telegram to this day. It's very short. "To Grachev, Kulikov. From 00 hour on 1st June cease the use of aviation. No explanation of reasons. Yeltsin."
>
> The reason was obvious. On the eve of this telegram, the MVD overheard Maskhadov on the radio demanding that his commanders hold out until midnight and then create a real "symphony" for the federals. "I am conducting talks about this matter," Maskhadov was yelling into the phone.
>
> Who among Yeltsin's people was conducting talks with the Chechens remains a mystery.[2]

From this account it sounds as if on the Russian side there was a similar process to ours, only the president and a narrow circle were informed. The paragraph concerning Maskhadov yelling into the phone is not accurate, but the account seems to confirm that there was an effort to arrange a cease-fire.

From June 2–12, 1995, the Russians had taken the war to the mountains and overrun three key strongholds that we expected to have held out much longer: Nozhay Yurt, Vedeno, and Shatoi. They attacked Vedeno first; they went around Serzhen Yurt, unable to break resistance there, which was being held by Shamil's battalion. In Vedeno we could see helicopters landing on a mountain range one after another and dropping off paratroopers. It seemed like an endless quantity of men and as soon as they landed they began to fire at us with mortars. Maskhadov sent reinforcements from the east, but it was not enough to form a front line. Some units were panicking and when Maskadov went to see Dudayev, who was in a different area in the southwest, a rumor spread that Maskhadov had fled apparently because he crossed through Dagestan. It was all that the commanders could do to try to prevent panic among their men. Maskhadov returned on horseback because all the roads were blocked and they had to navigate through mountain trails to get back to the vicinity of Vedeno.

I left Vedeno on foot with a small group of men, and we ran into tanks on the road to Dargo, which were totally unexpected at that altitude. There were helicopters swooping down on us and groups of fighters striking out in different directions without any coordination. On the outskirts of Dargo the elders met us and asked us not to enter their village. They thought that if we didn't come, they would be spared Russian bombardments. They demanded that anyone who entered the village disarm and take off his uniform. In some cases they did disarm individual fighters, in other situations fighters opened fire over the heads of villagers. Desperate and aggravated fighters were confronting a terrified civilian population that was willing to be deceived by Russian propaganda.

Shamil negotiated terms with the elders of Dargo, telling them that, "The Russians will bomb your village regardless of whether we enter it or not. Have you not heard what they did in the plains? Do you think they will behave differently in the mountains?" In the end they did let us into Dargo but on the condition that any defensive positions would be at a distance of 1.5 kilometers from the village. During the night, enthusiasts in the village went to Russian positions to negotiate. The terms were always the same: if the villagers promised to surrender all the fighters, the Russians would spare the village. In our case, the bombing of Dargo started almost immediately, and one of the houses that was destroyed belonged to the man who had led the negotiating team. This bombardment brought the population to our side; they were not even given a chance to carry out their part of the bargain.

The quintessential story of a village in the plains that attempted to make a deal with the Russians was Samashki. It became famous in April 1995 because it suffered one of the first horrifying massacres of the war and there were several neutral witnesses who were able to bring the story to international audiences. In Samashki, unlike most villages, the full story can be pieced together from accounts by outside observers. Tom Goltz, an American journalist, stayed with the fighters in Samashki. He was filming a documentary and later wrote a book about the village titled *Chechnya Diary*.[3] Tom left Samashki on March 27 with the peace march composed of several dozen activists, soldier mothers, Buddhist monks, Russian Orthodox, and Jews; the action had started in Moscow and the goal was to walk to Grozny. They were stopped on the road outside of Samashki and detained for the night by Otryad Militsii Osobogo Naznacheniya (OMON, that is the police special forces), as the village was being destroyed:

> They hold us in the bitter ice cold while Samashki is mercilessly bombed and strafed. A brutal tactic. They are terrorizing the civilians because they know so precisely that there are so few fighters inside. The goal is to root out all resistance.[4]

Russian troops moved into the town after the bombardment on April 7, and went on a two-day killing spree. The report by Memorial, the Russian human rights group, details the circumstances of the deaths of dozens of civilians, most of them by artillery bombardment, shooting, or grenades. Among the first people to enter Samashki after the killings was Viktor Lozinsky, an observer with the Ryazan branch of Memorial. When I met him seven years later in Boston, he showed me a warped piece of porcelain; it had once been a saucer, but had melted. "The temperature at which porcelain melts is 1000 Celsius," Viktor explained. He held in his hand direct evidence that flamethrowers were used in Samashki.[5] Viktor published photos of the remains of bodies and the melted dishes as he had found them on a table in a home. "Who knows how many people sat around that table?" he asked. The name "Samashki" subsequently became a synonym for massacre; actually, not just a massacre, but an operation for terrorizing the population as well. It represented a new line that the Russians had crossed from aerial bombardments to actual punitive operations against the civilian population.

When Vedeno fell, those of us in the General Staff were told to go first from Dargo to Benoi, and then to Sayasan. It was really terribly bleak; I no longer saw any reason to be part of the General Staff, and if I had to die, I wanted a combat death. I saw Shamil briefly in Dargo, and he asked me, "Where is Maskhadov sending you?" I told him, "Sayasan." He replied, "Then that is where you should go." I insisted, "I want to return to the battalion." But he was adamant, "No. You go to Sayasan." He could have drafted me to go with him on the raid he was planning; instead he chose to preserve me. Just as Shamil had told me to leave the fighting in Grozny and help Maskhadov to organize the General Staff, here again, he wanted me to stay alive because I had a solid education. Many of the Chechen highly educated professionals who had many career opportunities left the republic, so among our ranks my education was highly valued.

Several days went by, and I went up to Sayasan. It was very cold and overcast; artillery and aerial bombardments had paused. I was getting very sick, and beginning to suspect that my affliction was more than a recurring cold. After days of intense movement, I had terrible coughing fits and was incapacitated in a field hospital. We returned to Dargo and I think it was on the June 15, 1995 that I saw on television Shamil's extraordinary interview from Budennovsk. It took me a little while to comprehend what had happened and my account here is based on subsequent conversations with Shamil and several of his men.

Some analysts have linked Shamil's dramatic raid into Budennovsk with the bombing that killed his sister and ten others, who were distant family members in Vedeno. I was in Vedeno that day—I think it was in May before the Russian offensive—at six in the morning when a bomb destroyed the home of Shamil's cousin, Khalid Basayev. I helped to dig out the remains of the family. We spent hours sifting through all the rubble and Khalid stood at the edge of the crater, he was so solitary and calm, in a world of his own. The youngest of the dead was a nine-month-old baby.

That evening a man asked me to take him to Shamil so he could express his condolences on the death of Shamil's sister. Shamil didn't let the man complete the customary words of consolation, "My sister died like thousands of others, they are victims of this war and they will go to heaven," Shamil said. He did not want to hear the condolences; he had a different approach to death than the rest of us. Shamil emphasized the difference between war and blood feuds. War is impersonal, whereas murder is very personal. These are completely different situations, in the former there is a readily identifiable murderer. In war it is impossible to unmask the perpetrator; war is political, and impersonal. On several occasions, I have heard Shamil emphasize this difference to his men. More than that, it would be utterly inappropriate to use the fighters, the scarce resources of the resistance, to execute a private blood feud. As a military commander Shamil was very pragmatic, more so than Dudayev or Maskhadov and so it is impossible to imagine that Shamil went to Budennovsk for personal revenge. Shamil went on this mission to end the war and save us all.

Soon after I saw him in Dargo, Shamil had gathered about 119 fighters and told them he needed volunteers to carry out an operation in Russia. I can imagine how they felt: we were surrounded on all sides and Russian propaganda was blaring that they would wipe out all of us, once and for all, and Shamil is saying, "I'm going to take the fight to Russia. Who wants to come with me?" All of them stepped forward except for one man; he had a blood feud, and was the only male in his family. He had to focus on his blood feud, and this was understood by others.

They boarded two Kamaz trucks and a car that they painted to look like a police car. Abu Movsayev, a former policeman, drove the car and handled the police checkpoints. They were driving in the direction of Mineralnye Vody, and Shamil had claimed on several occasions that his goal was the military airport there. I don't think this was true. I've heard him discuss the details of this raid in a narrow circle of trusted people, for instance just Shamil and Maskhadov, and he never gave away his real destination.

My impression is that Maskhadov did not know in advance; it was news to him to find out that Shamil was in Russia. As Shamil explained, he swore not to discuss the intended destination of this mission in case he had to do it again.

Budennovsk was not the intended destination and the attack on the hospital there was improvised. The highways in Russia have checkpoints on the way in and out of cities and the convoy was stopped as it was leaving Budennovsk. The group pretended that the car was accompanying two trucks with bodies of Russian servicemen, "cargo 200." Abu Movsayev, who was dressed in a Russian police uniform started explaining to the police that it's sacrilegious to poke around soldier's corpses. The questioning policeman was asking for documentation to show that indeed this was "cargo 200" bound for the morgue. Shamil related to me later that he was lying on the sleeping shelf in the Kamaz and making eye contact with Abu Movsayev. When the police ordered the convoy to turn around and proceed to Interior Ministry headquarters, Shamil nodded in agreement. The convoy turned back to Budennovsk, accompanied by the traffic police. There again Movsayev tried to dissuade the police from examining the trucks, but they kept insisting. As Shamil described it, there was a moment when Abu Movsayev said to the policeman, "I told you not to do this." This was a signal to the others; Movsayev pulled out an assault rifle from under his jacket and all the others jumped out of the trucks. The fighting at the Interior Ministry headquarters did not last very long. Shamil's men did not try to storm the building and the policemen went to the top floors of the building and shot from there. There were about ten casualties on each side and several wounded. The main consequence of this stand-off was that it exposed the fighters, and required Shamil to stage his main attack in this town.

Shamil ordered the convoy with his wounded to the nearest hospital, which turned out to be a maternity hospital. Shamil remained there while two groups went out to sweep the neighborhood and bring in additional hostages. The second group went to the military airfield and on the way destroyed a bus that was shuttling pilots to the city; some of the pilots were taken prisoner, brought to the hospital, and executed. Shamil estimated that in addition to those who were already in the maternity hospital, the men brought in up to 2,000 additional hostages from the neighborhood. The groups barricaded themselves inside the hospital. They understood that they were not far from the front line, there were Russian military units nearby and it would not take long for them to gather.

Yeltsin was attending the meeting of the G-8 in Halifax, Nova Scotia, and rather than interrupt the conference, he authorized Prime Minister Victor Chernomyrdin to deal with the situation. An Emergency Headquarters was formed that included all the major security services, the *spetz-naz*, the Interior Ministry, and the Federal Counterintelligence Service, the successor to the KGB. The hospital was surrounded. The Russians made three attempts to storm the hospital, with support from tanks and helicopters, which failed to dislodge the Chechens but killed over 100 hostages.

Shamil demonstrated his leadership abilities. He shut off all possible access in and out of the hospital; underground passages and sewers were sealed off. There was no possibility of successfully storming the hospital without killing hostages. At the same time Shamil articulated his political demands: (1) An immediate cessation of military activity, (2) a cease-fire, (3) the withdrawal of Russian forces from Chechnya, and (4) the start of peace talks on Chechnya's long-term political status. Shamil also made it clear that he was completely on his own, that he was operating without any prior approval from Dudayev or Maskhadov. Indeed, the latter commented that he knew nothing about this raid while President Dudayev said that he would have Shamil court-martialed. By stressing his independence from them, Shamil was preserving their political credibility.

Shamil and Chernomyrdin spoke on the satellite phone that belonged to one of the journalists on the scene, and Shamil insisted on his political demands. There were several attempts to offer him money and safe passage, but he turned them down. These conversations were published in the Russian press and broadcast on television.[6] The Russians reverted to their traditional methods: they brought Shamil's relatives, including his brother Shirvani, to Budennovsk, but Shamil did not back down one iota.

The handling of the crisis was different from that of the Nord Ost and Beslan terrorist acts, which followed in 2002 and 2004. The Russian government had not yet stepped into the authoritarian abyss that it did later under Vladimir Putin. I think the personality factor is very important in evaluating this situation. There was no state policy for handling situations like Budennovsk—it was the first such situation—and Chernomyrdin, with all his many faults, displayed some degree of humanity. He was not a "hawk." The security services behaved along the lines of traditional Soviet practice, which held that everyone including the hostages and hostage-takers must die and thereby destroy any full record of the incident. The security services tried to storm several times. They shot at the hospital from a tank and from helicopters, but they never achieved complete control of the situation and this also made a difference. When similar hostage situations occurred in Moscow's theater Nord Ost and in a school at Beslan, the top political leadership was determined to protect the "honor" of the services no matter what. In both cases the security services chose to conduct raids killing hundreds of hostages, whereas in 1994 Chernomyrdin chose to negotiate and most of the hostages survived.

Russia under Yeltsin, although hardly a democracy, was responsive to public opinion and television was independent of the state. Chernomyrdin and Shamil had reached an agreement during a conversation that was broadcast on television. They agreed that Shamil would release most of the hostages, in exchange for the commencement of peace talks. However, some hostages would remain with the fighters until they reached Grozny. Several dozen volunteers substituted themselves for the hostages, including Sergei Kovalev, Andrei Babitsky, and others from among prominent human rights activists and journalists. The FSK headquarters demanded these people to sign statements stating, "I, ____ voluntarily join the bandit group of Shamil Shamil to travel to Chechnya, in full cognizance of all the possible consequences of this action."[7] The FSK at the Emergency Headquarters in Budennovsk considered what sort of consequences there might be later if they killed all the hostages that day.

I can't put Budennovsk in the same category as other acts of terrorism. I view it in the context of Samashki where Russian soldiers carried out a brutal massacre with the deliberate aim of terrorizing the civilian population. At Budennovsk there was no cruelty toward the hostages; there were no cases of rape, or other types of abuses, the civilian casualties were victims of the attempt to storm the hospital and they were killed by Russian "friendly fire." Unlike Nord Ost or Beslan, where the hostage takers deprived the hostages of food and water, in Budennovsk the hostage-takers took risks to get water from nearby stalls because none was being supplied. Of course, they took hostages, and they endangered their lives for political ends, but at the same time there wasn't the element of cruelty and terror toward the civilians; the hostage-takers did not abuse the helpless hostages. Shamil's attack was carried out to stop a greater evil: massive Russian war crimes. And certainly the Russian forces in Chechnya perpetrated far more cruelty and broke all standards of humane or ethical behavior.

The raid led to a cease-fire and the commencement of negotiations; thereby halting military activity and sparing thousands of lives. Budennovsk was very important for us in that it boosted morale and the cease-fire that followed permitted us to regroup. Shamil became even more of a popular hero.

However, from today's vantage point, Budennovsk is viewed mainly as the harbinger of much more terrible acts of terrorism. The precedent of massive hostage taking that it established caused more damage than any temporary advantage that it brought us at the time. I don't think that this cease-fire was crucial for the ultimate outcome of the war. If Shamil had not gone to Budennovsk, we still would have ultimately defeated the Russians, although it would have probably demanded greater efforts and more casualties from our side. I recall commanders in the mountains, who even as we were retreating, were talking about how to stage another offensive in Grozny. It was after all a little more than a year later, in August 1996, after a conventional battle in Grozny that we finally achieved victory over the Russians.

Although the negotiations that were initiated after Budennovsk were broken off a few months later in September 1995 they created the infrastructure, the foundation of contacts and procedures, which became the foundation for the Khasavyurt Peace Treaty in 1996. When the political moment was ripe, General Aleksandr Lebed and Maskhadov, were able to sign a document within days, because this foundation had already been developed and needed only to be reactivated.

The peace talks began in Grozny on June 19 with the participation of the OSCE assistance group, which was headed at the time by Sandor Meszaros. The talks were inconclusive because neither side was willing to make political compromises on the status of Chechnya; however, the experience of negotiations, of resolving practical questions jointly, is a confidence-building measure that is a basic precondition to eventually arriving at a negotiated settlement. The talks created mechanisms for trading prisoners and resolved technical disputes, which were significant steps toward peace. The Russian delegation was headed by Nationalities Minister Vyacheslav Mikhailov, Yelstin confidante and businessman Arkady Volsky, General Anatoly Kulikov, and Nikolai Semenov, the director of the territorial directorate of the Presidential Administration. The Chechen side was headed by Usman Imayev, the General Prosecutor, Aslan Maskhadov, the Chief of Staff, and Akhmed Zakayev, Minister of Culture. The first session was extremely tense and according to Imayev, it was due to the efforts of the OSCE mediators that the talks continued. Both sides wanted to use the talks to support their version of Chechnya's status, and at the outset could not agree on terminology. The Russians called us the "Chechen Republic" whereas we called ourselves the "Chechen Republic Ichkeria" and they called our army "illegal armed formations." This remained a problem for the duration of the negotiations, but was mitigated at the suggestion of the OSCE representatives, by creating two sets of original documents, with the preferred terminology for each side. Although the first round was tense and tedious for both sides, it did produce a moratorium on military activity and a decision to develop a framework for continued negotiations. Although minor incidents continued—Russians occasionally continued to bomb us and our forces occasionally attacked them—we developed effective mechanisms to stop these incidents before they escalated. We had a system of notification from any point of conflict to the Joint Control Commission, a team of officers charged with monitoring the implementation of the moratorium. Information was transmitted rapidly and this system was effective, exhibiting good will on both sides.

The second round of talks commenced on June 27 and in three days reached important decisions: prisoners would be exchanged on the principle of "all for all," a portion of Chechen forces would be disbanded, and the others would form new local self-defense units. The majority of Russian forces would be withdrawn and free elections would be held.

There were two incidents early in the process that could have derailed the proceedings completely. Arkady Volsky, on a secret mission from Yeltsin offered Dudayev to resign his office and move to a third country, which was angrily dismissed. The second was the murder of a Chechen family, seven people including five young children, whose bodies were carried to the center of Grozny by relatives sparking a spontaneous rally, which the pro-Russian police was getting ready to disperse.

On June 20, the sides signed a protocol determining the range of items that the negotiating teams would work on. They included military issues (such as stationing Russian forces in Chechnya, cessation of military activities, and prisoner exchange), political issues (conditions for holding elections and the status of Chechnya), and economic issues (restoration of the economy and support to the elderly and war victims.) The agreement stipulated inadmissibility of the use of force, and that all further disagreements must be resolved through peaceful means. On July 23, the sides reached a comprehensive agreement, "On the Regulation of the Crisis in the Chechen Republic," which was comprised of political and social measures, and the military block. Separate teams of negotiators were to work out comprehensive agreements in each of these areas. Unfortunately, the processes stalled after this point and only the military block agreement was fully elaborated, and finally signed on July 30, 1995.[8]

The talks on the military block proceeded painfully, with the delegations headed by Maskhadov and General Romanov arguing vehemently over seemingly minute points. Maskhadov complained that the Russians frequently paused negotiations to call the Kremlin for guidance; they were unwilling to make even minute decisions on their own. The agreement called for creating a Joint Monitoring Commission (of which I became a member along with Husein Iskhanov, Maskadov's adjutant), exchange of prisoners, gradual withdrawal of Russian troops contemporaneously

with the disarmament of Chechen armed formations, end to terrorism and diversionary tactics, and formation of self-defense units
from among those Chechen formations that were not dissolved.

There was an interesting intrigue around a provision in the
military block that condemned terrorism and all diversionary
tactics and stated that the "[T]he delegation of the Government
of the Chechen Republic Ichkeria condemns the terrorist act in
Budennovsk and will assist the Russian side in apprehending and
arresting Shamil and his group, which are accused of this terrorist act." For the Russians this was a necessary face-saving measure, which we signed, with the unspoken understanding that it
would not be fulfilled. Maskhadov told me that during a break in
the proceedings, Shirvani Basayev, Shamil Basyev's brother, had
come up to him and told him that Shamil understood that the
Chechen delegation had to agree to this term, and that Shirvani
had passed a similar message to Dudayev. Shamil assented to this
quietly, and let them know he understood that they needed to
state this publicly; at the same time it was understood that this
provision would not be implemented.

I attended a meeting of the General Staff during which
Maskhadov spoke in very glowing terms about the Russo-
Chechen agreement on military arrangements calling it an
important achievement. So it came as a shock to all of us when
Dudayev at a meeting of the State Defense Committee gave a
very negative assessment of this agreement, denounced Usman
Imayev, the head of the delegation, in the most abusive language, and abruptly fired him. I think there were probably several contributing factors for Dudayev who was not participating
in the talks became suspicious of Imayev and thought that he
made too many concessions. Imayev made substantial political
concessions by agreeing to disband the government, form coali-
tions with the pro-Russian opposition, and organize elections
on the basis of the Russian and Chechen Constitutions. We
could accept the principle of free elections, but we could not
agree to have them on the basis of the Russian Constitution.
Maskhadov once commented to me that, "We caught Imayev
just in time before he could sign a federative treaty with the
Russians." Nevertheless, it's very hard to believe that Imayev
betrayed Dudayev, and the story became murkier when Imayev

disappeared without a trace the following year after going to hold talks with the Russians. All efforts by his relatives to locate him were fruitless.

I suspect that Dudayev may have understood earlier than the others that the Russians had developed a tactic of using the elections to get us to accept a status within Russia. Despite Dudayev's vocal criticism of the proceedings, Maskhadov had remained firmly behind the "Agreement on the Military Block of Questions" and insisted that it be implemented. I don't think that Maskhadov failed to notice that the political block had stalled, but through forging ahead with the military block he permitted the cease-fire to remain in place for four months, which probably saved thousands of lives. Maskhadov's tenacity in pursuing these talks testified to his willpower and his faith that negotiations would eventually be successful. Dudayev hoped they would resolve all questions quickly, and when he saw that the Russians were playing games, first by attempts to bribe him, and then by trying to use this concept of the elections based on Russian Constitution, he started to focus on keeping the cease-fire in place while building up the capacity of our fighters. Maskhadov was dragging out the negotiations as long as possible, to maintain the cease-fire.

Dudayev named Khozh Akhmed Yarikhanov, the Minister of Education, to replace Imayev as Head of the negotiating team. Yarikhanov had frictions with Maskhadov because Dudayev was trying to slow down the military negotiations. From the Russian perspective, if Chechen units disarmed, Dudayev would lose control. Even if Moscow complied with the promise to withdraw militarily from Chechnya, they could roll back in at any time.

In early July, Husein Iskhanov, Maskhadov's adjutant, and I received permission to visit our families, who lived in the same district of Grozny. It was a very surreal experience for us to return home. During combat in the winter we were so preoccupied with the death and violence all around us that we barely noticed what had happened to the city. As we walked, I could not recognize the city where I had grown up and lived my whole life. It's not enough to say that buildings had been destroyed, I couldn't tell where in the city I was, the familiar landmarks were all gone, it wasn't the same city, and everything was covered in deep layers of dust.

A couple of months earlier my family returned from Gekhi-Chu where my mother and sisters spent the winter with my uncle. Everyone was home when I arrived. In Chechen families no one is supposed to show emotion, but of course my mother and sisters broke down in tears. Soon several neighbors came over to compare stories and to hear about the negotiations. It was a bittersweet reunion; I listened to their painful recollections and heard how they suffered. I slept in my own bed that night in a deep calm that I had not experienced since the start of the war.

The negotiations were proceeding with certain gains for our side. Among the points of contention was the issue concerning which Chechen units should disband. The Russians were insisting on all of our units and we were saying only the guerrilla units that had formed at the beginning of the war. The more the Russians insisted on this point, the more Maskhadov and Dudayev focused on the so called "self-defense units" which, according to the agreement, would be formed out of the units that had been dissolved. Most Chechen volunteers came to the front in groups of ten to fifteen from a particular village. It was not a problem for them to disband and then reconstitute themselves as "self-defense units." Under the terms of the agreement, the Russians would provide them with weapons. The reason the Russians permitted this, as far as I can tell, is that they had an inflated sense of the size of the Chechen forces, which they estimated to be between 10,000–15,000 men. They considered the smaller self-defense units the lesser of two evils. In reality we never had more than 3,000–4,000 fighters at any one time, which the Russians were now arming for us.

The program for buying arms from the general population was doomed from the beginning because the government offered by far less for weapons than their market value. If one wanted to sell weapons, they would fetch a better price at the arms market. Both sides maintained the ritual for the sake of appearances, the commission traveled to a town or village, the people's representatives handed over old useless items, for the most part hunting rifles, but sometimes we'd come across real "antiques"—like a German World War II-era submachine gun and other rarities. A detailed list was compiled and then the weapons were placed in a pile and a tank drove over them. On some occasions the pile was exploded. Journalists were invited to report on the proceedings.

The process of exchanging prisoners was complicated to the extreme by our very different interpretations of what was happening in Chechnya. For the Russians there was no war, there was no state of emergency, there was no special legal regime of any kind. They were "restoring constitutional order" and wanted to avoid giving Chechen combatants the status of prisoners of war at all costs. Anyone taken prisoner in Chechnya holding weapons was accused of having taken part in an insurrection or illegal possession of firearms, and similar charges. Chechen combatants were considered felons. Of course, even this is an idealization; many prisoners were executed on the spot. Russian servicemen held prisoner by the Chechens were also not considered prisoners of war, they were considered hostages. At one point, the Russian side presented us with a list of 1,400 Chechens who had been arrested throughout Russia prior to December 1994. This list was rejected outright, but it exhibited the type of maneuver that the Russians were trying to employ. In the end, I think the final list contained roughly 1,400 Chechen prisoners, including combatants and civilians who were rounded up at "filtration camps." The Russian side had an inflated notion of how many Russian prisoners there were because they would not accept the documents that were taken from dead soldiers and they insisted we had taken them from living men. It was very difficult to identify bodies because of the mayhem in the city. Because the Russians refused to consider a humanitarian cease-fire, many bodies decomposed in the streets, and were eaten by stray dogs. Many others were buried in mass graves that in some cases were marked and later disinterred, but in other cases were lost.

Our government was trying to prove that it was worthy of recognition as a state, hence, our parliament ratified the Geneva Conventions. Maskhadov issued orders to ensure strict adherence to the protocols governing the treatment of prisoners of war. We were trying to demonstrate that we were an army, not a rag tag group of fighters, and in the beginning made many goodwill gestures, such as freeing prisoners, which the Kremlin chose not to reciprocate, calling such overtures "propagandistic speculation." It was an attempt to encourage Moscow to accept civilized rules of engagement, but the Kremlin could only see political maneuver behind it.

This stalemate could not be resolved though normal legal channels. During the nearly four months that our commission was functioning only nine prisoners were exchanged through official channels, four Russians and five Chechens. This unsatisfactory situation created a whole network of informal trades and eventually led to the sale of prisoners and later the development of a kidnapping industry that flourished during 1996–99. After a particularly inappropriate instance of a Russian buying a prisoner, Maskhadov stormed out of a commission meeting, and said, "When will you stop encouraging this slave trade?"

On October 5, General Romanov's car and an accompanying APC were blown up, probably by a remote-control mine in Minutka Square, resulting in the deaths of three soldiers, wounding ten others, and putting the general in a coma. I had a friend who claimed to know one of the people involved in the attack, and according to him they were all from Samashki and most of them were avenging relatives who had been killed in the massacre committed under Romanov's command. On October 8, Russian planes bombed the house in Roshni-Chu where Dudayev had spent the night. He was not hurt, but several family members living in the house were killed. This attack was supposed to signal Russian revenge for the attempt on General Romanov and the resumption of war.

On October 9, I went home to see my family, thinking that I should take this opportunity before leaving the city again. I spent the night at home but in the morning I woke to the sound of APCs rumbling down the street. I looked out the window and saw a whole armada of vehicles and soldiers. I checked my submachine gun; I had an ammunition clip and five grenades, and for a few seconds I thought about how to position myself. But then my mother and sisters came into my room, my mother soundlessly was mouthing, "They will kill you, they will kill you!" and I realized that I couldn't return fire because that would bring retribution down on my family. I gave my submachine gun to my sisters and told them all to hide in the shed, not to approach the Russians, and definitely not to plead on my behalf because that could only embolden them. They did as I said, and I sat in my room and waited. These may have been the worst moments of my life. I was sure they would come for me and I couldn't defend myself, if I tried to fight they would kill my whole family, and probably the neighbors too.

I sat there for fifteen to twenty minutes and then the street seemed to come alive, one after another, eight APCs rolled past my window and were gone. I stayed at home for another couple of hours; my sister went outside to find out what had happened. The Russians had apparently arrested someone for the assassination attempt against Romanov. On my way back to the mission it was hard to get a taxi to take me through Russian checkpoints; no one wanted to take any chances.

I can't remember if there were specific events that signaled the resumption of the war. I think the Russians started to intensify their bombardment of our positions and we started to attack their garrisons, checkpoints, and columns of vehicles. Both sides were slowly getting involved in full-scale combat once again.

I remained in Grozny until the end of October. When one of my friends heard my cough, they insisted I get a chest x-ray. We went to the hospital and I was told that I had a very advanced stage of tuberculosis. The doctors did not think that I would live very long. I was very lucky because Sophie Chihab and Mayrbek Vyachegaev, a well-known analyst and activist, happened to come to see me. Sophie was a reporter for *Le Monde* who had come to Grozny to interview Maskhadov and Mayrbek had accompanied her. I had a terrible coughing fit in their presence, and seeing my condition Sophie offered to take me back to France for treatment. Mayrbek helped me travel to Tours where I was treated, and then spent the next several months recovering in Paris.

CHAPTER 4

MASKHADOV IS ELECTED PRESIDENT

The credit and glory for the battle of Grozny belongs to two men, Shamil Basayev and Aslan Maskhadov. Maskhadov was the strategic thinker, the one who developed and planned our strategy and Shamil was the head of the garrison, which meant that everyone bearing arms in Grozny was under his command. Everything the Chechen fighters accomplished was the result of Shamil's leadership. The character and talents of these two men complemented each other during the war and both were indispensable to our victory. The authority of General Dzhokhar Dudayev, whom both men served loyally, and the necessity to overcome differences in order to wage war effectively, overrode any competitive instinct. However, after Dudayev's death the differences between these two war heroes took on a fractious character during the Presidential election.

General Dudayev was killed on April 21, 1996 near the village of Gekhi-Chu in the western part of Chechnya while talking on his satellite phone. The Chechen leadership kept his death a secret for two days, while they discussed who would succeed him as President. Top leaders including Maskhadov, Shamil, Gelayev, Zelimkhan Yandarbiyev, and others met and some of them wanted to keep Dudayev's death a secret because it would undermine morale. Others, including Maskhadov and Shamil wanted to announce it right away. There was no debate over who would succeed Dudayev; it was understood that it would be Yandarbiyev, whom Dudayev had appointed Vice President in the spring of 1993. However, there was some concern because no official decree specifying his appointment existed; so a decree was written and back dated, and it reflected Yandarbiyev's status and position. The announcement of Dudayev's death and Yandarbiyev's appointment as Acting President was made on April 23, 1996. The death of Dudayev was a major blow to morale, but it did not have a substantial impact on the unity of the resistance, its tactics, or overall effectiveness.[1]

In March 1996, the Chechens had taken back Grozny for two days. The resistance entered the city, shot over everyone's heads, made a lot of noise, and left. This was a reconnaissance mission. It had been planned by Maskhadov together with the head of the operational staff, Mumadi Saidayev. To prepare for the major attack to come later in the year, they studied the locations of the Russian garrisons, the check-points, and commandant's offices. Throughout February small diversionary units had tested the defenses of the garrisons by nuisance attacks and imitations of ambushes, they also investigated possible routes that Russian forces could use for bringing in reinforcements.

Ruslan Gelayev, the Commander for the Southwestern Front was in command of the operation in the city. Gelayev's unit staged a diversion in the large village of Sernovodskoye, which is close to the administrative border between Ingushetia and Chechnya. Early in the morning on March 6 roughly 350 fighters, including those who spontaneously joined the operation, entered Grozny from the south, north, and the southwest. For two days they held most of the city, including the neighborhoods of Zavodskoi, Oktyabrskii, and Staropromyslovskii. In the course of the operation the local pro-Moscow police departments were completely destroyed, and most of the police either surrendered or ran away. The Russian soldiers were entirely on the defensive; they barricaded themselves in commandant's offices and other sturdy buildings, and broadcast desperate pleas for help over the radio. After a couple of columns were ambushed on the roads into the city, the Russians gave up trying to reach those who had been pinned down. After these two days, Maskhadov ordered the fighters to withdraw and they left in an orderly fashion without any resistance from the opposing side. Several diversionary units remained in the city and continued intermittent fighting through March 12.

This operation preceded our capturing the city in August 1996. Maskhadov had learned everything necessary to plan the next attack. The key mistake the Russian command made was that from March until August it did not change anything in the way it defended the commandant's offices, in positioning the garrisons, or in the system of check-points and communications. There were no lessons learned about tactics to repel an attack, and no improvements were made in the way Russian units communicated and cooperated with each other.

The Chechen resistance struck a devastating blow against the Russian forces in Grozny on August 6, as President Boris Yeltsin was being sworn into office for a second five-year term. The 1996 Russian Presidential elections required two rounds of balloting. After the first round on June 16, Yeltsin invited the charismatic paratrooper General Aleksandr Lebed, who had come in third in the voting, to join his administration as Security Council (SC) Secretary and Presidential Representative to Chechnya. Lebed's support was crucial in securing Yeltsin's victory over Zyuganov in the second round on July 3. The strike against Russian garrisons in Grozny was timed to coincide with Yeltsin's second inauguration both for its anti-Moscow impact and because many senior Russian commanders left Chechnya to attend the celebrations in the capital. Up to 7,000 Russian troops were trapped inside the city, which fell to Chechen fighters in those early August days.

The division of labor between Maskhadov and Shamil was the same as it has been in January 1995. Maskhadov developed strategy and Shamil commanded on the ground. Shamil was extremely disappointed on August 23 when Maskhadov agreed to General Lebed's offer of a cease-fire and began negotiations that would lead to the signing of the Khasavyurt Agreement on August 30. At the time, Shamil had several Russian garrisons fenced in and pinned down and for him this was not the right moment for a cease-fire. As the ground commander, Shamil felt certain that with another few days of active fighting, the core of the Russian army in Chechnya would collapse. He wanted to press the attack until the Russians admitted defeat, which would force them to recognize the Chechen state. For Yeltsin, it was convenient to burden Lebed, the charismatic paratrooper General, with responsibility to end a war that was unpopular and embarrassing for the Russian President. In his testimony to the Russian Duma, Lebed commented that he saw thousands of Russian soldiers surrendering.

> When I arrived there the Russian Group of Forces was on the verge of defeat—1181 men were trapped without food, water, or medicine. Ammunition was running out. Units were starting to surrender. Not just eighteen-year-old soldiers, but the whole army, the Krasnodar OMON, a police battalion from Tolyatti.... Was it really worth carrying on in such a situation?... There could be no talk of victory.[2]

On August 20 General Konstantin Pulikovsky, the Commander of Russia's Group of Forces, made his famous ultimatum that in forty-eight hours he would bomb Grozny so hard that nothing would be left. Terrified civilians began streaming out of the city. But Pulikovsky was helpless on the ground; he couldn't stop the disintegration of his army. During those days in August, Shamil and Maskhadov had real differences, possibly for the first time. Later, when the two men became political rivals, this topic was debated repeatedly in public. Maskhadov's judgment was that although the Russian army in Chechnya may have been on the brink of collapse, more Russian armies were not that far away—a few more days of fighting would not have broken Russia's political will, but would have only brought greater retribution against Chechnya's decimated and exhausted population.

The peace treaty was signed by Lebed and Maskhadov in the presence of the OSCE assistance group representative, Swiss diplomat Tim Guldimann. Since 1995 the OSCE Assistance Group for Peaceful Resolution had an internationally mandated presence in Chechnya. Guldimann who started to head up this mission in January 1996 was particularly active and skillful at bringing the sides closer together and played a very constructive role in this process. The treaty contained a great deal of "constructive ambiguity" that was instrumental to bringing an end to the hostilities, but provided an imprecise framework to guide subsequent

negotiations on the question of Chechnya's status.[3] The main provision of the treaty stipulated that:

> The treaty on the fundamentals of relations between the Russian
> Federation and the Chechen Republic to be determined in accor-
> dance with generally recognized norms of international law shall
> be reached prior to December 31, 2001.

The Russian government continued to insist that Chechnya was
part of the Russian Federation; we Chechens continued to insist
that we were de facto independent. The sides were temporarily
willing, for the sake of expedience, to conduct talks and reach
agreements without determining the question of status.

The Khasavyurt Treaty established a joint commission to be
comprised of representatives from the Russian Federation and the
Chechen Republic that would oversee the withdrawal of forces,
coordinate crime-fighting and counter-terrorism efforts, restore
fiscal and budgetary relations between Russia and Chechnya,
and coordinate humanitarian relief efforts. The treaty stipulated
that the question of Chechnya's status would be decided through
negotiations over a five-year period, but significantly did not out-
line a process for decision making. The joint commission was not
empowered by the Khasavyurt Treaty to define the relationship
between the two entities. In effect the Khasavyurt Treaty ended
hostilities by postponing all the difficult questions and without
establishing clear processes for resolving them. Would the negotiations last five years? How would the parties reach decisions?
Would there be referenda? What would happen if talks between
the sides broke down? Would there be international mediation or
observation of the negotiation process? The Khasavyurt Treaty
was silent on these crucial procedural questions.

After the battle of Grozny was over, Shamil announced that
his work was done and he retired to his beehives in Vedeno.
During the war he had said that if he lived to see the end of it,
he would become a beekeeper, and Maskhadov had asserted that
he would become a gardener. Instead, Maskhadov became the
Acting Prime Minister and coordinated the joint activities of the
Chechen and Russian armed forces in Chechnya. Shamil took

on a nominal position as director of border guards and customs; what had been his central command became the bureaucracy of customs officers and border guards. He was responsible for setting up the customs posts on the Chechen borders but he rarely left Vedeno. Instead, his subordinates would visit the new posts and report back to him.

Shamil had suffered a leg wound and it needed medical attention. He spent his days at home in Vedeno, where he had hundreds of visitors. His visitors included relatives of fallen fighters in search of friends or family members, Dudayev's ministers who had made themselves scarce during the war and now wanted to come back to government; this was so even for civil servants such as tax collectors who wanted to reclaim their former positions. And then there were the soothsayers and faith healers who came to tell him about their premonitions. He listened patiently to all these people and tried to sort out their situations. Sometimes he got annoyed and chased everyone out of his house, but most of the time he spoke with dozens of supplicants who had a variety of questions and requests.

On a couple of occasions Shamil and I visited Atagi, where Rizvan Lorsanov lived and where several meetings between Maskhadov and Lebed had been conducted. These meetings had resulted in the Khasavyurt Treaty. Next to Lorsanov's house was Yandarbiyev's house, which had been seized by campaign activity.

After Dudayev's death in April 1996, Yandarbiyev became Acting President and presumed he would be favored for the Presidency. He was the elder figure from the armed resistance; he was involved in the 1991 congress, which declared independence, and he wore the mantle of continuity with Dudayev. Somehow his men managed to procure a Chaika, which was the favored car of government officials in the Soviet Union, and three months before the elections, Yandarbiyev's aides were buffing and waxing his Chaika. Shamil and I smirked; there they were fussing over a Soviet status symbol and behaving as though they had already won the race. Shamil met with Yandarbiyev several times; I was rarely present and on those occasions when I was in the room, I did not speak.

During this time, articles in the Russian press started to favor Maskhadov. They were writing about him as though he already was the President and this was a real disservice. The press made him sound as though he was the dove and those comments had a Soviet flavor: they included quotes from fellow officers from his Soviet army days about what a good officer he was. The Russian press cast Maskhadov as the most conciliatory of the Chechen elite to conduct talks with Russia. These articles annoyed Shamil and, of course, did not help Maskhadov with the Chechen public. The first time that Shamil mentioned that he was thinking about running for president was after reading an article about Maskhadov, "What if I try for it?" he asked.

"You can run, but you have to realize that there are real obstacles in your path," I responded. "First, you are only thirty-two years old, which is younger than the constitutional age requirement of thirty-five; second, there are political factors. I doubt that Yandarbiyev will win because I don't think that the average person likes him very much, but in the mind of the voters all that they associate with you is war. People are exhausted by this war and Maskhadov can run as a peace-maker. It's hard to say how it will turn out, but we can try." Shamil decided very quickly, probably within the course of this conversation, that he would run despite my reservations.

He summoned a dozen of his closest associates for a meeting in Shali at the home of "Big Aslanbek" (Aslanbek Abdulkhadzhiyev). Among those present were "Little Aslanbek" (Aslanbek Ismailov), Abu Movsayev, Khunkharpasha Israpilov, and several mid-level commanders from the Buddenovsk raid. Most were enthusiastic about his candidacy, but Khunkharpasha and I voiced our concerns. Khunkharpasha argued that we should stay out of politics and I said that Shamil's electorate was limited to those who fought and it would be difficult to expand beyond that circle. We started thinking about who else his constituency could be. All of our commanders represented the southeastern region. There were also considerations of *teip* and of Sufi orders, these were important channels. We began considering which contacts and networks we could activate to reach out to other sections of the country.

A candidate in Chechnya does not declare himself; rather his circle nominates him, and becomes his campaign team. Little Aslanbek became the head of the campaign staff and it was decided that we would persuade the parliament to adopt an amendment to the constitution to lower the age threshold for the presidency.

There were already sixteen candidates for the presidency and the key players were leaders of the resistance: Yandarbiyev was the leading candidate, then Maskhadov, then the younger tier of commanders: Shamil, Arsanov, and Zakayev.

Each had his own slogan: Udugov's was "Islamic Order" and he had the best posters. There were no adequate printing presses in Chechnya and posters were printed abroad and imported. He had enormous glossy posters of himself in a lambskin hat, the *papakha*, gazing up toward the heavens. I learned later from Boris Berezovsky, a businessman who was influential in Russia, that he had supported Udugov and Zakayev during the elections. At the time we noticed only that they seemed to have a limitless supply of expensive posters. Zakayev had posters saying: "Warrior, Leader, Patriot," among the jokers this quickly became "Actor-Warrior" because Zakayev had been an actor before the war, and we joked that even in his fatigues he looked theatrical.

Vakha Arsanov turned out to be the cleverest politician. His alliance with Maskhadov became a winning combination: nearly 60 percent of the electorate voted for them out of sixteen candidates. Arsanov had been a member of Chechnya's first parliament in the early 1990s and became a famous commander during the war. Although Arsanov was not as talented as Shamil or Gelayev, he had tremendous authority among his men who were drawn largely from the mountain *teip*, the Chaberloi. He managed to form a highly disciplined unit, with highly competent commanders at the mid- and junior levels. In 1996, Dudayev had appointed Arsanov to command the northwest front, and although they were involved in only one major battle, near the village of Dolininskaya at the beginning of the war, Arsanov's unit had earned a reputation for a great degree of daring and careful planning.

Arsanov represented the Cheberloi; which is the largest of the mountain *teips* and some of the smaller mountain *teips* followed them. Many of the Cheberloi had moved to the lowland, to the fifteenth Sovkhoz and other towns, so they were able to bring along some of those districts. This was a much wider electorate than the armed resistance; it was an entire region. Arsanov was smart, and he was aware of his limitations. After declaring his candidacy, he went to Maskhadov and struck a deal—he agreed to bring along the Cheberloi if Maskhadov would put him on the ticket as his Vice President. From Maskhadov's point of view this was a good alliance. The move sidelined other young commanders because they could not do the same; their honor would not permit them to accept positions inferior to a young commander.

Yandarbiyev's strategy was to arrange meetings with candidates and explain to them that the armed resistance should endorse one candidate. I wasn't present in those meetings, and although the commanders did not laugh in his face, they laughed later. A pious speech about a "united" candidate and the assumption that this candidate could only be the old lion Yandarbiyev could not earn their respect. Yandarbiyev understood that these young ruffians were his most serious challengers and he also saw that they were mocking him. Yandarbiyev's significant advantage was that he was the presumptive heir who represented continuity with Dudayev, a claim that every faction wanted to make.

After Shamil announced his candidacy the number of visitors to his home doubled. Journalists and businessmen streamed in from Moscow. The businessmen wanted to sponsor him and claimed to have in-roads to the Kremlin. These men had information, contacts, and money. Some were Chechens from Moscow, but there were also Russians and plenty of other post-Soviet nationals. I can't blame Shamil for being interested in these men; we could not offer him financial help or new information. He asked me to stay out of this "nuthouse" and write his election platform. I didn't have a formal role in his campaign, we were friends and he thought that I could articulate his ideas in a clear and diplomatic style.

I attempted to write something very general and to make few promises because it was obvious how difficult the situation would be. It was a fairly laconic document, several pages long. The main points were: continuity with Dudayev's policy; post-war rehabilitation; building a democratic and independent Chechen state; and establishing transparent relations with Russia. The document stressed that the Chechen state should protect basic rights and freedoms and be in accordance with international law. Our position on relations with Russia was that we should obtain full diplomatic recognition and build normal, equal, interstate relations. Shamil was open to currency and customs union, joint border patrols, and, if need be, dissolving the Chechen army; but all of that would come only if Russia recognized Chechnya's sovereignty. The formula was something like: "We must take ordered steps toward establishing equal, transparent, and neighborly relations." Shamil stressed that he would seek compensation from Russia for the damage sustained to the infrastructure and economic potential of Chechnya. To rebuild and develop Chechnya, he would also seek international investment.

Shamil spoke frequently all over the country and crowds turned out to hear him speak, which created the impression he had a huge following. Campaign events were held in any large public space that was still standing: mosques, university buildings, schools, and places of business. The audiences seemed to enjoy his improvised presentations and he was comfortable with the crowds, made jokes, and was very charming. In contrast to the pathos-filled slogans and messages of most other candidates, Shamil's slogan "2 +2 = 4," was characteristic of his style to mock the overblown slogans of the others. Unfortunately, as the campaign season progressed his speeches became increasingly aggressive against the other candidates, particularly against Maskhadov. In the end, this had a negative impact on his performance in the polls.

On one occasion, Shamil, a few other fellows, and I were sitting around talking about this problem: How best to assert continuity with Dzhokhar Dudayev? And someone had the idea of bringing in Vakha Ibragimov, who was with Dudayev the day he was killed and had sustained a wound. None of us knew him, we had fought on a different front; all we knew about him was that he was one of Dudayev's advisors and was with Dudayev at the end. Shamil asked someone to go find Ibragimov and said, "On the way, find out his first name, and ask him to be Vice President on the ticket." This particular improvisation turned out to be a grave error.

Vakha Ibragimov broke a taboo among the top commanders. They did not permit their internal disagreements to spill over into the public, whereas Vakha started to publicly attack Maskhadov. His main complaint was that Maskhadov was acceptable to Russia, and how could we place our future with a man who was acceptable to the country that had drowned us all in blood? I was bitterly opposed to this whole line and thought it was a big mistake. Such statements cast Shamil as the war-time President. Maskhadov had given the people peace and for that we were attacking him? Shamil had an argument, too. He could have said, "I brought the peace because I did all the dirty work." In Budennovsk it was Shamil and in Grozny it was Shamil. This could have been the message; instead it was all slander against Maskhadov. There were a few initial joint statements from the Shamil-Ibragimov ticket, over which I protested to Shamil, but no one was listening to me any more. The rest of the group, the two Alsanbeks, Vakha, Shamil started to meet without me. I saw what was happening and I distanced myself from this inner circle. To Maskhadov's credit, he never responded in kind and Shamil's political immaturity was very much evident. As the campaign wore on the rhetoric worsened, and they improvised to make Maskhadov look bad, to needle him in some way.

On New Year's Eve in 1997, Shamil came up with an idea, "Let's go to all the other headquarters and wish them a Happy New Year." I stayed behind because I never liked these little outings, but they came back laughing and very pleased with themselves. "I have seen 'Islamic Order'—it's an Islamic orgy," exclaimed Shamil. Apparently, champagne was flowing at the Udugov headquarters. Shamil had quit smoking and even quit drinking coffee and there was definitely no alcohol at our campaign headquarters. He understood very well that some of us might drink privately, but he did not tolerate our drinking in public. Shamil brought up the "Islamic orgy" in a campaign speech, and Udugov said about Shamil, "Do you really want that petty dictator to be President?" They displayed contempt for one another, so I was very surprised when I saw Udugov at Shamil's house around the time of Shamil's resignation as Prime Minister in 1998 and the fateful beginning of the Congress of Nations of Ichkeria and Chechnya. I had never seen Udugov in Shamil's company before, although it's possible that he may have visited when I was not there; I just remember being very surprised to see him.

The Presidential elections were held on January 27, 1997 and were deemed free and fair by an OSCE team of seventy observers. The leader of the OSCE assistance group, Tim Guldimann said that the elections were "exemplary" and "reflected the will of the Chechen people." Tim and his group did a great deal to make these elections possible. The OSCE provided funding and technical support so that the process would go smoothly; they facilitated voter registration, printing ballots, campaigning, and the counting was completed in a short amount of time by people who had little experience conducting elections.[4] There was enormous enthusiasm among the population; this was the first truly free election, and it heralded a new beginning.

The day the results were announced we were at the campaign headquarters. There were probably twenty of us in a basement, a large space that housed our computers, printers, and copiers. Russian and Chechen television announced that the counting was over and Maskhadov had almost 60 percent, Shamil had 22 percent, and Yandarbiyev had 10 percent of the vote. Voter participation was nearly 80 percent.[5] Shamil came down to thank the technical personnel for their efforts during the campaign, "The Central Electoral Commission says that we got only 22 percent of the votes. Personally, I find consolation in the fact that the best 22 percent of our society, those who are the most determined and committed to our independence believed in us, and gave us their vote. For me, and I am sure that for all of you also, this is sufficient honor and reward."

There was a brief pause before the others started speaking. Each wanted to know what Shamil would do next and what all the rest of us would do. Shamil was not responding to questions and comments; he sat down on a chair and did not speak at all, he wasn't making eye contact with anyone. He sat like that for an hour. Each one of us expressed our opinion about what should happen next. Some said, "We have to appeal the election results." Others said, "We came in second place, let's ask for a portion of the ministerial positions." Vakha Ibragimov was in this group and was angling to become Foreign Minister. Another idea being bantered around was to seize power by force; another idea was to ask for a recount of the votes, or have new elections. Shamil took no part in this discussion; he just listened to the different arguments.

I said, "What I am hearing scares me. I had said at the start of this campaign that you cannot win by attacking Maskhadov and now it is not his fault that he won. The Chechen state is in its infancy and today we are standing at the source of its political life, and you are saying, 'Let's not recognize the results of the election and stage an armed revolt?' You do this today and someone else will topple you tomorrow. If we cannot help Maskhadov, at the very least we should not hinder him. The political strategy is simple, if we are not in the government, we should take out our pencils and write down all the mistakes of this government and in five years we base a campaign on their real mistakes, not on our petty squabbles."

Shamil just sat there, I don't know if he was listening; he didn't respond to what was being said. When he finally spoke, he asked for a Koran and someone brought him an old tome. He took this Koran, stood up, and said, "Let's go." We didn't know where we were going or why. We were joined by various supporters Shamil's bodyguards, the two Aslanbeks. There must have been seventy or eighty fully armed men in a dozen cars. I had Shamil's old Niva with a bullet hole from a sniper shot; and I had to push it to get it started. Most of the others had Jeeps by then, so I let everyone pass before me, so the column would not stall every time I did. Once we were on Staropromyslovkoye highway I understood that we were going to see Maskhadov. He was staying with relatives in Pervomaiskoye; his own house had burned down completely.

When we arrived, we found five guards in front and Maskhadov's wife, Kusama came out to greet us. She was a little nervous, but she was very polite and invited us to come inside. Shamil responded that we would wait outside for Aslan. "He's not here, I'll send for him," she sounded a little uncertain.

I did not know why we were there, and neither did the guards or Kusama. We stood around making small talk for about half an hour, when Vakha Arsanov and his guards, roughly fifteen men, appeared. When they came up, Shamil congratulated Arsanov, and only then did Maskhadov appear. The guards explained that Maskhadov came through a back door, but I didn't see anyone drive up to the back of the house. Most likely Maskhadov's guards kept him out of sight until Arsanov and his men arrived.

Shamil congratulated Maskhadov, who asked us to come inside, but Shamil refused.

"We will come back another day for a social visit. Today we have a different purpose," and with that Shamil raised the Koran, "We came to swear to you and for you to swear to us that we will travel together on one path. While we all have one goal—our independence; while you permit no one to deceive you; so we honor the dead and we swear our allegiance to you."

When Aslan first appeared he had a rather cautious expression. I think that until Shamil raised the Koran, Maskhadov and those around him, expected only trouble from our visit. Shamil's words that he and his comrades in arms were there to swear loyalty to the legally elected President and wanted to hear a similar oath in response was a total surprise for Maskhadov. Shamil's words released the tension from the situation and Maskhadov responded in kind. Standing in the center of the semicircle of men, placing his hand on the Koran that Shamil held out to him, Maskhadov responded with his own oath:

> Addressing you, and with Allah as my witness, I will say what I intend to say to the whole Chechen nation. I swear to my unwavering faithfulness and loyalty to the values of Islam, to the ways and traditions of our ancestors, and in the indomitable striving of our nation to freedom and independence.

Maskhadov was visibly moved and it occurred to me that I had never before seen him nervous. I was proud of Shamil that day. He had disregarded the crazy ideas swirling around that basement, and made the right decision, which became binding for all of us. His gesture of reconciliation was very much in keeping with Chechen tradition and seemed, at least for a time, to reunite our camps.

CHAPTER 5

MASKHADOV'S IMPOSSIBLE QUANDARY

The last Russian army unit left Grozny on New Year's eve 1996, and of course we were euphoric. Maskhadov had won the elections and the Russian President had sent a letter of congratulations that recognized him as Chechnya's President. From now on all of our outstanding issues were to be resolved through negotiation and compromise, or so we thought. Chechens expected that their lives would return to normal; that there would be reconstruction, employment, and security. People thought that the deprivations of the war were over and a more stable and secure future was at hand, and they expected the government to provide a framework for the attainment of these goals.

The politics of the republic included unpredictable combinations of traditional, Soviet, Islamic, and democratic institutions and ideas. We needed to find a balance between different ideologies and traditions in public life, and craft institutions that reflected the complexity and variety of values present in our society. Landlocked and internationally isolated, we knew that to establish a functioning state we needed to normalize our relations with Russia, but as it turned out the corridors in Moscow were too long and people's patience in Grozny was too short.

It soon became clear that for post-war reconstruction to occur we'd have to rely almost exclusively on our own means, and we lacked the social and political organization to mobilize our very limited resources. The institutions and values of traditional society—the elders and our customary law (the *adat*) had been weakened by the war, while the institutions of a modern democratic state—parliament, media, rule of law—were at an embryonic state of development.

Under these circumstances all the questions of national policy became the responsibility of the President. Maskhadov had enormous responsibilities: to provide for post-war reconstruction and employment, build the institutions of the state, normalize relations with Russia, obtain international recognition, and formulate the ideological basis of the state. And all of this had to be accomplished quickly, before his political rivals used these problems against him. To seize the initiative he had to articulate and implement a strategy to address the momentous political, social, and ideological challenges facing the republic. Instead, he was continually distracted by challenges from various armed units.

I had been able to observe more closely Maskhadov's style of leadership in the General Staff than that during his tenure as President. He he did not like to share his positions and views to his subordinates, he preferred to remain silent, and when he had to speak on an issue, he did so calmly and diplomatically. Maskhadov's political style was by far more open and democratic than Dudayev's in that the former let different views percolate among his staff.

As President, Maskhadov wanted to maintain unity, which meant including the opposition, the minority who lost the elections. He invited members of the opposition, including Shamil, into the government and adopted elements of their program in an effort to bring them into the political process. Maskhadov expected that they would make similar compromises and the experience of doing so would teach even the radicals to become responsible. Instead, because they did not make similar compromises, his compromises became one-sided concessions and every concession Maskhadov made emboldened them to become increasingly more brazen and rebellious.

The Presidential inauguration was held on February 12, 1997. For Chechnya at that time, it was a fairly grand affair; it was appropriately solemn and attracted a great deal of public attention. It was attended by Ivan Rybkin, as President Yeltsin's official representative, General Lebed, and a delegation of Russian regional leaders, which indicated the significance the Kremlin attached to the event. The OSCE was represented and a few other international organizations and foreign guests were in attendance.

In front of 1,500 guests, President Aslan Maskhadov swore an oath on the Koran, many speakers made congratulatory remarks, and the overall atmosphere was solemn, optimistic, and patriotic. The one bit of excitement came when Rybkin's bodyguards were alarmed by the Chechen custom of shooting guns into the air in celebration. This is part of any joyous occasion in Chechnya, particularly weddings, which has led to many accidents, but remains irrepressible. Rybkin's bodyguards didn't expect the shooting, covered him up, and spirited him away. Despite the killings of six nurses from the International Committee of the Red Cross in December 1996[1] and various abductions that took place later, the inauguration and those first few months stand out as upbeat and calm.

Thus, Maskhadov became responsible for a republic that was in total ruin, and could not count on any humanitarian aid from abroad. Unlike Sarajevo, Mostar, or Pristina, which sustained comparatively minor damage, Grozny never received funding for reconstruction. Maskhadov had to find a golden mean: he needed professionals and contacts in Moscow; he had to draw in his own commanders; he had to please his election supporters and his clan, but most importantly he had to satisfy the veterans of the war.

Maskhadov understood that the rest of the world was very far away and this meant that he needed people who could accomplish things in Moscow. Most of us understood that recognition was still a long way off and that organizations like the OSCE, the World Bank, the Red Cross, and a whole array of international donors and relief agencies would not be able to help us, without Moscow's acquiescence. To reconstruct Chechnya meant establishing better relationships with Moscow, but, it turned out that this could not be achieved without compromising our independence.

The overriding challenge for Maskhadov was to form a government that could begin to address these problems. On what basis should he make appointments? Should they be made on the basis of loyalty or professionalism? Almost every minister from the Dudayev government had gone over to the Russian side or had left Chechnya during the war. The new authorities were the field commanders, who claimed that during the war they had

executed the basic functions of a local government in their jurisdictions. Naturally, many viewed appointments through the prism
of rewarding loyal commanders for war-time achievements. There
was widespread belief that courage and competence during the
war compensated for lack of professional qualifications. I remember Shamil saying that if you could lead a unit in the war then you
could run a factory. This is how we wound up with factory direc-
tors in military uniform and unemployed engineers. Our post-war
patriotism pushed us to adopt policies that were harmful to our
development.

Everything in Chechnya, including a trial in a shariah court,
finding a job, or obtaining an education was seen through the
prism of your participation in the war. This was a terrible mistake, because the majority of the population, who were not
directly involved in the war, were consequently disenfranchised
and marginalized.

A lustration law was debated on television and in parliament—it
was borrowed in a vague and superficial form from the French
post-war experience to determine who was a Nazi collaborator
and who was not; and therefore should not be permitted to hold
government office. In our version of the lustration law, com-
mittees were formed that had to approve ministerial level and
mid-level appointments. We called them *troikas* (three-member
commissions that sentenced people under Stalin) and they usually
included a former fighter and a religious authority. All candidates
for middle and high-level positions were interviewed by these
commissions and the proceedings were televised. Typically, questions focused on the degree of religiosity of the candidate, specifically how many times a day they prayed.

I remember watching Umar Khanbiyev, a highly regarded doc-
tor who became Minister of Health, go through this screening.
I don't remember one person on the troika who remotely had
the medical qualifications to evaluate Khanbiev's competence for
this position. They wanted to know if he fought in the war and
whether he was religious. Most people, myself included, regarded
these commissions a humiliation and an affront.

Chechnya is a small place and high-level appointees are known
personalities. People usually know whether a person is devout. The
population watched people they respected make patently false claims

about their beliefs and practices. Chechnya is different from Russia and many parts of Central Asia. We may have lacked religious education, but we always had faith. The wildest drunkard or the most determined party member—any Chechen at all—will say that he is a believer and has faith in the Almighty. People do not want to see those they respect be humiliated and they don't want to see a mockery of their religious values. The public spectacle of these commissions was another blow to our self-image. Moreover, we understood very well that everything depended on patronage. Someone with a suspicious background could get the job, if an important commander vouched for him, saying for instance, "When he was serving the Russians he was actually spying for me."

When he formed the first government, Maskhadov put all the defense and security ministries in the hands of his top commanders, who were also members of his electoral team. Magomed Khanbiyev became defense minister, Kazbek Makhashev became Chief of the Police Ministry (MVD), Turpal-Ali Atgeriyev became head of the Security Ministry. These appointments made perfect sense. What undermined them, unfortunately, was the rapid growth in semi-official security structures. Soon there were as many security departments and guard services as there were mid-level commanders.

Several appointments annoyed the veterans but were accepted due to a dearth of better qualified professionals. Alkhazur Abdulkerimov was a former police investigator, who in the 1990s moved to Russia and made a fortune. Maskhadov made him director of Yuzhnaya Neftenaya Kompaniya (YUNKO or Southern Oil Company). Another personality was Musa Dokhshukayev who had a position in every post-1991 government, from Dudayev's to Zavgaev's to Maskhadov's to Kadyrov's. Maskhadov appointed Nuzhden Daayev to run the department of roads, the acronym of which was "AVTODOR." He had very good connections in Moscow and was able to organize construction work. Chechens joked at the time that we had two industries, *avtodor* and *nakhbador*, the latter means "kidnapping." They stood out from the rest; their attitude was different, they had money, and they had contacts in Moscow. In the context of overall unemployment, the presence of these characters in prestigious government positions irritated people.

Shamil was very critical of these appointments because he feared that through them Russians would gain undue influence. Ministers traveled to Moscow all the time, and this also came under unfair criticism.

There were mass protests against this government in February, and by April Maskhadov had formed a second government that included Shamil and Ruslan Gelayev. Maskhadov wanted Shamil in government to offset these appointments and because he hoped that Shamil would control the proliferating number of private armies. Maskhadov needed Shamil to neutralize the criticism of the government (that was coming from unruly elements) and to impose order.

Shamil was appointed Deputy Prime Minister in April 1997 and remained in this position for four months. The negotiations between him and Maskhadov were conducted chiefly by Atgeriyev, although others such as Zakayev and Makashev may have also played a role. When Shamil became Deputy Prime Minister several of his close associates came with him into government.

Despite the bitterness between Shamil and Maskhadov, they needed each other. For Shamil it was not embarrassing to join Maskhadov's government: he was in opposition only in the sense that he had competed for the presidency. Their ideological differences had not yet crystallized. Shamil swallowed his pride and worked for Maskhadov who defeated him in the election simply because in the larger picture both men were on the same side.

Although Shamil claimed that all he wanted was to tend to his beehives, he simply could not leave politics. He had huge reserves of energy and political ambition. He was a significant national leader, by virtue of who he was, regardless of any government appointment. Of course he was disappointed by his defeat in the Presidential elections; he was a war hero at thirty-two and this appointment gave him an opportunity to prove himself as a politician.

Contrary to Maskhadov's expectations, Shamil did not want to be simply an enforcer, "a torpedo" that sails forward and breaks heads. This had been his role during the war, but as Deputy Prime Minister for Industrial Reconstruction, he no longer sought such a role. He wanted to be a politician, and his concept was that government institutions should perform their functions: the courts, the parliament, and the police; each institution should play its role. He believed that the government had to prove its strength and that as Deputy Prime Minister he had to find ways of reviving the industrial sector.

At this time, I was an informal assistant to Shamil. I did not want to be appointed to a formal position and go through interviews and commissions, but I did help him with specific tasks as necessary. Usually he would ask me to respond to correspondence, or help someone resolve a particular problem. I did not receive a formal salary, but there was an understanding on compensation. Shamil gave me money when he had it. It was not very much and I frequently had difficult periods like almost everyone else, but he always remembered me when he had money.

Shamil was not well educated. He had attended the Agriculture Institute in Moscow and never finished his university courses. As with many people who are very intelligent but not well educated, he had respect for education, sought advice, and listened carefully. On many occasions he invited me to sit in on meetings and later questioned me about how the meetings had gone and what I thought.

I sat in on many meetings with the representatives of the Russian ministries that came to see him. Among them were the representatives of ministries of transportation and roads, construction, industry, and others. The subject of the discussions was always the same: What was the degree of destruction? What would it cost to reconstruct? How could this be achieved? What needed to be done to restore a particular facility? I know that this sounds contradictory given Shamil's image in Russia as an implacable enemy, but in the meetings that I attended he was practical and flexible. Although he did not have specialized knowledge in these industries, I could see that he was genuinely trying figure it out.

However, all these efforts resulted in nothing because of Chechnya's political status. It was simply impossible to resolve the practical issues of our economic revival without resolving our political status. The Russian ministries were frequently willing to include Chechen facilities in their plans and programs and Shamil could try to work out an arrangement with a particular ministry. As individuals they could reach agreement on specific practical issues. The Russian government could subsidize one of its own ministries to facilitate the reconstruction of a facility in Chechnya and the particular elements of the deal could be negotiated. But, as soon as they had to write down an agreement on paper, they hit the question they simply could not resolve: Is this an agreement between the federal government and one of its jurisdictions, or is it an agreement between two equal entities? Would these technical agreements establish precedents that we would not be able to live with later? When these questions arose, neither Shamil nor the other party could compromise. They couldn't go back to Moscow with a piece of paper that dealt with Chechnya as a state entity, and he couldn't sign something that dealt with Chechnya as a subordinate part of the Russian federation.

If a public figure, like Maskhadov or Shamil, made what could be construed as even a hint of compromise on the question of Chechnya's independence, he would face a whole storm of criticism. There were, and still are, some very shrill guardians of our independence who will not give an inch, even in rhetoric, in exchange for really important gains like reviving our industrial sector. My impression is that it would have been possible to work out arrangements with individual ministries, only if our status was already defined, or if we had a very specific process in place for how our status would be determined in the future.

The Khasavyurt Treaty specified that our status would be determined by 2001 and the Peace Treaty of May 1997 contained a block of socioeconomic measures. What undermined both efforts was the absence of political mechanisms. There was no standing commission whose function it was to write an agreement acceptable to both sides. Needless to say there was no international mediation or conflict resolution expertise. It was Moscow's policy to refuse to provide economic assistance unless we gave up our sovereignty. At the same time, there was stupidity on our end as well. We placed too much emphasis on formalities and labels, and let these things override more immediate concerns.

When there is no official sponsorship from international institutions or foreign governments, the way is left open for informal personal arrangements. How such arrangements functioned can be seen from the famous contribution from Russian businessman Boris Berezovsky to Shamil in support of our industry.

In the summer of 1997, I was in my apartment when Shamil's guards came by and said that he was waiting for me outside. When we were already on the outskirts of town I asked him, "So where are we going?" He smiled, "We're meeting Boris Berezovsky." This was a controversial name, and Shamil wanted me to be a witness to their meeting, because as he put it, "Everyone believes what you say." It was risky for him to meet privately with any Russian politician, but Berezovsky in particular was viewed as a powerful insider, and Shamil did not want to be accused of conspiring with him.

In 1997 Berezovksy was one of the richest men in Russia. He controlled several companies, including the Russian airlines Aeroflot, the country's largest automobile manufacturer Avtovaz and the largest car dealership Logovaz, and had control over the television station, ORT. Berezovsky represented in large part the money, the media, and the strategic vision behind Yeltsin's Presidential campaign and like other influential businessmen who had contributed to the campaign, he was appointed to government office after the election. Yeltsin rewarded Berezovsky with two appointments—Deputy Security Council Secretary and Secretary of the Commonwealth of Independent States—and in these capacities he traveled all over the Caucasus. Berezovsky was negotiating deals with Azerbaijan concerning so-called "early oil," which was supposed to travel along Russian pipelines from the Caspian Sea to Novorossiisk. This pipeline traversed Chechnya and he wanted to have influence in Chechnya as he was putting this deal together. Overall, I think Berezovsky sought influence in Chechnya to remain close to Yeltsin. Berezovsky seems to have supported two Chechen Presidential campaigns: Akhmed Zakayev's and Movladi Udugov's, to the great annoyance of the two frontrunners, Maskhadov and Shamil.

When we arrived at the summer house of the President of Ingushetia, Ruslan Aushev, Berezovsky was already there. There was a park nearby, and Berezvosky proposed that he and Shamil take a walk alone. Berezovsky and Shamil walked along the alleys while their guards sat on the benches by the park. They remained in plain view but their conversation was inaudible. I don't know what they talked about.

While Berezovsky and Shamil talked, Aushev and I went inside and he gave me a tour of the residence. It was recently renovated and I was very impressed. I was living in rubble, and Aushev assured me that we would have the same comforts soon, "This doesn't take very long" he said. He asked me about my family and I told him that during the deportation our fathers were acquainted. Aushev's father was a mechanic in the same car pool in Kazakhstan where my father was a driver. I also let him know that my younger brother Idris also served in Afghanistan and that Aushev, when he was still a major and battalion commander, figured prominently in my brother's letters. Our family knew all about Aushev long before he got the "Hero of the Soviet Union" medal for personal bravery. The award became a joke under Yeltsin who rewarded his bodyguards for palace intrigues and under Vladimir Putin, too, when he bestowed the medal on Ramzan Kadyrov, which is an outrage from the perspective of what it is supposed to signify, an extraordinary contribution to the nation.

I am not sure how it came up; it must have been when I was praising his house that Aushev asked me about the cement factory in Chiri Yurt. This factory used to produce high-quality cement and was the primary supplier for all of the North Caucasus. In 1995 it came under heavy bombing, the Russians found greater resistance there than they had anticipated, and when they could not take it they bombed it almost into the ground. There was very little left of this factory. Aushev took an interest in this because he was organizing many construction programs in Ingushetia including the so-called "Euro-city" for which, he explained they were buying lower-quality cement in Nalchik. We talked like this for less than hour, probably about forty minutes, when Berezovsky and Shamil joined us in the house.

The table was set for five and and the table setting was lovely, complete settings of delicate china, crystal wine and water glasses, and gleaming silverware. I don't know when I had last seen this kind of elaborate table setting. The conversation was mostly banter. We talked about current events and told jokes. There wasn't any specific subject that was being discussed. At one point, Aushev asked Shamil, "Does your reconstruction program include the Chiri Yurt cement factory?"

Shamil responded, "No. We do not intend to restore it, it would cost too much."

Berezovsky interjected, "How much would it cost to rebuild it?"

Shamil responded, "Ten billion rubles." This was in pre-devaluation rubles and was not as much as it would be today.

Berezovsky was chewing but he looked up from his plate and said, "Put me down for two million green ones." And he kept chewing and Shamil also kept chewing.

I thought that I should try to speak up to formalize this, so I asked Berezovsky if he was willing to sign something with us to that effect, so we wouldn't forget about this after we finished lunch. "*Za bazar ya otvechayu*," was how Berezovsky responded. The phrase is jargon for "I'm responsible for my words."[2]

Later, many legends grew from this incident. General Anatoly Kulikov got wind of it somehow, and the whole matter was blown out of proportion. From what I saw, all of it unfolded spontaneously and at Aushev's initiative. The contribution from Berezovsky was not the purpose of the meeting; Berezovsky and Shamil had their private discussion earlier. The two million dollars for the cement factory was not some secret arrangement between Berezovsky and Shamil; in fact Shamil took pains to make it transparent.

For me the most interesting bit of conversation over lunch was that Berezovsky confirmed his support for Zakayev and Udugov. It was rumored widely that he had funded their Presidential campaigns, but I actually heard him confirm it. In a typically direct manner, Shamil asked, "So why are you giving money to Akhmed and Movladi?" Berezovsky responded, "They're good guys and you have to support good guys."

A couple of days later I was again summoned to Shamil's house. In the middle of his study there was a large duffle bag, filled with packs of one-hundred dollar bills. "Is this from Berezovsky?" I asked.

"Yes."

"How much is there?"

"One million"

"But he promised two."

"This is all for the moment. It leaked into the press, which is screaming that Berezovsky is arming the bandits."

We took this duffle bag and went to see Maskhadov. When Shamil explained its origins, Maskhadov was not pleased. Maskhadov always had total contempt and distrust for anything even remotely involving Berezovsky. However, Maskhadov had just brought Shamil into the government he didn't want to provoke a fight. So, while he was not at all grateful for this bit of financial support, he was not going to turn it down and cause an argument with Shamil. Maskhadov told us to deposit the money in the central bank, which we did immediately. We saw the bank attendants place the bag in the vault. The cement factory was never restored. But a sugar factory in Argun was rebuilt and Shamil took particular pride in that.

In the years since this incident various versions surfaced. First, while Berezovsky had initially promised two million dollars, Shamil, to my knowledge, received only one million. Second, the Rusian media claimed that Shamil admitted at a parliament hearing that he appropriated a portion of this money for himself. I can't imagine this to be true. It would have been very complicated for him to withdraw a portion of this money from the bank once he had deposited it. Shamil had an image to maintain and he could not have withdrawn from a government account for his own personal needs without this becoming public knowledge immediately. Third, there are occasional efforts to link this money with Shamil's incursion into Dagestan in 1999. I believe this is completely inaccurate. There was nothing in the context of the summer of 1997 that even remotely hinted in that direction; the project of the North Caucasus Khalifat was born about a year later. Finally, as far as I know, this episode was the only instance that Shamil received money from Berezovsky.

Shamil was only in the government for four months during which petty conflicts arose with Maskhadov, most of them pertaining to personnel policy or development contracts. The major conflict between the two occurred over the Peace Treaty of May 1997, which, perhaps for the first time, exposed real differences in their politics.

After the Khasavyurt Treaty of August 1996, which postponed the resolution of the main issue, the status of Chechnya until 2001, a commission was formed under Ivan Rybkin, the Secretary of the Security Council, to try to normalize relations in specific areas, such as banking and the airports.[3] Maskhadov needed to use this process to exhibit concrete achievements in post-war reconstruction and to do so without sacrificing our claim to independence. In my opinion, for Maskhadov's political success, all the technical questions had to be resolved in those early months. The first protests in Grozny broke out in the summer of 1997; huge crowds gathered in front of government buildings demanding payment of wages. The demonstrators were mostly women who had worked in brigades to clear the rubble in Grozny and the spectacle of these female workers being dispersed was unsettling.

The peace treaty turned out to be a public relations success; Maskhadov and Yeltsin signed a document proclaiming that both sides would henceforth decide their differences exclusively through peaceful means. However, the treaty had no practical application. Maskhadov insisted that during their initial discussion Yeltsin had been willing to resolve the political status issue in Chechnya's favor and it was his advisors who stopped him. According to Maskhadov, when the two of them were alone, he was able to persuade Yeltsin that there was no point in waiting for 2001 and that the political status of Chechnya should be resolved right away. According to Maskhadov, Yeltsin was willing to sign the version that Maskhadov's delegation had brought with them, which recognized Chechnya's independence.

Regardless of whether it achieved anything concrete, Maskhadov could point to the treaty as a success because it signified that the Russian President accepted him as an interlocutor. In Moscow's point of view it was an effort to bolster Maskhadov. For Yeltsin, the Presidential elections were over and he didn't need the agreement for his own internal needs. For the Kremlin, Maskhadov was an acceptable figure but there was nothing substantive that they would give him and the treaty was an empty symbol of that fact. Shamil made skeptical comments about the treaty and this became an additional point of contention.

When I participated in a discussion of the peace treaty at Grozny University, I commented that it contained only one useful article; the one stating that henceforth Russia and Chechnya would determine their relations in keeping with international law and would not use force against one another. I said that the agreement contained no obligations and that it was purely declaratory. It was good that Russia promised to abide by international law, but the treaty contained no mechanisms to ensure that it would do so.

The articles pertaining to the economy that promised assistance to Chechnya were also empty declarations with no implementing mechanisms.

The last straw for Shamil was the appointment of a person he did not approve of to take charge of the airport. The Sheik Mansur airport was important to us; it was our window to the outside world. Under Dudayev there were many duty-free flights to Turkey that facilitated commerce and made Grozny a center of trade for the North Caucasus. In 1997, there were plans to restore the airport. The airport had been occupied early in the war by the Russians and did not require much repair. Creating a tariff-free zone to stimulate trade seemed like a viable option, and was also acceptable to the Russians. Who would head up the airport became a very contentious issue.

Maskhadov appointed Viskhan Shakhabov, a controversial figure. He was chief of staff under Dudayev, before Maskhadov took that position. Shakhabov was appointed by Dudayev and confirmed in the rank of Major General by the Chechen parliament in 1994, but when the skirmishes started in the summer of 1994, Shakhabov refused to suppress the anti-Dudayev opposition. On the eve of the war with Russia, Dudayev fired him and Shakhabov moved to Moscow, where he began working for *Rossvooruzheniye,* the state weapons exporter.

Maskhadov's reasoning was straightforward: he once worked for Shakhabov and knew him well. Shakhabov was a former pilot and had excellent contacts in the Russian military and political establishment through his work in *Rossvooruzhenie.* This appointment was logical from the perspective of restoring the airport with the fewest obstacles from Moscow. Shamil's position was also understandable: Was it wise to appoint to an important strategic position someone who betrayed Chechnya and profited from the war? There were strong words between Maskhadov and Shamil. I wasn't there when the appointment was decided, but I saw Shamil very soon after and he was still shaking with rage. Shamil resigned as Deputy Prime Minister very soon after this argument.

Apart from the presidency and the cabinet of ministers, an important state-building role could have been played by the parliament. The initial round of parliamentary elections was held at the same time as the balloting that elected Maskhadov President. In February 1997 soon after the Presidential inauguration, Shamil called a meeting of all his election supporters in a movie theater in the Oktyabrskii district. The theater was packed, even after it was known that he had lost the election. There was still talk that the election was falsified and that the Russians had installed Maskhadov. However, Shamil behaved correctly. He said, "I have conceded the election and I have congratulated Maskhadov on his victory and I hope that he will remain on the path of President Dudayev. At the same time there is 22 percent of the population that supported me in this election and I think we represent an active portion of society and I would like us to participate in public life and prepare for the next round of the parliamentary elections." And then to my astonishment he motioned to me to join him on the stage. I was standing in the wings and signaling, "No!"

"I would like to form a political party and nominate Ilyas Akhmadov as the chairman of the party. He is very well-educated and smart and we went through the entire war together." He went on for a little while describing my credentials for this position.

I have shunned public roles for my entire life, beginning with the Komsomol, which I tried to avoid at all costs. I found this new offer embarrassing but it was even more embarrassing to refuse publicly. So I agreed, and he presented me at this meeting as the chairman of our new political party *Marshonan Toba*, which means Freedom Party. When just a few of us were left at the end of this meeting, I tried to back out but there was no way to decline the appointment.

In the first round of parliamentary elections only five of sixty-three districts elected representatives. There were 900 candidates running and a candidate had to have more than 50 percent to win on the first round. Hence, in the spring of 1997 there were several subsequent rounds of voting and a parliament was finally seated, in which the dominant factions were Maskhadov's Independence Party and Udugov's Islamic Path. Our party had five or six representatives including Turpal-Ali Kaimov, Tutak Vagapov, and Aslanbek Abdulkhadzhiev.

Shamil had to do something to keep the party members actively involved but these people thought that because they had supported him they should get appointments in the local administration. It's hard to say what the membership of our party was. We issued roughly 4,000 party cards but discontinued because people were trying to use the proof of party membership to resolve common problems and get out of sticky situations. I stopped issuing party cards after police complained that people were using them to try to get out of paying speeding tickets. I think we had fewer than 10,000 members, who were spread all over the republic and represented different segments of the population. Shamil's election headquarters became our party office where we employed about a dozen people.

We continued to advocate for items that were part of Shamil's party platform: the law on lustration, which required candidates for public office to declare any previous work in the Russian or Soviet military, security, or governing structures (which our representative Abdul Khadzhiev pushed through parliament), various forms of support for veterans of the war, definition of our position vis-à-vis Russia, and criticism of Maskhadov's personnel policy.

Of course, it was easy to complain and criticize, and much more difficult to accomplish anything. As time wore on I became concerned about the aggressiveness of the members of our party. For instance, they demanded positions in local government, and asked me to write statements on their behalf. I tried to explain that we had no right to demand this. It goes without saying that the President appointed people from his own party into the bureaucracy. I tried to explain that this was to be expected.

It was very difficult to calm them down; there were no jobs and people hung on to party membership as something that might improve their situation. I always felt bad for those who came at their own expense from remote districts for our weekly meetings. We had representatives from everywhere, including traditionally pro-Russian districts such as Nadterechnyi. Our weekly meetings typically involved Shamil and the parliamentarians; particularly at first but less so as time progressed.

We were effective at helping people resolve specific problems such as when a member of the party needed medical treatment or university education. People were swarming to our offices, especially when Shamil was the Deputy Prime Minister. Some needed help finding employment, some wanted to get us to resolve some local squabbles that were a total headache for me but I tried to listen and give my best advice. Sometimes they brought drafts of statements that they thought we should put out; one party member thought we should make a statement condemning the U.S. imposition of the "No Fly Zone" over Iraq. We didn't have a stable political culture, which meant that people went to the party with all kinds of requests and concerns.

Once I was summoned to quell a rebellion in Argun because the members of my party had taken over the mayor's office and were menacing the mayor. When I arrived, Kazbek Makhachev, a former Interior Minister, was already there trying to hold back a crowd of irate women who had surrounded the mayor. When they saw me, they left the mayor alone and turned to me. I said, "Please come outside to have this discussion and leave the government building." I was just as surprised as the mayor and Makhachev were when they actually quietened down and calmly walked out to the square in front of the city administration. They listened to me, despite my youth.

I started to tell them that, "I don't want to discredit the government by staging a chaotic rally in the city administration. I also don't want to discredit Shamil, who is right now chairing a meeting of the council of ministers. Shamil is part of the government that you are attacking. I would suggest all of you go home except for the party leader. I and the party leaders will go to the office and you will calmly tell me what the problem is and I will try to represent this to the mayor, who hopefully will do whatever he can to resolve the problem, so that such scenes don't happen again."

We sat down in the office and wrote up a list of complaints, including that the local administration was discriminating against our party members in their hiring procedures; local officials were demanding bribes; and local officials were seizing real estate from party members. These were typical problems for post-Soviet countries. I told them that their methods were wrong they shouldn't take over government buildings. The list of demands was transferred to the mayor. I don't know whether he resolved the issues, but I never had to go there again.

There was tragedy in all this. Shamil couldn't send everyone abroad for medical treatment; he couldn't solve every problem, nor could the government. People were in Shamil's house night and day; there might be fifteen people there in the middle of the night. Sometimes he demanded to be left alone; the constant demands frustrated him and made him feel ineffective. It was a shame to betray the enthusiasm of these people. They were active and, of course, we wanted to keep them on our side but it was impossible to find jobs for all of them. I had no program to offer them. What was I supposed to do, discuss policy issues with them? It was very difficult for me to explain that the problem was not that Maskhadov's mayor wouldn't give them a job; the problem was our catastrophic rates of unemployment.

We had very open and stormy meetings, the party members demanded to know why Shamil left the government and tried to prevail on him to remain involved. They didn't see the intrigues, they just saw that he was giving up and wanted him to remain engaged in government. These people were united by a very strong belief in independence. As the months wore on, I found myself holding fewer and fewer meetings; I hated the idea that we were deceiving our members. I wanted to disband the party, because I felt as though we were not making any progress.

In 1998 when political competition between Maskhadov and the opposition became more confrontational, Shamil joined the Congress of Nations of Dagestan and Ichkeria and many of our party members left for that organization, while others joined Salman Raduyev's Path of Dzhokhar party. I was trying to keep our members away from both the Congress and Raduyev. I did try to shepherd them toward normal political activities, but as the situation started to unwind, I persuaded Shamil to dissolve the party. The party without Shamil was useless. I didn't need my own party, particularly as my main preoccupation became trying to persuade the membership to employ only legal political means. I finally dissolved the party in the winter of 1999. The dissolution of the party was a symbol of our failure to pursue political goals as an opposition party, through legislative and electoral strategies.

The Congress of Nations of Ichkeria and Dagestan, which played a fateful and terrible role in Chechnya's history, emerged later as a union of many small armed groups. They originated in the small splinter groups that were left out of the Defense Ministry, the Interior Ministry (Ministerstvo Vnutrennikh Del or the MVD), and the customs and border guards. Outside of these main government departments there were various smaller units, many of them splitting and multiplying. During the war there had been one Islamic Battalion, under Islam Khalimov, but now we had dozens of *dzhaamats*. They were financed from abroad and were the ideological opponents of Maskhadov and secularism. There were commanders that supported Shamil during the elections and many of them fought on other fronts and were his ideological allies. After he lost the election for President and had few appointments to hand out, he lost control over many of these mid-level commanders.

Each commander wanted to enter the government, but only in a top position and only with the members of his unit; they weren't interested in being subordinate to another commander. There were "Wolves of Islam," "Shariah Guards," and many, many other different security groupings, some of which were called *dzhamaat*. A *dzhamaat* is a village community that lives according to certain religious values, but in our parlance, it became a politicized gang, a private army. Authority was splintered among them into thousands of little pieces, so that in the end there was no real authority.

When institutions did not function, people relied entirely on personal networks. An influential person could make the system work for them. If a person was arrested, their relatives went to Shamil or Gelayev. For instance, I became involved in resolving a situation when the family of an incarcerated man appealed to Shamil. I went with his relatives to the National Security Service (Sluzhba Natsionalnoi Bezopasnotsi, SNB), which at that time was under Magomed Kariyev. I had been Shamil's adjutant and this was an important status; typically for something like this you needed twenty men to stand behind you with submachine guns. All I had were letters from Shamil and the relatives explaining the situation. This man had been incarcerated for two months, but there was no case and no file on him whatsoever. The leadership of the SNB knew nothing about it. How did he land up in jail? It was over a personal dispute; a member of the SNB felt that this man owed him money, so he put him in jail for two months. This was not a rare occurrence, it was a fairly standard situation, and it illustrates the impotence of the state. If a person was considered pro-Russian, and his family couldn't appeal to

Shamil or Gelayev or another important commander, he simply had no recourse.

If you listened to our leaders talk on television about the future, you would have thought the way to restore Chechnya was through its capacity to extract and refine oil. I can't claim any professional expertise in this field, but I always have had the impression that this was a false hope. I've spoken to various specialists at different times, both in Chechnya and abroad, and they say that there simply is not enough oil in Chechnya. As far as Chechnya's ability to refine oil, refineries were built before World War II and were technologically backward even then, and although the Russians may have tried to spare the oil facilities during the air raids, they were damaged during the war. The idea that you could rebuild Chechnya using revenue from oil was a myth—but this myth was universally professed at the time.

All of the major industrial plants in Chechnya, which had been the primary employers, were in ruins. Krasnyi Molot, a machine-building plant, and Elektopribor, an electronics plant, were facilities that had serviced their sectors for the entire territory of the Soviet Union. The cement factory at Chiri Yurt serviced the North Caucasus region. The idea that these complex industries could be revived by handing them over to people whose only qualification was that they fought well, would mean suicide. Certainly Maskhadov understood this, but Shamil did not.

The workers of these various factories still attempted to work there, they tried to stick together and to restore things, and get help from the government. These people were preyed upon by various armed groups. There were many of these private armies and Maskhadov tried to bring most of them into government structures, but it wasn't possible to control them.

These units started seizing factories and stripping them for parts. Chechnya became a market for construction materials for the entire North Caucasus region. Some commanders claimed that this was not thievery, but rather an attempt to prepare for a new war. This was condemned by both Maskhadov and Shamil, but to no avail.

War is the most extreme experience a society can endure, and people often feel that they are strong and brave during war which calls for extraordinary effort. Now they were scared of returning to their former lives. Maybe this sounds cynical, but twenty months of war is long enough to acquire a taste for it. If you survived, you faced real monsters, you discovered your own strengths, and now you were faced with going back to an ordinary life. And what was meaningful to you in your former life? Was it your tractor, or your university textbooks? What if you held no position in society?

The majority of the male population changed into uniform. During the war you could not find these items, now they were on sale in every stall, you'd see uniforms hanging next to Pampers. During the war there were three or four of us who had NATO uniforms. After my unit was dissolved, I took mine off and put it on only for special occasions when it was unavoidable. My family never liked me in uniform and I did not need it anymore. I wore civilian clothes and didn't carry any weapons. I could afford to do this: I was Maskhadov's former aide and Shamil's former adjutant, and everyone knew me. I didn't run into problems in the street but there were bands of young men with weapons, whom I did not know. I thought I knew everyone, but there were new people out there. Most men wore some sort of military uniform to protect themselves; looking tough has deterrent value.

The government tried several initiatives to limit the spread of weapons among the population: there was a program to buy weapons, and in some cases weapons were seized. Another idea was legalizing the possession of weapons but making it illegal to carry weapons in the streets. Yet another proposal was to have official stores of weapons in each village or town, so that one could deposit their weapons in a central location. None of these efforts worked.

The practice of seizing weapons was doomed from the start. If you have a column of jeeps full of guys armed to the teeth with grenade launchers driving around the city and no one dares to question them, and then the police confiscate a pistol from some ordinary person, who is just trying to protect himself, it's really hypocritical. Maskhadov and some of his ministers, for instance, Kazbek Makashev, the Minister of Internal Affairs, tried to institute policies for buying and confiscating weapons. Shamil wore a suit and appeared on television making jokes about these newly uniformed warriors. None of this worked and of course this was a huge failure for us. Shamil did seek ways of battling against this, but it's one thing to seize weapons and a another to stop them from being sold on the market the day after they've been seized. Shamil too was powerless when it came to this problem. These bands of uniformed armed men were an omnipresent symbol of the anarchy reigning in Chechnya.

Shamil and Gelayev, the two most significant commanders, disbanded their units. Shamil's units for the most part went into the border guards or the army. Shamil told them, "I am not your commander any more." Gelayev did the same. The main problem was the mid-level commanders, who had fifty or sixty men, who didn't get a government appointment, and weren't going to enter into someone else's unit. Every commander wanted to remain a commander.

If you were a mid-level commander, how could you disband your unit? If you disbanded your unit, you would be just another man unable to find his place in this new reality. And if you held on to your unit, how would you feed and supply them? There were four obvious routes: first, were bodyguard services—any man who was known outside his own block felt he needed a bodyguard; second, one could take over a factory and strip if for parts, ripping out pipes and selling them; third, one could act as an intermediary who could settle scores and collect debts; and fourth, one could take hostages and demand ransom.

We lived in two parallel worlds: on the one hand, there were long speeches on television about plans for our future, recognition of our independence, talks about economic reform and reconstruction, and on the other hand there was the reality of our lives when nothing seemed to be improving. Over the ensuing three years, most Chechens—somewhere near 70 percent—remained unemployed. I still don't completely understand how we survived. There was no famine, no acute hunger. People subsisted on vegetables from their gardens and the shuttle trade with neighboring republics.

Dudayev had stated at the beginning of the war, "I am horrified to think what I will do with 300,000 armed Chechen when the war ends." He was wrong only about the numbers. At most, even if you count those who only fought a few days, there were only 12,000 fighters. But in principle he was right. Of course, the

Chechens were not the first to experience this, a French General after World War I had said that the most painful consequence of any war is the veteran.

Ironically, Maskhadov facilitated the emergence of the commanders as a political entity. In 1997 he started to convene the council of commanders, which included those who had served during the war but were not currently in government positions, clearly an extra-constitutional body. He convened this body to discuss current problems and essentially ratify government decisions. Maskhadov unwittingly created a parallel structure that laid the groundwork for the dual government that emerged later.

In formal terms Maskhadov had everything: a government, a parliament, a constitution, and a judicial system. Where did this council of commanders fit in? Seeking the consent of this council of commanders contributed to the weakness of the formal institutions. Politically it made sense, one shouldn't leave so many armed people outside of the system, but they weren't going to permit the government to become stronger. From Maskhadov's perspective, he was trying to involve them in the new system. But they were playing their own game, and for Maskhadov it became a dangerous balancing act, because each time he made a deal he gave up a little bit of his authority.

Repeatedly, Maskhadov employed the same maneuver, and it proved to be fatal. He tried to implement his opponents' program. It reminded me of the Soviet government during the 1980s, which after seeing the tide of popular opinion shift in favor of democratic process and national movements, declared sovereignty for their republics. This began in the Baltic States, but then spread to the Caucasus and Ukraine. In each place it was the old Soviet party bosses that declared sovereignty in 1990 when they tried to take over their opponents' program, but this maneuver did not work, all of them were swept out of power by authentic national democratic movements within a two-year period. What Maskhadov was trying to do reminded me very much of that. He could see that certain ideas were becoming popular among some active segments of the population and he tried to win them over by implementing portions of their program. He created the council of commanders, he brought radicals into government, and he eventually proclaimed sharia law. He did these things reluctantly.

He did not believe that they were best for the country, but he made compromises with political and ideological opponents because he sought unity.

The foundation for all of our future tragedies was laid during the first year after the Khasavyurt Treaty when no strategy was created for managing these various armed groups. The government couldn't do anything to curb the spread of weapons among the population or to disband or control the private armies. In 1998 these forces combined into the Congress of Nations of Dagestan and Ichkeria, which staged incursions into Dagestan in August 1999 creating a formal pretext for the second war.

What should Maskhadov have done? This was Makhadov's impossible quandary. He was walking a tightrope; every time he tried to do something constructive, all the splinter groups united against him. No matter what he did, they accused him of collaborating with Russia or permitting sin to triumph in Chechnya. Some claim that Maskhadov was a weak politician, but I find that misleading. Maskhadov could not employ the maneuvers that Dudayev used, which were authoritarian but peaceful. Because we were a post-war society, taking on the opposition in an aggressive manner would have meant killing them. So to accuse Maskhadov of weakness is to blame him for not becoming a ruthless dictator and physically destroying his opponents. Maskhadov tried to use political methods, he tried to seize the initiative; he tried to be moderate, fair and democratic, and the situation that he inherited was so complicated that I doubt very much that another politician would have done better or achieved more.

CHAPTER 6

THE HOSTAGE TRADE

To begin a discussion of the hostage trade we need to discard the two most popular explanations for it. The explanation prevalent in Russia is that Chechens have a cultural or historical predilection for hostage taking, and that it's somehow in our blood. The second notion, popular among the Chechens, is that the hostage trade represented a conspiracy by the Russian Security Service (Federanaya Sluzhba Bezopasnosti, FSB). In my view it's wrong to assume that the leadership of the Interior Ministry (Ministerstvo Vnutrennikh Del, MVD) or the FSB hatched a devious scheme to instill the hostage trade into Chechnya. These are both exaggerations and simplifications when the truth is much more complicated. To examine some of the key features of the ugly history of the hostage trade, we can pick out some of the more famous cases, specifically those cases about which I had some first-hand information.

Historically, Chechens used hostage taking the same way many other armies have throughout history. For instance, Russian armies took hostages during the nineteenth century wars as did the Red Army during the civil war of the 1920s. In principle the tactic of taking hostages is not new or exclusive to the Chechen war.

The massive growth of the hostage trade in the 1990s was an unintended consequence of the Russian ideological position that the war in Chechnya was not really a war. Initially, the hostage trade grew out of the treatment of prisoners; Russia regarded Chechen prisoners of war as common criminals and Russian prisoners of war as hostages. The Russians could not treat Chechen prisoners as prisoners of war because that would imply recognition of Chechnya as a warring party, this would contradict the official line that we were simply bandit formations, and the Russian army was simply restoring constitutional order. So it followed that Chechens taken prisoner during the conflict were considered criminals, and that Russian servicemen held prisoner by Chechens were hostages. This bordered on the absurd. I remember reading a list of names that the Russian side had prepared, which included a prisoner who was being held in jail in Russia. He was supposedly "arrested" in Grozny in January 2, 1995 for financial crimes. But this was absurd because in Grozny in those days there was heavy fighting and no one was being arrested; people were taken prisoner during military operations. The absence of legal status and legalized procedures for exchanging prisoners created an informal market, a system of intermediaries, which facilitated exchanges.

The Russian army had a practice of taking hostages from Chechen villages to build up their *obmennyi fond*, which are reserves of hostages to trade for Russian soldiers who had been taken prisoner.[1] If there was some chance of officially trading prisoners; those who were taken prisoner with arms in their hands in Grozny had some chance of making it into the official lists. But those people taken hostage for the *obmennyi fond* were held secretly and their relatives could only get them back by going through unofficial channels and by paying ransom, or making a trade. So, for instance, the Russian unit would tell the relatives of a person they were holding that they would exchange him for a soldier who was being held by a Chechen commander. The Chechen commanders traded or sold their Russian prisoners to Chechen families who were trying to get their relatives back from the Russian side. This market in human beings was established during the war but it was invisible to most people. After the war it grew at a catastrophic rate.

The first time that I had first-hand information about a kidnapping was that of Mauro Galligani, who came to Grozny with another Italian reporter named Francesco Bigaze, to report on the Presidential election. Their contact in Grozny was Andrei Mironov, a human rights activist with the Memorial Human Rights Center. Their car was surrounded in the middle of

Grozny during the day by armed masked men who pulled Galligani out of his car and into theirs and sped away. Soon after this happened, I ran into Andrei and Francesco on the street. I had known Andrei since the first days of the war and offered to help them. I took them to see Shamil, and he also agreed to help. He suggested two things, "Take Ilyas with you and go see all the other major figures, he can help you arrange meetings with Khunkharpasha and the MVD. I can't investigate what happened, but if you come back and tell me, 'He's being held in that house,' I'll go and storm it."

There was a real danger that Andrei and Francesco would also become targets of hostage taking and I made sure that they had guards that I knew who would be responsible to me personally. We went to see all the major players, we saw Khunkharpasha Israpilov, the head of the antiterrorist unit, at the antiterrorism center and Kazbek Makhashev at the MVD; these agencies were newly formed and, of course, they lacked professionals. Khunkharpasha had been an investigator before the war and the men working under him were the men he fought with. The head of MVD had been a major in the penitentiary police. At best, in all of our agencies there were only a handful of professional investigators with experience in these matters. Moreover, we didn't have any laws. Was there a criminal code or a procedural code to underlie the criminal code? None of this was in place in any meaningful way. For the most part, the men working there were operating on intuition.

Neither the lack of experience nor the lack of legislation were the most serious obstacles for fighting the hostage trade. The fundamental problem was our tradition of blood feuds. If an investigator at the counter-terrorist center participates in a raid to free hostages, and in the course of fulfilling his professional duty, kills one of the hostage takers, he could incur a blood feud. The state could not protect against the possibility that by fighting bandits a policeman might bring a blood feud upon himself and his family.

The members of the antiterrorism center appeared on TV and declared that a blood feud against any of them would bring retribution from the rest. But what does this have to do with the state? It demonstrates that no effective institutions were left after the war, there was no law, the elders were discredited, and even *teip* loyalty declined in importance. Traditionally, the elders have to approve a blood feud. If you feel you have been wronged, you tell the elders of your *teip* and they determine whether the case deserves retribution and only then can you carry it out. Elders went on television and explained that a policeman carrying out his official duties is not subject to a blood feud. But this was meaningless for us, and it would not restrain anyone. The only thing that had meaning was who fought next to you during the war. This lack of protection made law enforcement timid and uncertain. Investigators lacked everything, legal experience, training, and most importantly, motivation. Everything militated against such crimes being solved.

When we were looking for Galligani, we didn't know any of this. We were very naïve. We went to every government agency I could think of and talked to everyone. Khunkharpasha told us not to negotiate with anyone and that if any information became available to let him know. He said, "Don't bargain, don't even permit that possibility. If you let on that you might pay even a small sum that will only inspire them to raise the ransom demands." Our goal was to put pressure on Chechen law enforcement to conduct an investigation, find Galligani, and release him—by force and with Shamil's men, if needed. In April 1997, after three months in captivity, we saw on television that Galligani had been released in Moscow. No one had even approached Andrei and Francesco. The deal was struck totally outside of our circles; there were intermediaries and negotiations, somewhere far away.

The kidnapping of the ORT television crew in January 1997 became very famous because it was the first case when Berezovsky took credit for arranging the release of ORT journalists Roman Perevezentsev and Vyacheslav Tibelius who were held for about six weeks. I don't think it was necessarily inappropriate for Berezovsky to get involved; he was after all on the security council and was Secretary of the Commonwealth of Independent States.[2] Moreover, the state could not create official mechanisms to resolve these situations when thousands of Russians and Chechens were being held as prisoner or as hostages. There needed to be some mechanism to release them. Wasn't it natural that someone like Berezovsky would come along and find a semi-official solution? If the state structures were lacking, something had to fill the void.

I think the media image of Berezovsky as an evil genius holding all the strings is overblown. His behavior was typical of Russian officials: He simply attracted more media attention than the others. What wasn't reported in the media is that even minor Russian officials, any *krai* Duma Deputy, FSB chief of any region who met with Chechen leaders would ask, "Can you release a prisoner to me?" It's important to stress here what they were asking: that a prisoner be released to them personally, outside of any normal channels. I was at these meetings with Shamil or Maskhadov during and after the war. In Russia, it was a matter of prestige: every careerist policeman or regional-level politician wanted a prisoner release on his resume. Perhaps Berezovsky outperformed the others, but it was fashionable at the time for officials to try to further their careers by persuading people in power that they had special connections among the Chechens. I think that the primary motivation for Berezovsky must have been to solidify his position as a Kremlin insider. By demonstrating that he had influence in Chechnya, he could court favor with the small circle of people around Boris Yeltsin. Inadvertently, this competition among different Russian politicians, security services, and government agencies, each of them competing to release a prisoner, spurred on the hostage trade—it was a vicious circle.

In other cases, enormous sums were apparently paid in ransom, and from my perspective this was outrageous. All that is needed to take a film crew hostage is thirty to forty armed men. If you pay a million dollars once for a hostage, you can be sure that the hostage takers will never go lay bricks at some construction site. The very next thing they will do is to plan the next one. Did Yeltsin understand this at the time? Were the Russian officials who paid these ransoms deliberately feeding the hostage trade, realizing that it would politically destabilize the Chechen republic?

Of course, the actual hostage takers are the most primitive part in the whole machinery of kidnapping. The more sophisticated ones are the mediators: those who learn how much ransom can be demanded and have the contacts to conduct the talks. You can't conduct the negotiations from Chechnya, nor can you gather information about the financial assets of your potential victims. If you spent the war in Chechnya fighting, you did not have the contacts in Moscow to hold these negotiations. Imagine this chain: the victim, the kidnappers (who usually held the hostage themselves, or through a subsidiary group), the mediators, and those paying the ransom (relatives, a government, a media or humanitarian organization). In this chain, seizing a hostage is the easy part; plenty of groups in Chechnya did that; what was complicated were the ensuing negotiations.

Officially, of course, there was never any ransom payment. The official statements were always the same; the hostage was freed as a result of a special operation. It is implausible that Russian Security Services were conducting special operations in Chechnya in 1997 and 1998 because Russian troops were withdrawn in 1996 as a result of the Khasavyurt agreement, and certainly this was impossible without the cooperation of Chechen units, but any Chechen involvement was never mentioned. Let's say I'm wrong about that. Let's say that the Russian MVD really was carrying out special operations in Chechnya and freeing hostages by raiding places where they were held. And in some cases they went so far as to show video of these raids. For the sake of argument, let's pretend that this is all real. Why then didn't they ever publicly identify and formally charge the hostage takers?

There are very few reliable sources of information about the hostage trade. Apart from a couple of journalists such as *Vyacheslav Izmailov* of *Novoya gazeta*—a retired MVD Colonel who had participated in prisoner exchanges—and staff of international NGOs who compiled field data about hostage taking to protect themselves, there are no credible firsthand accounts. What is particularly cynical, is that even the victims, after being released never revealed publicly who held them.[3] Of course, Chechnya is a small place and people infer based on what they see, but there is never specific information. You never really *know* who was responsible for which hostage taking and you never *knew* what ransom was actually paid.

The media picture that emerged in 1998 or 1999, was that there were three or four "barons" of the slave trade: Arbi Barayev, Sulim Yamadayev, and the Akhmadov brothers, and Baudi Bakuyev fed into this. It's easy, particularly now that Barayev is dead, to hang everything on him. But it does not represent reality, which is far more complex. The media distorted the stories and exaggerated the impact of these colorful personalities, thereby creating "brand names." Often a person was kidnapped and held in some Russian region, let's say Perm, but the hostage takers would use Barayev's name to claim a larger ransom than they could have obtained otherwise. Barayev would sit down and make a video, for which he would receive a cut based on that tape. But that was the extent of his involvement. What role did Barayev play in these situations? He wasn't the hostage taker; he was a spokesman, the most feared "brand name" in the business.

By way of comparison if you look at the smaller cases, which involved Chechens and not millions of dollars; once in a while those cases were solved. When Shadid Bagrishev replaced Khunkharpasha, he led several operations and those were filmed and televised and the perpetrators were arrested. Bagrishev was blown up by a car bomb in October 1998, and I saw it happen. Probably it wasn't over a particular kidnapping but in general to stop what he was doing. He was very active in small cases, usually involving Chechens, or others from North Caucasus. In the cases that he solved, he announced publicly who was responsible for the hostage takings. I don't remember any instance when a major kidnapping was officially solved and its mechanisms revealed publicly.

The next major kidnapping after the ORT case was that of the film crew of NTV and Elena Masyuk in May 1997. Masyuk became notorious after Budennovsk, where she had reported from the field and she became friendly with Shamil. She had access to him and Aslanbek Ismailov, which in effect meant access to everyone. I wouldn't say that her reporting was unusual for the time, there were many journalists who reported objectively. But she certainly spent a lot of time in Chechnya and had many contacts. I can't say that I knew her very well but I would often be present during her meetings with Shamil. He liked to hear my opinions after the meetings and compare notes.

On this particular day when Masyuk came by, Shamil wasn't there. He didn't have his own house yet and lived either in his father's house in Vedeno, or in several different apartments in Grozny. There was one which had a computer, and I would sit there and try to work, and that's where Masyuk found me.

She wanted to ask Shamil for bodyguards to accompany her as she researched a story about the illegal oil industry. The underground refineries were a topic of considerable discussion. There are places where the oil, or the so-called condensate of oil, is so pure that it requires very little processing. The story circulating was that this business was fueling all of the North Caucasus and was very profitable. This coincided with the court case against Beslan Gantemirov, former mayor of Grozny, who went to jail for stealing proceeds from the oil business. Masyuk wanted to do a story about the condensate deposits in the Zavodskoi rayon.

When I explained that Shamil was out of town for several days, she asked me if I would take the guards and accompany her, and I refused. I tried to tell her that this was incredibly dangerous and I wasn't going to take people in there without Shamil's explicit instruction to do so. My advice was for her to wait until he returned. She left and I heard two days later that she and her crew had been taken hostage.

Although she did not have Shamil's blessing in this particular situation, overall she was perceived as being under his protection. He knew this and saw this hostage taking as a personal affront. He offered money for information about her whereabouts. I think he raised the sum several times and the end amount was in the neighborhood of $100,000. Both Shamil and Khunkharpasha Israpilov saw this as a matter of honor and they set about trying to find her. I saw in one Russian newspaper a version that claimed Shamil had taken Masyuk hostage, which was absurd. Shamil was a hero and men came up to him in the street and asked to touch his shoulder. He regarded himself as a national leader and did not need to get into the hostage trade, especially not in the case of Masyuk.

First of all, Shamil didn't need the money. Chechen businessmen gave him money, hundreds of thousands of dollars, and cars, hoping to buy influence. He gave most of it away to people around him. He eventually built a house and enjoyed a nice lifestyle but was not involved in business himself. He took care of the men around him, for instance, sending many of them to Turkey for medical treatment. That was where most of his money went.[4]

I don't know if Shamil and Israpilov or Aslanbek Ismailov ever figured out who held Masyuk. I still do not know and I have never heard any account of what actually happened to her. The official version was that there was a special operation leading to her release. What I find particularly frustrating is that the victims would not say who held them. Masyuk knew everyone; she knew all the commanders; she knew many of their fighters, and she would know who was responsible for her kidnapping. The fact that she didn't speak out later to name her captors suggests that silence was one of the conditions of her release.

Berezovsky's next major success was to arrange the release of Camilla Carr and Jon James, British citizens volunteering with a small Quaker charity, Center for Peacekeeping and Community Development (CPCD). They were abducted in Grozny on July 3, 1997 and released in September 1998. Without giving away too many specifics, Berezovsky admitted that he had arranged the deal:

[O]n the request of the then [British] ambassador in Russia Mr [Andrew] Wood, I used my relations with [Akhmad] Zakayev and with Movladi Udugov and appealed to them with a request for them to find out where these people were being held and to help in their release.[5]

The CPCD had developed good relations with Khunkharpasha Israpilov. He genuinely tried to find and release the hostages and had stormed a house in Urus Martan to free them, but they had been shifted elsewhere. The hostages were being kept in a village and lots of people were involved in guarding these precious goods. Everyone knew all about this case, but at the same time, it appeared that no one knew! Any person could see on television that there had been the release of a famous hostage, and shortly they would see who now had a new jeep, and draw conclusions. But no one could prove anything.

There were three main black holes of the hostage trade: the town of Urus Martan, which practically belonged to Arbi Barayev and the Akhmadov brothers who were considered Wahhabis. In Gudermes, the next most famous hostage taker was Sulim Yamadayev, who later became the head of the United Russia Party under Akhdmad Kadyrov and a representative of Chechnya in the Federation Council. Then there was the State Milk Farm No. 15, which was controlled by people close to the Vice President Vakha Arsanov.

I was directly involved in a different case, with less famous personalities, but it reveals the key features of the business. In the winter of 1998, Chechen television invited Shamil to a round-table in Moscow organized by the weekly magazine *Novoye Vremya*. He asked me to represent him and I agreed, thinking that it would be an interesting experience and would give me, who once had pretensions of being a political scientist, a chance to brush up on my skills. This was an interesting event, where I met Valeria Novodvorskaya, a famous dissident and opposi-tional intellectual. Chechen-Russian relations were a hot topic and there were lively discussions. After I spoke, Novodvorskaya ran up to me, gave me a big hug, and said she was overjoyed to finally hear a real Chechen speak. I went outside to smoke and was approached by Alexander Dzasokhov, a Duma Deputy from North Ossetia. Dzasokhov had a great reputation. He was regarded as practical, balanced, and a serious politician—even then, before he became President. I was very flattered that he liked my remarks and he gave me his card.

When I returned to Chechnya I must have bragged about this because a few weeks later, I was summoned by a Chechen family who needed to contact Dzasokhov. There was an old feud between a businessman from Chechnya and a businessman from North Ossetia. Once upon a time, they had been business partners; then had a falling out and in retribution they had taken one another hostage; this happened repeatedly over several years. The Chechen and his companion had been taken hostage in North Ossetia and the family wanted to know if I would call Dzasokhov. I did not feel comfortable doing this, but I gave the brother the visiting card and said, "Go ahead and call from my name." By this time Dzasokhov was already President and I did not think that anything would come of this. I gave them the contact information and left.

Later in the day I was driving in Grozny and noticed that Shamil's guards were trying to catch up to me. They said, "Go immediately to Basayev because Alexander Dzasokhov is trying to reach you." I spoke to someone in Dzasokhov's staff who said that the hostages had been found and released and that we could meet the North Ossetian FSB General at the checkpoint on the Ingush-Ossetian border and the hostages would be released to us. This entire episode from the kidnapping to the release took one day.

The hostage's brother and I went to the checkpoint. We didn't take guards; I never liked to have guards. It was already one in the morning and we approached from the Ingush side. On that border there were the Ingush police, federal MVD to keep the Ingush and the Ossets from shooting each other, and then the Ossetian police at the Ossetian checkpoint, called the Chermen checkpoint. There were two Ingush policemen who checked my identification. My card read, "Adjutant to Division General Basayev, Captain Akhmadov." They commented, "You're the first Chechen captain to go through that border post. Every Chechen is a colonel or a general." They did not want to know very much about why we were there. They ignored our presence and we waited for the Ossets.

The Ossets arrived in a column of ten cars, everyone piled out, most of them in uniform and masks with automatic rifles. In front were two very tall men in civilian dress. They introduced themselves as Director of the North Ossetian FSB Major General Vladimir Bezuglyi and Major General of the FSB Yuri Bzaev. Later Bzaev became the Secretary of the North Ossetian Security Council. They told me that on Dzasokhov's orders their directorate had freed the hostages, the perpetrators were under arrest and their case was being prepared, that the victims and I could have access to the materials of the case as it went forward. I was so impressed by all of this because I had become accustomed to hostage taking being a hopeless reality and here they had resolved the whole affair in less than one day. They brought out the hostages, the businessman had been badly beaten, and they apologized for this. His companion had not been beaten.

After the hostages were transferred to our car, Bezuglyi asked if he and I could speak privately. We stepped aside and he began by pointing out that they had done what we asked and had done so very quickly and professionally. This was absolutely true and I thanked him for it. He then asked me if I could talk to Shamil about helping them win the release of two agents of the Ingush FSB, Yuri Gribov and Sergei Lebedinski, who had been abducted in Nazran in the fall of 1997 and were being held hostage in Chechnya. They were ethnic Russians who had been sent to work in the Ingush FSB and were kidnapped soon after their

arrival. Bezuglyi wanted me to relate to Shamil that his directorate was working on the case and he was interested in having
them released to him. I told him in general terms what I thought
of hostage taking: that it was an evil that we had to fight against.
I said I would tell Shamil about this conversation and would seek
his support.

I went to see Shamil the following morning and he said to me,
"Remember, early on I told you that either you are in a position
to actually do something to free people, or these good intentions
of yours will sooner or later turn you into an intermediary."

"Shamil, look at it from a different angle," I countered. "They
released those hostages in four hours. This is a shock for me.
Shamil, what's more they are open to our participation in this and
they are doing everything in a forthright manner. It's embarrassing to compare what they did to what goes on here. And they are
approaching you officially, you are Deputy Prime Minister."

"All of this is well and good," he replied, "if they were civilians
but this is the FSB and I don't want to go near the FSB."

"They are approaching you officially," I continued. "They are
our neighbors and they just made a very graceful gesture and they
are looking for a similar gesture from you." I tried to reason with
him, but Shamil shut me down and changed the subject.

A few days passed and I got a message from the Chechen businessman. He owned a computer store and had a cell phone, a
rarity at the time; very few people had cell phones. Bezuglyi had
called him and asked that I come to Vladikavkaz for a meeting. I
was very cautious about this because I always tried to steer clear of
any and all security services. Once you make contact with them
they can involve you in things that you can't understand; you
become a pawn in some game that you can't see. However, I went
to see Shamil who said simply, "Go ahead. You should listen to
what he has to say."

I met Bezuglyi and his escort at the Chermen checkpoint and
they took me to the Vladikavkaz FSB building and we had lunch
at a nearby restaurant. I told him Shamil's position on the matter. Bezuglyi understood how to approach me; his last name is
famous in Grozny, because his uncle was the editor-in-chief of
Grozninskii rabochii, the main newspaper of the republic. The family had lived in Grozny for many years and Bezuglyi had grown

up in Grozny, knew Chechen, and generally understood how to approach me. I felt that he was being sincere. I was ashamed that we were not helping him and that our government couldn't do what he had done. But I was between a rock and a hard place. We were suspicious, rightfully, of everything that had to do with the FSB. I had warned Shamil, "Letting the bandits sell these hostages means strengthening the business, and you know there will be a ransom and a big ransom." I thought the stronger arguments were for helping Bezuglyi.

Bezuglyi explained to me that, "It is important to me personally, I want it to be my directorate."

I asked him, "Why is this your concern? Why isn't the Ingush FSB taking pains on this case?"

"I know that the Ingush will not be able to do it. And I don't want Tolboyev in Dagestan to release them." The different FSB directorates in the North Caucasus were in competition with each other over who would release Gribov and Lebedinsky. This meant that the bandits had a choice about whose ransom payment to accept. Magomed Tolboyev, a former Soviet kosmonaut, was at this time the Secretary of the Security Council of Dagestan, and was emerging as an intermediary, together with Nadir Khachilayev, a representative of the Lak nation of Dagestan. The two men had already arranged some releases of hostages who had been kidnapped in Dagestan and taken to Chechnya.

Bezuglyi had said to me very candidly, "I am personally interested in this case because it will have a direct impact on my career." He went on to say that they had $1 million, but the hostage takers were asking for $4 million. He wanted Shamil to persuade them to accept $1 million.

"Why are you willing to start this negotiation? Don't you understand that this is your fundamental mistake?" I asked.

"Ilyas, you have a point when it comes to civilians, but these are FSB agents and we're afraid that they'll just kill them."

I understood what he was saying. This conversation revealed the competition among different services, but also between branches within a service. He told me they had funds for the purpose of ransom payments. I don't know where the North Ossetian FSB Directorate came up with $1 million, but I know other situations where Chechen businessmen in Moscow were shaken down to contribute to ransom payments. As the different "customers" compete, they drive up the price. It's an ideal situation for the bandits who end up with all the trump cards in their hands.

When I returned, I did approach Shamil about this, but he wanted absolutely nothing to do with it, so I dropped the topic. In the end, Gribov and Lebedinsky were ransomed and released at checkpoint Gerzel on the Dagestan-Chechnya border. I talked to a man who was a witness to the trade and he told me that part of the ransom payment was in sniper rifles with silencers. The FSB was giving hostage takers weapons equivalent to those of the special forces! The hostage takers were incomparably ahead of our police in their weapons, cars, and communications.

In the fall of 1998 there came a whole series of hostage releases, suddenly one after another, of people who had been held for many months. What you saw on Russian television or in the official releases, was that the MVD was conducting these brilliant operations.

In one case I have information from two different sources that the release in December 1998 was actually staged. This was the case of Vincent Cochetel, head of the UN Human Rights Commission office in Vladikavkaz. He was from Tours, France. That's where I was hospitalized in 1995 and treated for tuberculosis. I felt some connection to him on that basis and paid attention to his case. He was taken hostage in January 1998 in Vladikavkaz. The hostage takers, in two or three cars, had to go through six or seven checkpoints to deliver him to Chechnya, so there must have been some degree of corruption. My two sources said that the MVD had hired people, paid a separate sum to act out the release scene, filmed it, and put it on TV. The scene closely resembled the release of Valentin Vlasov in which masked security services ambushed the hostage takers.

There were also two kidnappings of the Russian President's representative in Chechnya. The first was of Valentin Vlasov, in May 1998 and the second of Gennadi Shpigun in March 1999. The contrast in the way the political elite and the media handled these cases is striking. Vlasov's kidnapping did not change the tone of Russian-Chechen relations and there weren't bellicose threats or confrontations over the hostage taking. It was seen as one is a series of crimes, but not a reason to go to war.

It's probable that Baudi Bakuyev held both men, that's the name usually associated with kidnappings. The main piece of information about the release of Vlasov in September 1998 was that Bakuyev's men rapidly acquired white jeeps and the local villages started calling these vehicles "Vlasov mobiles." It's rumored that astronomical sums were paid for the release.

The Russian federation had a representative living in a compound at the airport in Grozny. This representative was usually an MVD General, who was changed every few months starting in 1997. When Shpigun's name was first mooted for this position Shamil came out strongly against the appointment. During the war, Shpigun had been in charge of the Glavnoe Upravlenie Operativnykh Shtabov (GUOSh). These were "filtration camps" where thousands if not tens of thousands of people were tortured and humiliated. I wonder if the Russians understood how many people in Chechnya would like to see this man dead. It's not clear to me how on earth Shpigun got assigned to this position but he became a sitting duck.

On March 5, 1999 Shpigun was taken out of his plane as it was approaching the runway for takeoff. This was something out of an action movie; several cars sped onto the runway and forced the plane to stop, then gunmen burst inside and pulled the General out. According to rumors current at the time, as soon as they left, another group arrived and also started looking for Shpigun. How did they do this without meeting any resistance and no shoot-out with the guards around the airport? Magomed Khatuyev was the head of customs and border guard and was close to Shamil. Vyacheslav Izmailov reasons that Shamil was behind this. I don't think that Khatuyev or Shamil deliberately planned anything, but the Chechen guards of this airport were not going to fire on other Chechens to defend the former head of the filtration camps. Why was this turn of events surprising to anyone?

The Vlasov release reveals the difference in the political mood. In March 1999 there were really bellicose statements from both sides. Russians were talking about this being an insult to the honor of the Russian state, and threatening to stage special operations to free the General. Maskhadov called it a provocation by the Russians, that it was the work of the FSB. The rhetoric became very heated and it was disproportionately shrill compared to any previous hostage taking.

Apart from the four telecom workers, Gennadi Shpigun was one of a handful of high-profile hostages who was not recovered and died in captivity after the start of the war, probably when the airport was bombed. According to official Russian sources, all the hostage releases were the result of special operations, but never once were the hostage takers named. I think it was entirely possible to ransom Shpigun and apparently Bakuyev had been trying to negotiate such a deal but the war started, and that made everything much more complicated to arrange. It's also possible that the Russian side thought that they would free him in the course of the military operations. I don't think there was a deliberate political motivation on the Russian side to use Shpigun as a *causus belli*, but certainly when it happened it generated an enormous amount of very bellicose rhetoric.

As to the four telecom workers from Great Britain and New Zealand, I did not have direct knowledge of what happened. But as with Vincent Cochetel I was getting information from someone who was a witness to some aspects of it. It's impossible to keep secrets in a place as small as Chechnya and I am now relating the version that was being discussed at the time. I think I was given correct information and in comparison with the other version available, my version is more logical and coherent.

All the high-profile cases ended in ransom except for those of Shpigun and the telecom engineers. The killing of the engineers was particularly grizzly, they were beheaded and their heads were left on the road. It was so terrible and outrageous and there were so many loose ends and coincidences that all manner of theories abounded. This happened in December 1998 when internal power struggle between Maskhadov and the opposition commanders had reached boiling point.

The employees of Granger Telecom were brought to Chechnya in 1998 by several businessmen who sought to set up a cell phone company. The monopoly on mobile telephones was being controlled by Movladi Udugov; he had set up Chechnya's only cell phone company. There were no land-lines for telephones and there was only one cellular phone company. Most of the population relied on the old central telephone exchange, where you prepaid for a particular amount of time, and you went to a booth to make a phone call. The Chechen government made arrangements with Udugov's company and wound up owing them obscene sums of money. All Chechen government officials had cell phones with Udugov's company, but they didn't understand how expensive the deal was and that the phones should be used sparingly. The government ran up a bill that it couldn't pay, and Maskhadov terminated the contract, in effect leaving the government without phones.

In 1998, a group of businessmen from the *teip* Melkhi invited a British company, Granger, to set up a competitor cell phone company. The engineers had been in Chechnya for several months and their work was almost complete. They were testing the system, when they were kidnapped by Barayev's people in October 1998. It's universally understood that they were held for a while and were eventually killed by Barayev's gang in December 1998.

There are several versions explaining why this case ended in beheadings rather than ransom. One version is that Udugov had something to do with this because of the business competition. I find this implausible. Udugov's goals were ideological; he was instilling certain ideas and he sought political goals. He did not need money the way that the bandits need money; he needed money for his ideological and political campaigns.

The other version—that the killing of the telecom workers was meant to discredit Maskhadov on the heels of a trip to the United Kingdom where he had met Margaret Thatcher—is also dubious. The United Kingdom is very far away. For Barayev, sitting in Urus Martan, in a state of permanent paranoia, ruining Maskhadov's international image was not a high priority. Moreover, Maskhadov had taken several trips, including to the United States. Nothing ever came of those trips and there was no reason to suppose that the visit to the United Kingdom would be more worrisome for the Russians than Maskhadov's other trips.

I have a different version that is more about banditry than politics. The Melkhi decided to take on Barayev. They armed themselves and all their relatives and kidnapped three of Barayev's men, one of whom was some sort of low-level "commander," a person who was directly responsible for leading hostage-taking raids. Obviously Barayev did not carry out hostage takings himself. His guys were Wahhabis and cultivated long beards. According to what I heard, the Melkhi humiliated them by forcing them to shave with a piece of glass. The message went back to Barayev, "Free the hostages or your three guys will have a very bleak future." There were negotiations, but Barayev did not accept their terms. Consequently, the Melkhi cut an ear off the "commander" and sent it to Barayev.

You have to imagine this situation from Barayev's perspective: he was a cold-blooded killer with an image to maintain. He was the "General" of hostage taking and suddenly some lousy businessmen had come after him on his own turf, using his own methods. Barayev had lots of enemies, *krovniki*, and our security services. He was sitting in Urus Martan armed to the teeth and getting paranoid.

Barayev could afford to lose the ransom payment. The reports were that $4 million was being offered by Granger. The next day, he could take more hostages and sell them for $10 million. What he absolutely could not afford to lose was his name and his status; and that's what he was looking at with the Melkhi. They had three of his guys, and for him his gang was his *teip*. He was no longer a Chechen in the traditional sense; he had crossed over too many lines. From his perspective, cutting off the commander's ear meant that someone was coming into his territory and trying to beat him at his own game. That raised a question of honor for Barayev. For his men, he was a charismatic leader who had to demonstrate that no one could control him. So he scuttled the game, broke all the rules, and showed he was out to win at any cost. That's why those engineers were executed in such a shocking and terrible way: four heads lying on the icy road. This makes sense in terms of the bandit's mentality and, I think, is the most credible explanation.

The representatives of our government, Turpal Ali Atgeriyev, the MVD Minister, Islam Khalimov, and Maskhadov himself said that they would take the most decisive measures against hostage takers. It looked like Maskhadov had abandoned his caution as the fight against hostage taking became an absolute political imperative. However, in reality it was the Melkhi that took the lead.

Later, propagandistic explanations started to grow like mushrooms after the rain. The Kavkaz Tsentr website ran videos where the engineers confessed to being spies against Ichkeria. Why would Barayev care even if they were spies? He had a full-time job as "General of the slave trade." He made a video for propaganda purposes; and one can imagine Barayev's "investigation" and "sharia court." Barayev was at war with Ichkeria. Then after September 11, 2001, the Russian media come out with the version that Osama bin Laden had paid Barayev $1 million for the killings. This was opportunistic Moscow propaganda. It was a convenient lie meant to persuade the Americans that Chechens were connected to Al-Qaeda. There was no reason to think that Osama bin Laden had anything to do with this.

The supposed link to Osama bin Ladin was Khattab, who ostensibly fought under him in Afghanistan. However, Khattab was never known to be involved in hostage taking. His forty-five-day course in Serzhen Yurt was financed by the Middle East and had Arab instructors. This course accepted anyone who came and was free of cost for the student. You had to pass a test, and some those who failed to follow all the rituals were dismissed. That was very important to these camps. They taught specific military skills, sniper, grenade launcher, mining, and explosives. Once the students finished his course, they were free to go. They had a fearsome image: long beards, fatigues, and supposedly, a righteous way of life. Some of these trainees wound up among the hostage takers, but not Khattab himself. If he had gotten involved in either the ideological battles or the hostage trade he would not be able to pursue the central mission of his life—the jihad.

I don't believe in the conspiracy theories that paint elaborate networks between Chechen hostage takers leading back to the Kremlin. I think the primary motivations in any particular hostage taking were much more about banditry than about political manipulation. Of course, the hostage trade had political consequences: the enormous ransom payments ensured that the worst elements in our society, the most unruly and cruel units, would have the best equipment and resources. A great deal is said about financial support from Arab sources to spread jihad in the North Caucasus. But who knows which one was more destabilizing for our society—the Wahhabi money or the ransoms?

What is clear is that while extremist and criminal units received subsidies from abroad, no one supported our official structures. No one was interested in bolstering the capacity of our government to ensure security and stability. The Russian propaganda machine blamed all Chechen leaders for the hostage trade, which became a convenient way of discrediting all of us. The ransom-demand films showing terrified victims with severed fingers became Russian propaganda films. How could these barbarians be taken seriously in their claim for statehood? And most outsiders felt no need to draw distinctions between our government and the gangs; it was easy to dismiss all of us as guilty of involvement in this hostage trade.

CHAPTER 7

CRISIS WITHIN CHECHEN SOCIETY

In 1998, a myriad of armed units and splinter groups formed an opposition bloc and sought to impeach President Maskhadov. The confrontation with Maskhadov built up gradually out of minor scuffles between different units, but by the end of 1998 it had grown into a political struggle between the two ideologically distinct camps. During that spring and summer two camps began to emerge: those who supported the President and were nationalist and secular in outlook, and the opposition that was radical and sought power by removing the President. The conflict culminated in a six-day battle between these groups at Gudermes in July 1998 and a subsequent assassination attempt on Maskhadov.

The disparate elements in the radical camp needed an influential leader from among the political elite, and found such leadership in Shamil, who was disenchanted with his position in the government. His final break with Maskhadov came in the summer of 1998 when he left the government and aligned himself with the radical elements.

The result of the political struggle was mixed. President Maskhadov reluctantly adopted elements of the opposition's platform, but they could not force him out of office. Though the opposition was very vocal, active, and well-armed, it was a minority that could not speak for the nation as a whole, and Maskhadov proved repeatedly that he had broad public support. By the summer of 1999 it was clear that Maskhadov would retain the presidency and survive any future challenge to his authority. However, the opposition groups distracted him from building state institutions and we lost valuable time in these power struggles. The radicals foisted a radical religious agenda on him and continuously challenged his authority. At the same time they discredited themselves and their ideology by failing to observe the very sharia that they introduced into the country. To build a viable state we needed a government that would assert itself against these elements, and with evident public support Maskhadov was trying to do exactly that. The group that staged the August 1999 incursions into Dagestan had already lost Chechnya's internal power struggle, and sought to recoup their political fortunes by inciting a wider rebellion in the North Caucasus.

One of the obstacles Maskhadov faced in creating state institutions was a lack of consensus about basic values, chief among them was the relationship between religion and law in the new Chechen state. The Islamic code of law, sharia, had been present in Chechen society for 300 years, but had never been instituted as a legal system representing the state. There were two short-lived attempts in our history to create states governed by sharia: the Imamate of Shamil in the nineteenth century and the Emirate of Chechnya and Dagestan in the twentieth century. The Emirate was proclaimed by Uzun Khaji, the last living *naib* of Imam Shamil, during the chaos of the collapse of the Russian Empire in 1918. In the 1990s there were several legal codes operating: the official law was Soviet, but the law that governed most civil matters was the Chechen customary law, the *adat*, or sharia.

Our first attempts at instituting sharia law after the Soviet experience was during the war, when court martials started to render judgments on that basis. I witnessed one such trial. A Russian policeman had visited a Chechen policeman at Gudermes and the two got drunk. The Russian said, "I'd like to see a real Chechen fighter." "I've got cousins in the mountains," replied the Chechen cop. In a state of total inebriation they managed to circumvent Russian checkpoints and wound up in areas controlled by Chechen fighters near Vedeno. They were promptly delivered to the local headquarters and had to appear in front of a sharia court. The Chechen policeman received forty lashes and the Russian none, because the judges deemed they had no jurisdiction over him. Moreover, they let the Russian go, because he had trusted the Chechen, whereas the Chechen was charged with aiding the enemy. It was a sad spectacle. All these sharia courts usually did was dole out lashes to alcoholics. Moreover, the sharia courts coexisted with the secular judicial system, and it was not always clear which institution had ultimate jurisdiction.

During the war, several Arab emissaries came to Chechnya; the most famous was a Saudi guerrilla fighter named Ibn al-Khattab. He arrived from Afghanistan where it was rumored that he had received training in diversionary tactics from the CIA. He certainly taught us many new tricks and became a fearsome symbol of the international jihad. I saw Khattab several times and although I do not claim to know him very well, he certainly seemed smart. He had a funny accent, in Russian and his speech was not completely grammatical. I remember him saying, "I don't tell you what to do. You live as you think right. Chechens don't take an interest in jihad. You take an interest in jeep or a Stechkin pistol."

Khattab never took a stand on issues of internal Chechen politics and he never proselytized publicly. He remained in Chechnya after the war and lived according to his own rules; people who trained with him in his camp near Serzhen Yurt learned these new norms and rules of behavior. He ran a forty-five-day course that was free and available to anyone who came. Some did not last all the way through, but everyone had an opportunity to try. It was essentially a boot camp featuring intensive exercise and basic training in shooting and fighting, and even more important, the basic norms, values, and daily rituals of the Salafi Muslims.

This could be seen in the intense debate over head scarves. It would have been utterly inappropriate for Khattab to make a public stand on the issue, and he understood our mentality, that we would reject him if he started commenting on our way of life. Instead, Khattab stayed out of all of these discussions; he just showed an example of what he considered a righteous life, and taught this in his camp. This approach was very effective.

Even though Khattab was not in the public eye, there were plenty of Chechens who went on television to proselytize. Our television station would allow anyone who wanted to speak to appear, provided they had a gun or two. One could go to the studio, sit down and start talking.

Meanwhile, the factories were at a standstill; agriculture was destroyed; the fields were mined; the university was barely functioning; and most secondary schools were closed. There were armed bands preying on the population. How could one make a name for himself? Simple: join a sharia court, or force women to wear headscarves, or segregate buses along gender lines. The introduction of alien religious norms represented a sphere of activity where any young man who wanted to be noticed could show that he had initiative.

Traditionally, Chechen women did not wear head scarves prior to marriage; married women wore a thin ribbon around their heads. Suddenly this became a political issue and all women had to start covering their heads. This became state policy; a woman could no longer enter a government building unless her head was covered.

Then came the controversy over buses. The Ministry of Transportation received a proposal to divide buses with partitions, and women were to use the front entrance and men the back. However, someone noticed that most of our buses had only one door, so it was resolved that buses would henceforth become single-sex. But then another problem arose: what was to be done if a whole family needed to travel together? Was the woman to board the bus with the children and the man board the next bus? And then they would have to wait for him someplace? This whole inane debate within the Ministry of Transportation was televised, and in the end came to nothing—men and women would continue to ride the bus together.

The elderly, who had a degree of knowledge and education in these matters, kept their distance. All of our sharia authorities were young men, who supposedly received religious education abroad in Saudi Arabia or Egypt. One never knew if they really had qualifications—but who among us was in a position to judge? Those who were educated in Russia used the Russian translation of the Koran by Iganati Krachkovsky. That was a rather minimal basis for undertaking something as ambitious as the introduction of a legal code based on sharia law into a post-Soviet society.

It is important to draw a distinction between different meanings of the term "Wahhabi." There were a few religious emissaries from Arab countries: Arabs and some ethnic Caucasians, including Chechens like Fathi and Abdurakhman, who were descendants of Chechens who had fled to the Middle East in the nineteenth century. They were adherents of Salafism, or pure Islam, and their small circles consisted of truly devout people. Who we referred to as "Wahhabis" in casual conversation were enormous men with long beards, draped with garlands of ammunition and grenades, who used the concepts of righteousness as a primitive excuse for criminality and political ambition. The Chechen Wahhabis at best had a few quotes from Krachkovsky's translation of the Koran which they used as needed to fit their needs at any particular moment. They took advantage of the tremendous ignorance of religion in Chechnya.

So it was that any man with a beard and a uniform could consider himself a guardian of moral virtue. Any man in camouflage could take it upon himself to stop couples in the street and ask if they were properly related. They would break into rooms in the public bath houses to see who was there. This was never considered normal in Chechnya. The war against alcoholism and the televised spectacle of lashings was also totally unacceptable according to the way that I was raised. But it was impossible to tell who was really affiliated with the government. Did these people have any authority to enforce these rules? The common man did not know what do in these situations. If a person were considered to be pro-Russian or only passively in favor of independence, or if he did not have the patronage of a powerful commander, he became doubly vulnerable.

These Wahhabi groups were behaving provocatively, and small, sporadic confrontations between them and the authorities began in 1998. The first violent confrontation occurred after the government sought to break up the rallies sponsored by Salman Raduyev's "Army of General Dudayev" or "Path of Dzhokhar." Raduyev had fought in the war, been seriously wounded and had reconstructive surgery done on his face. During the war he became famous for the hostage taking in Kyzlyar, where he seized a hospital. It was a less successful version of Shamil's raid on Budennovsk. Raduyev sought to repeat Shamil's example but had obtained no political concessions. During the Presidential elections he was very active in Yandarbiyev's campaign. After the elections when many others—including some from the opposition—went into the government, Raduyev and his party remained in opposition.

Raduyev had his own television station, Marsho, and he used it to spread his message. He was a gifted speaker and his speeches were impassioned and lengthy. He mostly complained and I could never quite understand what he wanted; other than flinging invective against the government, he offered no positive political program. He had a few dominant themes: first was how terrible everything was (this at least was true, and everyone knew it). Second was that Maskhadov had made too many compromises, that we should have no relations with Russia at all, and that we should not recognize any of the agreements that we had made with the Yeltsin government. The only positive suggestion, if it can be called that, was a very amorphous scheme about Caucasian unity, a confederation of the Caucasus nations. Another dominant theme was that all world politics were somehow being played out in Chechnya. His worldview placed our little battles at the center of the universe, portraying us as far more important than we actually were.

It was always hard for me to see Raduyev's speeches as anything other than demagoguery, but he had a large, stable, and committed following. Raduyev had people out on the street in the middle of the city in the square across from the Reskom (Republican Committee of the Communist Party), which is what we still called the Presidential palace, demonstrating against the government for almost a year.

Among the discontented people on the square were those who claimed that Maskhadov's policies were too secular. There were also radicals there, and a collection of criminals, all of whom made up the opposition. Usually the star of the rallies was Raduyev, but sometimes other opposition figures made statements and attracted basically the same mass of people.

The people who gathered at these rallies were the poorest, most desperate segments of the population, including the war widows and others who were deeply disappointed with their lives. There were odd characters among them, like the exotic religious figure Dati, who to me looked like a shaman, draped in talismans and amulets and pronouncing incantations. Dati had a charismatic authority over this crowd. Under his guidance the demonstrators started to build a clay tower, a bizarre memorial to the heroes of holy war. It was called "Gazotan bow," the tower in honor of the *gazawat*. This turned into an endless demonstration, continuing night and day. The government had repeated many times that this demonstration was unsanctioned, but took no measures to disband it.

In June 1998, Maskhadov grew impatient with the rallies and asked one of his own commanders, Lecha Khultygov, Director of the National Security Service, to resolve the problem. He was a former Field Commander, a very tough, direct man, and a highly effective ally of Maskhadov. Khultygov took his men, smashed the tower, and chased the demonstrators out of the square. The demonstration, of course, resumed the next day. Then Khultygov went to Raduyev's television station, Marsho, expropriated all the equipment and shut down the station.

But in addition to the weird crowd on the square and the television station, Raduyev had a very well-armed unit of between 100 and 200 men. I have never seen as many sniper rifles in one place as when Raduyev moved around the city with his unit; every other man with him had a sniper rifle.

On June 21, 1998, a day or two after Khultygov seized Raduyev's TV station, Raduyev's men seized the government television station and told the staff to leave.

Someone must have called Khultygov, who wasted no time getting to the station with his men. They burst in, and according to witnesses, Khultygov yelled, "All of you are under arrest, eat the floor." This is very insulting language; this was not a game of "cops and robbers," and among Raduyev's men there also were some very respectable people. One was Vakha Dzhaffarov, who was well-regarded in our circles, though what he was doing as Raduyev's Chief of Staff no one could understand. I had met Dzhaffarov only twice. He struck me as a normal person who was known for being calm and reasonable and had been on the political scene for a long time; he had first became famous after fighting in Abkhazia along with Shamil.

Precisely how a deadly shootout at the station involving Dzhaffarov and Khultygov started remains a mystery to me. Witnesses told me that Dzhaffarov shot and killed Khultygov; then one of Khultygov's guards shot and killed Dzhaffarov; and, finally, one of Dzhaffarov's guards shot Khultygov's guard. The miracle is that the dueling stopped there. I do not know who stopped them and how, and I cannot remember if there were any wounded—but there were three dead, and two of them (Dzhaffarov and Khultygov) were fairly substantial figures.

I heard what had happened on my hand radio set as I was driving through the city, and I hurried to the building, arriving within a half hour of the shooting. On the way, I connected with Shamil and his guards. When we arrived, there were five of us: Shamil, two bodyguards, one of Shamil's commanders, Dzhaambulat, in uniform, and me in civilian clothes. We were probably the least impressive looking of any of the people there.

When we arrived at the television station, even the front yard was packed with fighters. Everyone who had any influence was there. Most were armed to the teeth and it was impossible to figure out who was with whom. We went inside the building; it was a small space crammed with men. We could not walk through the building; there were loaded grenade launchers all around us. All I had was a pistol under my shirt. I made my way very carefully through the crowd, trying to show that I did not have a weapon in my hands, and moving people out of my way very gently. One wrong move and this powder keg could have exploded. It was surreal, going from room to room, and everywhere fighters were standing with weapons drawn. Down one hallway, I saw mourners starting to sing and perform the circular dance, the zykr.[1] Three men had just lost their lives in this space, all because of a few ill-chosen words. We could barely squeeze by the grenade launchers and sniper rifles, and people were already voicing funeral chants and dancing.

At the end of the hallway was a little entry-way and then the studio; again, these were very small spaces and people were crammed in. In the studio were Raduyev, a few of his people, and Vakha Arsanov, the Vice President. Shamil and Dzhaambulat made their way in. The bodyguards and I could not fit and we stayed at the entrance. Raduyev was extremely upset, yelling that his Chief of Staff had been killed and trying to recount the story from the beginning. Arsanov was trying to calm him, saying that this issue could not be settled through confrontation and we should go to the courts. Still, Arsanov was willing to listen to Raduyev's arguments.

But Shamil would not let Raduyev seize the opportunity to escalate the situation further. He cut off Raduyev pretty harshly, saying, "All of this has to be decided in the courts. If you try to find the truth here and now, you will provoke this situation, and all of our lives will be on your conscience. You seized the television station, that was a crime, and this needs to go to the sharia court."

He firmly told Raduyev, "What you are doing right now constitutes an attempted coup. You should lead your men out of here immediately. The killings will be judged by the sharia court. We are not bandits and we won't decide this right here and now. Your side and the opposing side will be heard in court. The only thing to be done right now is for you to leave these premises."

I think Raduyev must have realized how dangerous the situation was for us. He said, "I am willing to go to sharia court, but I declare that the blood feud for Vakha Dzhaffarov is on me!" And he started to move his men out. It took roughly forty minutes to clear the place.

When we were all outside, Raduyev gathered his men around him, "We are leaving but that does not mean that any of the issues will be left unresolved. The blood vengeance for my Chief of Staff, Vakha Dzhaffarov, is on me. We came to the station only to get our own station back and we will go to the sharia court to settle this issue." The whole crowd, including the singing women and sniper rifle-toting fighters, left in their usual theatrical mode, which included shouts of "Allah Akhbar"; but this time they did not shoot into the air.

Immediately after these events, Maskhadov proclaimed martial law and a state of emergency—but these were just an opportunity to say something rather than do anything. The government declared that people could not drive around the city at night. But who was going to stop jeeps full of fighters? A single car with civilians would be stopped at a checkpoint and turned back, but a jeep full of fighters would be stopped by no one.

The next set of violent confrontations involved the *dzhaa-mats*, which in its original meaning is a religious community or village, but in our context came to mean a group of fighters who proclaimed fervent religiosity. The sharia court had existed since the war and two units had been created in 1996 and assigned to the court. These units were Abdul Malik Mezhidov's Sharia Guards and Arbi Barayev's Islamskii Polk Osobogo Naznacheniya or IPON (Special Purposes Islamic Regiment) had been created in 1996 under Zelimkhan Yandarbiyev, who was acting president following Dudayev's death. Because these units were assigned to the sharia court one of their duties was to guard the prisons. It is completely unclear under what law they operated and what their jurisdiction really entailed. These units ended up only outraging the public and challenging the foundations of the state.

These guardians of public virtue behaved as they wanted; they stopped people for unclear reasons, such as "unbefitting appearance," they searched markets and seized alcoholic drinks. They humiliated people arbitrarily and provoked conflicts within society. Around this time, in May or June 1998, Barayev led a raid to destroy marijuana plants at Alleroi, Maskhadov's home village, where most of his closest associates (including Turpal-Ali Atgeriyev) were from. This was very provocative, and when First Deputy Prime Minister Turpal-Ali Atgeriyev found out that Barayev was conducting random searches in his home region, he tried to stop Barayev's column. One of Barayev's men hit Atgeriyev in the face with a rifle butt, and one of Atgeriyev's bodyguards was beaten. This incident was contained, but the frequency of such confrontations between pro- and anti-Maskhadov factions was growing.

The rifts in society were growing throughout the republic, but it boiled over in Gudermes in July 1998 from very trivial beginnings. One version of the story has the confrontation beginning when either Mezhidov's or Barayev's men tried to arrest a man for buying alcohol at the market in Gudermes. He was a former fighter who resisted, and was killed. Another version claims that a café owner who served alcohol was being arrested by the members of the *dzhaamat* and was killed while resisting "arrest." Regardless of which version is true, Yamadayev's people killed two Wahhabis in response.

Gudermes was under the control of the Yamadayev brothers, who were close to the Mufti of Chechnya, Akhmad Kadyrov. The Yamadayev brothers had their own scores to settle with the Wahhabis because the latter had already made several assassination attempts against Kadyrov. The quarrel between the Yamadayev brothers and the *dzhaamats* was essentially a turf war between rival gangs; they were continuously in conflict over the hostage taking trade.

The situation escalated rapidly when the Sharia Guard and the IPON released the prisoners from the main holding facility in Grozny and dispatched them to Gudermes to support the Wahhabis. At the same time, all the secular fighters who had scores to settle with the Wahhabis started moving to Gudermes.

The Wahhabis had annoyed many people, and it was impossible to argue with them because they claimed to speak directly for the Almighty. Their public beatings and searching of women for alcohol were deeply offensive to us. Their arrogant behavior caused countless grievances and many were eager to go to Gudermes and fight it out. The Sharia Guard would stop cars with couples and humiliate the man and woman inside, demanding to know their relationship. On what grounds were they being humiliated? Who gave these Sharia Guards authority to institute new norms of behavior through force and public humiliation? Even Imam Shamil faced rebellions among Chechens when he tried to institute public punishments.

The eruption of fighting in Gudermes gave everyone who had grievances against the Wahhabis an opportunity to take them on as a group; it was dangerous to go up against them individually. What ensued was a six-day battle employing all manner of weaponry, including mine launchers, which left over 100 dead. By different estimates, there were dozens of casualties, including some civilians, but mostly from among Barayev's and (to a lesser extent) Mezhidov's men. Significantly, Khattab and his fighters made no visible move to help the Wahhabis in Gudermes. Khattab never commented on internal Chechen power struggles: his line was that all of us are Muslims and should be united.

Maskhadov was waiting and watching, avoiding confrontation at all costs; he did not send anyone to Gudermes to participate in the fighting or to end it. Gudermes definitely showed that people were infuriated with the Wahhabis. Afterward, Maskhadov used the episode politically when he saw the anti-Wahhabi momentum rising.

During the fighting, I stopped in to see Shamil one dark evening. I saw a couple of men with long beards leaving his house; I assumed that they had come from Gudermes. The Wahhabis sought his support in ending this conflict, and they also sought out Vakha Arsanov. Shamil's position was that the government had to get involved and contain it, and that if we permitted this to escalate it could spill over into the other towns. It is important to emphasize that Shamil and Arsanov ended this conflict on live television as private citizens; due to their authority and charisma. Their influence did not derive from their government positions. Shamil tried to stop it but Aslanbek Ismailov, former Minister for Construction, and Abu Movsaev, former Chief of the Department of State security, and their men were there fighting against the Wahhabis. Both were commanders close to Shamil. In this instance (as in many others), their behavior was determined by personal factors.

Shamil's view of the situation was that the Wahhabis were sincere in their beliefs, which was good, but they were also fanatics, which was bad. He did not think that they had to be destroyed because they were young, idealistic, and served as fighters. From his perspective, the Wahhabis represented potential that could be channeled in a productive direction, particularly when we might be looking at another war with Russia. I assume that Maskhadov must have had a similar approach because he also had sought to bring the Sharia Guards, into government service.

In the end, I think these were political considerations, and the fundamental problem was that none of this was guided by the rule of law. The Wahhabis understood that they had strength and that for this reason people were negotiating with them. They could work out a deal and did not need to obey any laws. I watched the resolution of the fighting in Gudermes on live television: Arsanov spoke, followed by Mezhidov, and that brought the fighting to a halt.

Much of what was later written about Gudermes contained propagandist distortions. The distortions that were promulgated in moderate and nationalist circles were that the fighting in Gudermes represented Maskhadov's strategic campaign against the Wahhabis. On the other hand, the radicals, such as Doku Umarov and his Kavkaz Tsentr website, claimed that Yamadayev's were spies and that the fighting in Gudermes was a Russian provocation against Chechen unity. Whereas Maskhadov disbanded Mezhidov's Sharia Guards and Barayev's IPON in 1998, the two units were restored by Doku Umarov in 2007.[2] One of the Yamadayev brothers, Ruslan, who led the charge against the Wahhabis, eventually went over to the Russians, and became a Duma Deputy in December 2003. The second brother, Sulim Yamadayev, became the head of the special forces battalion "Vostok," which was particularly loyal to Russia and particularly cruel to the population. Both were awarded the top honor of "Hero of Russia," and both were killed in unclear circumstances in 2009. But in 1998 they were just unruly bandits with no particular political loyalties.

During these same days there was an attempted assassination against Maskhadov on the *Staropromoslyvoskoe shosse*. I drove by the spot not too long after it happened; my parents' house was not far from there. This was the closest of all the attempts against him. A parked car blew up as his convoy was passing, killing one of his bodyguards and wounding several others. Maskhadov was not traveling in the car that he usually used, and this saved him. He was immediately shown on television, with a bandaged arm and chest, and—if I am not mistaken—he mentioned that he harbored no suspicions against Zelimkhan Yandarbiyev and Arbi Barayev. Nevertheless, the procuracy demanded that they appear before the sharia court and swear on the Koran that they were not responsible for this assassination attempt. Yandarbiyev came to the court and was exonerated. Barayev did not show up but swore allegiance to the President.

When it became clear that popular opinion was on his side, Maskhadov used this situation to try to accomplish certain things: first the IPON and the Sharia Guard were officially dissolved (in reality they lived on, but were no longer part of official force structures); second, he called a partial mobilization of all the reserves, and appointed Shamil Deputy Commander-in-Chief; and third, he declared all Arabs *personae non grata* on Chechen soil. A list of those who had to leave the republic within forty-eight hours was published and included Chechens from the diaspora, like the Jordanian Chechen Abdurakhman, Khattab, the Avar exile from Dagestan, Bagauddin Kebedov (the spiritual leader of the Dagestani Wahhabis and one of the more prominent personalities around Khattab in Serzhen Yurt), and six or seven others. However, this decree was never enforced because Arsanov and Shamil again talked Maskhadov out of it. Aslanbek Ismailov, a close associate of Shamil, became Military Commandant charged with the implementation of martial law throughout the republic.

But the rule of law was still lacking. For his seizure of the television station Raduyev appeared at the sharia court, which found him guilty and sentenced him to several years in prison. He went to jail for about a week. At first he made a big show of how he accepted the authority of the court, but then he remembered his war injuries, and Shamil made an appeal on his behalf on health grounds. The sharia court granted him clemency because he was suffering from the after effects of his war injuries.

So what law was could be applied to Raduyev? He had seized the television station, which was a serious antigovernment action. Although he had not pulled the trigger, he had created the situation in which three killings took place. The sharia court was revealed to apply only to the defenseless, and this raised the most serious doubts about our ability to build a state. We lived in a space divided among tough guys, and with a government unable to defend itself against them. People saw such things happening every day, and the accumulation of such observations destroyed our morale. To build a viable state, our government had to assert itself decisively against the opposition, and failed to do so.

The summer of 1998 also marked Shamil's final break with the government. He had been Deputy Prime Minister for four months in 1997, and then returned as Acting Prime Minister for about six months in 1998, leaving in July on the eve of the Gudermes fighting. The first time he left was over specific policy disputes; the proximate cause was an appointment that he found offensive, although there were many other issues of contention as well.[3]

In the beginning of 1998, Atgeriyev offered Shamil, on Maskhadov's behalf, the premiership. My advice to him was to decline the position, "You are being appointed to share responsibility for the chaos. I doubt that you will be able to do anything now that you were not able to do before. I understand that Maskhadov wants you to share the responsibility for all these situations: the wars over oil, hostage taking, and overall chaos, but it's not possible to accomplish anything. The relations with Russia have come to a dead end, the attempts to organize reconstruction efforts have failed and there are no positive processes and you can't change anything."

For me it was not a question of personalities; it just did not matter if Shamil was Prime Minister, or if someone else was Prime Minister. Without normalized relations with Russia, which would permit the resumption of normal trade and transportation and facilitate international assistance for post-war reconstruction, no one could resolve these complex issues. What I said had no effect, and Shamil accepted the position and brought in a team of people: Vakha Ibragimov as Minister for Tax Collection, Aslanbek Ismailov as Minister of Construction, and Shirvani Basayev, his brother, as Director of the Yunko, the Southern Oil Company. Many criticized him for where he placed his brother, but Shamil had his own logic: "It's easier for me to control my brother than a different man." My sense was that by the time Shirvani got appointed, there was nothing left to steal. Udugov became Foreign Minister in this government, but Shamil had not brought him in; Udugov had been at a ministerial level in several governments under both Dudayev and Maskhadov.

In 1998 there were disagreements between Shamil and Maskhadov; Shamil was upset that the President didn't trust him with finances and refused to authorize spending for his programs. But this was not the decisive issue; the main issue was that Shamil lost faith that he himself could accomplish anything and felt he was treading water and not going anywhere. I knew before he told me that he would probably leave. He stopped coming to the office and increasingly lost enthusiasm for his work. He felt that he had failed. His office was elegant and stylish, but there were no portraits or paintings; the only ornament was an illuminated citation from the Koran that he had kept on his desk. Someone had sent him a massage chair, which he used frequently. This was the only thing that he took with him when he left. Shamil did not make any public statement or announcement when he left.

During 1998, Shamil moved closer to Udugov. My sense is that this was when the idea of "the liberation" of Dagestan was being developed. Udugov was Foreign Minister and had a television station, Kavkaz, which was propagandizing his views. He had a two-pronged foreign policy: to seek recognition from the Taliban and to foment rebellion in Dagestan.

Shamil and Udugov were never friends. During the elections in 1997, they were competitors and Udugov ran a tape on his television station that embarrassed Shamil. This tape was of a sharia tribunal in the summer of 1996 when an elderly man was tried and found guilty of providing information to the Russians that led to the bombing of a village, Makhety, causing a dozen deaths. Of course, Shamil was no judge or prosecutor; he argued at the time that he was relying on the rules of war. He had the court proceedings videotaped during which all the judges voted for the execution of the man. Shamil read the verdict and asked the man if he had anything to say, and he responded, "No. We will all meet again in the afterlife." Then he was tied to a tree and shot at by a firing squad. During very desperate times, there may have been logic to killing informants, but playing the tape during the Presidential elections was very embarrassing for Shamil. Udugov ran the tape without commentary, and in private conversations asserted that Shamil would become a dictator if elected President. However, during 1998, Udugov became a frequent guest at Shamil's house. I noted this because almost every time that I came by, Udugov was there.

In April 1998, I was driving in Grozny when one of Udugov's aides stopped me on the way and gave me six invitations to the April 26, 1998, founding Congress of Nations of Ichkeria and Dagestan to give to Shamil. They were printed on heavy, fine-quality paper and I thought to myself that Udugov knew how to throw a party. I gave them to Shamil and told him that I was keeping one invitation as a souvenir and had no intention of attending.

There was a little intrigue being played out at the Congress; it was not clear yet what the Congress would become but it was obvious that it was composed of the opposition. It would have been good for Maskhadov if they had elected him to some ceremonial position. There is a saying in Chechnya, "If a stable of horses is stampeding, run in front and steer them the way you want them to go." Similarly, if Maskhadov could have become the chairman of this group he would have had some chance of steering them in a different direction. Both Maskhadov and Yandarbiyev attended and probably hoped to be selected as leaders. As it happened, Adallo-Mukhamad Aliev, a poet from Dagestan, stood up and nominated Shamil for the chairmanship. Of course, this was all Udugov's show and it was arranged in advance. Maskhadov did not stay very long after he saw that Shamil was elected "Emir." Udugov, Adallo, and Bagauddin Kebedov were named his deputies. This group united malcontents from Dagestan and Chechnya and created a forum to advance their political ambitions under the banner of liberating Dagestani Muslims from the Russian yoke.

By 1998, Dagestan was emerging as the weakest republic of the North Caucasus. There was internal turmoil in Dagestan that had nothing to do with Chechnya; some of the conflicts were power struggles among nationalities, some were turf wars among criminal gangs, and overlaid on top of this was the conflict between traditional Islam as practised in Dagestan for generations, and the adherents of the "pure Islam." In December 1997, Khattab raided Dagestan, after which many of the local Wahhabis came under pressure and were forced to leave. Among them was Bagauddin Kebedov, a prominent leader of the Dagestani Wahhabis, who remained with Khattab in Serzhen Yurt.

Various delegations kept coming to see Shamil. Prominent among them was Nadirshakh Khachilayev, the leader of the Lak nation in Dagestan. These leaders and groups told Shamil that the righteous believers were being persecuted and that the overall environment was brimming with dissent and ready to rebel against Russia. Shamil was gradually stepping into the role of the informal protector of the believers in Dagestan. They were trying to suggest to him that he might be a modern-day Imam Shamil, which of course flattered his ego.

During this period, Udugov was Foreign Minister and stated many times that we should help our Muslim brothers in Dagestan obtain freedom from Russia. Udugov and his staff talked about Ingushetia and Dagestan as if they were foreign countries. I said at the time to Shamil, "There are no such 'countries' as Ingushetia and Dagestan. These are republics that are part of Russia." Udugov talked too much about the internal situation in Dagestan as we tried to improve relations with Russia. Why was he making such inflammatory statements?

In October 1998 the parliament summoned Udugov to question him about his statements. One of the deputies, Vagap Tutakov, asked him, "What is the nature of your special interest in Dagestan?" Without even looking in Tutakov's direction, Udugov responded, "I was just asked about Dagestan, and I forgot already; was it Vagap Tutakov or Tutak Vagapov?" That was the total extent of his comment. His behavior amounted to total contempt not only of the questioning deputy, but also of parliament as an institution; Maskhadov dismissed Udugov very soon after this incident.

Once, when I was at Shamil's home and we were sitting in the living room, he asked me, "Tell me, Ilyas, do you have a dream, a vision of our future?"

I answered, "Yes, I do have a dream. I don't have to be part of it, but I would like to look through a key hole and see on the other side that Chechnya resembles a state with normal political processes."

"You are an idealist, as are many among us," Shamil countered. "I used to believe this too, but now I can see, based on everything that I've experienced, we'll never be able to build a state."

"What do you mean? What have we been trying to accomplish all these years? And why have we made all the sacrifices if not for a Chechen state?"

"The Russians will never permit us to establish a normal state," he insisted. "We need to create a caliphate. The Russians will never let us be."

"Shamil, do you understand that a caliphate is an empire, a religious empire, but still an empire? Historically empires arise in one of two ways: if a state is so well run, prosperous, and beneficial to its citizens that its neighbors rush to unite with it, or if it is so strong militarily that it can conquer its neighbors. Right now we resemble a gang, and you cannot build a caliphate around a gang. Chechnya is a piece of land divided by rival gangs. We don't control our territory, we don't control our borders, there's chaos all around, and based on this you're going to build a caliphate?

"Your problem is that you are a hostage of your Soviet education," Shamil shot back.

"Okay. Let that be my problem, but I don't want my problem to become anyone else's problem. I don't pretend to understand these congresses and caliphates, and I don't think that they offer a way out, and I have no desire to participate in them. In any case, Shamil, in any endeavor that you undertake, if what you are doing is just and right in my understanding, I will always be your loyal companion and I will stand next to you, but I have to believe that you are on the right path."

He responded, "Each is free to make his own decisions and each will answer to the Almighty for his decisions and his actions."

This was probably the last time that I casually dropped by Shamil's house. After this we had very few meetings, partly because he moved to Serzhen Yurt and partly because our relationship changed. I think Udugov and Shamil were already hatching plans for Dagestan, and this is why they would quieten down when I entered the room, or isolate themselves from me.

After Shamil left the position of Prime Minister, he convened a meeting in July 1998 of those who had fought under him during the war. Most other commanders had called meetings of men who fought in a particular battle, or on a particular front, but we had never held one. Several hundred veterans, everyone who served under Shamil Basayev on the central front gathered at the training camp of the customs and border guards. Most carried pistols, as we usually do, but there was no particular effort to display weaponry.

Shamil had stopped wearing his uniform after the war, but now he was again in fatigues. He told us the following, "I have resigned as Prime Minister. I don't want to say too much publicly, but I left because in the given situation I could not accomplish very much. At the same time, I left quietly because I didn't want to hurt the chances of another person who might follow me in that position. Those of you who are in government service, particularly the border and customs service, should remain in your positions and remain loyal to the government. For me, my personal choice is to die in the cause of jihad."

When I heard him say this, I thought to myself, "*Where* does he intend to die for jihad?" In July 1998 the whole territory of the former Soviet Union was at peace. But he was not posing, though I had never heard him desire death in jihad before. After Abkhazia, Shamil had never taken a passionate interest in world events; he did not travel, we were very isolated from the rest of the world, and the idea that Shamil was going to fight and die someplace far from home did not seem likely. In retrospect, the most likely interpretation was that he intended to meet his end in jihad at home, and at the time, this phrase had a disquieting effect. I did not understand yet what it meant. I wanted to ask him to say more, but I did not think he would tell me. This discomfort stayed with me for a long time.

He was saying goodbye to us, at least in the capacity that we had known him in up to that point. After Shamil spoke, other commanders took the floor. They talked about all the familiar topics: anarchy in the republic, the lack of a social policy, and the absence of direction. There were no resolutions or conclusions drawn. The event lasted about an hour. Shamil had said goodbye to us so that he could pursue his personal quest to find his end in the path of jihad. A few days later, he left the city and moved to Serzhen Yurt, Khattab's training camp, where he remained until the summer of 1999.

I visited Shamil again in the camps in the late summer or early fall of 1998; I had not been in these camps since the war. They were constructed as summer camps for Soviet youth groups and factory workers and consisted of long rows of wooden cabins along the length of the river. This area made a convenient base for use during the war, and after the war Khattab made his training camp there. Initially it was a training facility of the Chechen Ministry of Defense but when Khattab took it over, Maskhadov issued decrees to dissolve it. The local population was annoyed with the camp, the war was over, but they still had to endure endless noise from shooting. The locals were the ones who most wanted the Serzhen Yurt base closed.

It was surreal for me to return to this place (where I had fought for several months) and find a checkpoint manned by an Arab and three Central Asians. I gathered that the Central Asians were of different nationalities because they spoke to each other in Russian instead of their native languages. I wore my fatigues and carried my wartime identification as Shamil's aide. I gave my identification card to the Arab, who called Khattab on the radio and received his approval. I then was permitted to drive up to the main gate, which had a second checkpoint and was manned by ten more Central Asians. I had never seen Central Asians in uniform in Chechnya. In a political sense, among Chechens, Shamil's career had ended, but here he was with people who were to us nobodies—they were foreign vagabonds and misfits, whom many wanted to expel from Chechnya. In a social sense the men now surrounding Shamil not only could not make a claim to political leadership in Chechnya, but could not even marry into a reputable Chechen family.

When I saw Shamil, the first thing I asked was, "Who are the Central Asians?"

"Don't worry, they're good guys," he responded.

I had come to ask Shamil to disband the party, "Marshonan Toba," which in Chechen means Freedom Party, of which I was the chairman and he the leader and the inspiration. I had repeatedly talked to him about disbanding it because we were not presenting the people involved in it with a real alternative; he had lost interest in the party anyway, and was putting a different strategy into place. He had agreed with me in principle but would not give me definite authority to officially disband it. I just held fewer and fewer party meetings. Shamil did not try to use the party in the coming impeachment effort or for the anti-Maskhadov propaganda that he engaged in.

After we discussed the party, he took out a folder that contained two or three sheets of paper and gave them to me to read. It was the draft text of an appeal to the parliament asking them to begin impeachment proceedings against Maskhadov. It was signed only by "initiative group." The charges were that

Maskhadov had exceeded his constitutional authority by not having a Prime Minister and that he made too many compromises with the Russians. It was written in the style of a Soviet-era denunciation.

I said, "This has the Komsomol drumbeat to it."

"Raduyev wrote it," Shamil said. I had hit the nail on the head: Raduyev had once been an activist of the official Soviet youth movement, the Komsomol.

"You need a little more to impeach a President than not agreeing with his policies, there has to be some serious infraction," I said.

"Well, take a look at this." And with that Shamil pulled out another piece of paper, which was a photocopy of an order from the representative of the Russian President, an Interior Ministry General. The order authorized issuing several thousand rounds of ammunition for Maskhadov's Presidential guards.

"Why is this a problem?" I asked. "Why shouldn't the Russians provide some ammunition? They provide training to the border guards, they occasionally hold various seminars. What's the problem?"

"This is just what I was able to get. Who knows what else there might be. This cooperation with the Russians might run much deeper," he replied. If he had any further information he did not share it.

I told him, "This is not going to work, because we don't have the institutions that might enforce it. Second, this is one more contribution to the chaos all around us and it can hardly result in a positive outcome." Shamil responded that this was his only remaining legal opportunity to change the government. I did not think that it was possible to dissuade him.

Shamil and the others held an evening *namaz* (prayer) outdoors in a field with roughly twenty people. Shamil invited me to join their meeting in one of the nearby barracks. Through the lighted window I could see garlands like New Year's decorations that were machine gun rounds. They were draped like decorations in the barracks. I refused the invitation, saying that it was getting late and that I had a long way to go to return to Grozny. That evening I learned that Shamil was just a volunteer, a student in Khattab's camp. He had gone there deliberately for religious instruction, to learn the Koran, not for any kind of military training. It was strange for me to see this transformation, for Shamil not to be a leader but just part of the group under Khattab's tutelage.

Shamil's competitiveness with Maskhadov was pushing him into strange alliances with people that he did not personally like; his departure from the government represented a final break and there was no longer any hope that he and Maskhadov would reconcile. In 1998, Shamil was thirty-four years old. He had already been a war hero and a national leader, but he was a failure as a Presidential candidate, a failure as Prime Minister, and he could not accept that his political career was finished. Although his premiership failed, the proposed Congress of the Nations of Chechnya and Dagestan opened up new possibilities for him to reinvent himself.

When the impeachment effort was made public in October 1999, I quickly recognized the text; it had not changed substantially. The initiative group consisted of Shamil, Salman Raduyev, Aslanbek Ismailov, Abu Movsaev, Khunkharpasha Israpilov, and Aslanbek Abdulkhadzhiev. In parliament it was introduced by Aslanbek Ismailov and gained no support; I doubt that it even came to a vote and I do not think it went to the Constitutional Court. The main consequence of this move was to insult Maskhadov.

Maskhadov sought to outmaneuver the radicals by overtaking their agenda. For this reason he declared full sharia law in February 1999. He thought that by doing this he could demonstrate that the opposition was really only interested in gaining power. If he implemented their program they would not be able to use the religious arguments against him, and would have to admit that they were simply seeking political power.

Maskhadov was still trying to co-opt the opposition by offering to create another extra-constitutional body, the Shura, which would include commanders and clerics. The opposition declined to participate in the President's Shura and created their own, Mekhan Shura, which for the first time united the entire opposition. The parliament issued a public statement saying that the President was overstepping his constitutional authority by proclaiming sharia law, but the opposition was undermining the foundations of the state.

Mass meetings were assembled in Grozny in which the government, together with the *muftiate*, always attracted bigger crowds than the opposition. The size of the rallies indicated that the public was behind Maskhadov and the secular state. During the summer, the fighting in Gudermes showed that the radicals were weaker militarily, and in the autumn they showed that they could not summon public support either on the street or in the parliament.

In 1999, Maskhadov declared a state of emergency twice to fight against theft from the oil wells. Armed groups seized wells, took what they could and left, or sometimes held the well for several weeks. The quality of the oil was low but it was cheap and it was popular in the North Caucasus. Television footage showed columns of oil trucks being ambushed. There was real fighting over this. Fighting broke out between Yamadayev and his own men; there were attempts to assassinate Maskhadov and Mufti Akhmad Kadyrov. There was constant tension because of numerous small-scale incidents.

For me personally, there was one positive result from Maskhadov decreeing sharia law in the republic: it provided the perfect pretext to officially disband the party. Political parties are contrary to sharia law, and Shamil had to accept this, and did. Ironically, we were the only party to disband; Raduyev's "Islamic Path" and Udugov's "Islamic Order," and other supposedly religiously-oriented parties remained active.

I called a meeting of the party to explain that it was being closed down. It was sad for me to see that we were disappointing people. In reality there was nothing that we could do for our supporters other than engage in political discussions. Still, they hung on to a feeling of being part of something bigger than themselves, to the hope for some degree of protection and patronage.

In July, on the eve of the events in Dagestan, I was offered the Foreign Minister's post. Husein Iskhanov, who had been Maskhadov's aide during the war and later became a member of parliament, came to see me with this offer. He explained that he along with Mairbek Vatchagayev had suggested my appointment to Maskhadov. Later when I met with Maskhadov to discuss the appointment (our first meeting since the war) he explained that Akhyad Idigov, who had replaced Udugov in the Foreign Ministry, wanted to simultaneously hold the office of Chairman of the Parliamentary Committee for Foreign Relations and the office of the Foreign Minister. Idigov would only leave the parliament if Maskhadov appointed him Deputy Prime Minister. Maskhadov was not willing to do that. "We already have more Deputy Prime Ministers than Russia does," he commented to me. I have to give Idigov credit for defending the constitution against the efforts to replace it with sharia law; he was one of the stalwarts on this controversy.

I told Iskhanov I was surprised by the offer of Foreign Minister. "I have not been doing very much," I told him, "I have been critical of the government, I'm just a private citizen and I doubt that I could be particularly useful. I'll think about it and I need to talk to Basayev about it. Prior to the congress, I was close to him and then I simply distanced myself, but I feel I should discuss it with him before I make a decision." A week passed and I could not force myself to go back to Serzhen Yurt. Then Iskhanov came to see me again and I felt uncomfortable, as if I were playing games, which I was not.

I started asking about Shamil and found out that he was at his father's house in Vedeno, and I went to see him there. I found Shamil alone at his computer. I think he already guessed why I was there.

"I am being offered the Foreign Minister position," I told him.

"And did you accept it?"

"I think I will accept it."

"Everyone will think that even my closest people are running away from me," he griped.

"No, Shamil, I've always been just a private citizen, and now I'm accepting an official position."

"So you also were always dreaming of high offices!" he retorted.

"Shamil, there were people who pulled you out of bed for patronage. In three years, I never asked you for any appointments. On the contrary, I turned down your offers."

"But you think you will change something?"

"I don't pretend that I will be able to change something. I just won't feel ashamed that I'm seeing all of this and not trying to do something about it," I said.

"I thought I would have an impact and twice I went into government and had no impact," Shamil responded. "You are one of the few people near to me who has not been tarnished. If you want my advice don't go into government now, wait a little while, the situation will change and there will be a place for you. But if you do go into government, you should expect that sooner or later they will make you the scapegoat for everything that has gone wrong."

"Shamil, I just came to tell you myself, so that you won't think that as soon as you left office, I went to over to Maskhadov to seek office. I value your opinion, but I intend to accept the appointment." On my way out, I stopped to talk to his father. We stood outside and chatted for a while; he was always very polite with me. And then I left Vedeno.

The next day I spoke to Iskhanov and accepted the position. I spent the next three days writing my concept of our foreign policy and on the fourth day I met with Maskhadov. He greeted me very warmly, hugged me, and said, "For seven months we spent day and night together and now for three years I don't see you." He scolded me for not visiting him and I responded that I did not want to trouble him. He invited me to his home the following night and leafed through my conception. He did not read it very carefully, just skimmed through it, and said, "Very good. You may begin your work." I was somewhat disappointed that he did not take a deeper interest in my foreign policy concept and discuss its specifics with me, but I understood that he had many other things on his mind. He had gotten to know me when I was helping him on the General Staff and during the post-Budennovsk negotiations, and knew that I shared his views, was well-educated, well-spoken, and had a diplomatic style. Maskhadov had solicited my views about possibilities of dialogue on many occasions in the past, so now when he was appointing me he was sure to know what direction I would want to pursue in office.

I was formally appointed on June 27, 1999, but was not confirmed by the parliament until September. One day when I came home from office, I found out from Malika, my wife, that my appointment had been made official. She told me, "A neighbor came by and said that on television they said you were appointed to something." I had not discussed the appointment with her or anyone else, because it was such a sensitive issue.

The first fact that I needed to grapple with was that we had no foreign policy. The first Foreign Minister after the war, Idris Akhmadov (no relation to me), was a writer and had made trips abroad but it is not clear that anything was gained from them. Then there was Movladi Udugov whose main preoccupation was diplomatic recognition from the Taliban. Finally, there was Idigov who traveled to the Baltics and perhaps other countries but was really very hampered by his dual appointments in the executive and the legislative branch. I met with Idigov prior to my appointment to ask his advice on how I might continue his work, but he offered no strategy.

I went with Ishkhanov to the ministry building. I was a little annoyed that no one had been alerted to introduce me to the staff. The building was totally bare: there was nothing inside, no furniture and no telephones. I did find a few staff people; one older man in the human resources department, whom I recognized from the days when I had been a very junior staffer in the early 1990s. I asked him to summon all the staff to the building. When I returned, I found that the conference room was full of people; everyone was standing because there were no chairs. I asked the old man, "How many staff members are there?" He told me 115. I introduced myself and laid out what I thought were the main starting points.

"I think that a staff of 115 for an unrecognized republic is a luxury we can't afford," I announced. "Especially because I know that you have not been paid in two years. I don't know whether any of us will receive salaries; we are unrecognized; there is no work flow. I think a staff of fifteen will be sufficient."

The general reaction was muted because the staff had lost all interest in the Foreign Ministry due to its inactivity. We talked for two or three hours. The main result was that Udugov's people demonstratively walked out and I did not have to fire them.

I continued, "I can see that many of you are armed. Please do not bring weapons into this building. I am not carrying a weapon and I don't have guards. This isn't a ranch and we're not cowboys, there is no reason to be armed in this building. I don't want to hear any talk about who fought and who didn't. I don't care what war you fought in, even if it was the Russo-Japanese War, save it for when you visit elementary schools on Patriots Day, because it has nothing to do with the work of this ministry. Finally, I don't want to hear anything about head scarves. If you come to tell me that this woman or that woman should be wearing a scarf, I will throw you out! Whether a woman covers her head is her business, to be decided in her family. I don't want to know anything about it."

After this meeting, I looked into my office. It had a desk and a broken bookshelf. I then visited the human resources department. There were no files there, no work histories. I thought there might be an archive of correspondence but there was none. There was no telephone, no list of contacts, and no computers. I was informed that while I was out, Udugov's people had come in and hauled away the large carpet on which the whole staff used to pray.

I went to Maskhadov's office and told him, "Look, I have no archive. There are no papers at all in my ministry; there's literally nothing there. How can there be no archive at the Foreign Ministry?"

"You didn't get an archive for one ministry," he snapped. "I didn't get a scrap of paper for an entire country. It's okay...just start working." I turned around and walked out.

This comment had a sobering effect on me. I understood that he had many other problems. I did not have a phone or a computer or a car and the only person who could help me was the President. There were two of us ministers without guards or jeeps: me and the newly appointed Apti Bisultanov Deputy Prime Minister for Social Programs. It was comical to watch government meetings disband; each minister would get into his jeep full of fighters with their weapons sticking out in every direction, like needles on a porcupine. It would take them a long time to maneuver their way out of the traffic jam in the narrow passage in front of the government building. Apti and I would walk together to the bus stop.

To obtain basic things, I had to sit for hours in the waiting room for Maskhadov while he held various meetings. My little triumphs were getting the phones connections activated and getting a driver. I held exams so that I could reduce my staff down to fifteen. Those who survived were mostly women, very well educated, some of whom had been there since Dudayev. They commented to me that this was the first time that they were actually engaged in something productive besides discussions about head scarves. I will not assert that we were a real Foreign Ministry but I want to think that, at least, we came to resemble the office of a small company. This was the condition we were in at the start of the next war, when the fighting erupted in Dagestan.

CHAPTER 8

INCURSIONS INTO DAGESTAN: WAR RESUMES

The first instances of fighting between Russia and Chechnya began in June 1999 with repeated skirmishes along our borders with Russian territory, along Ingushetia, Dagestan, and Stavropol. The most serious incident occurred when one of our customs posts was seized by Russians, who killed one of our guards, held the post for a day, burned it down, and then left. Another incident happened in the Sharoi district, near Dagestan; the Russians moved their post five kilometers forward. They claimed that this was in retaliation for an attack by Khattab's trainees, which is entirely possible. Because Khattab did not control the people he trained, it's possible that they learned basic skills from him and then applied them at that checkpoint.

On July 4, I had written one of my first press releases protesting a July 3 Russian air strike against a border post near the village of Lomaz Yurt, which wounded two border guards. That was the fourth air strike against Chechen territory in 1999. This attack represented an increase in such incidents compared to previous years. In 1998 there had been five air strikes and in 1997 there had been eight. In the second half of July there was a sharp escalation in the number of incidents on the Dagestani portion of the border including several nighttime exchanges of fire in the Kyzlyar and Khasavyurt sections. On July 29 there was an incident between the Russian OMON and Chechen border guards at the Krasno Oktyabrskii border post in the Kyzlyar section. The Russian side claimed that the Chechens had attacked their post; however, the one Chechen guard who was killed was found on the Chechen side of the border, at the border post that he had been manning.

In my press release, I made an official protest stating that the "provocations occurring on the border represent a prologue to a new round of military aggression by the Russian Federation against the Chechen state." I went on to say that the "Russian government either has no control over the situation, or these provocations represent a deliberate policy of Russia vis-à-vis Chechnya." I added that Grozny reserves the right to "take adequate measures to prevent such aggression in the future."[1] In Moscow, these were interpreted as "preventive strikes" and led General Ovchinnikov, the Commander of the Interior Forces, to respond that the Russian army was ready to launch its own "preventive strikes" against Chechnya.

The Congress of Nations of Chechnya and Dagestan was propagating the idea of the union of the two republics, although the details of their plans were not made public, it was clear that they would eventually go from rhetoric to action. In early August, Bagauddin Kebedov rushed home from Serzhen Yurt and by doing so made the overall scheme unfold in a way that was different from what had been intended. I drew that conclusion myself, but Shamil also had said that Bagauddin returned to his home village in Tsumadinskii *rayon* without informing Shamil. According to Shamil, President Magomed Ali Magomedov of Dagestan had sent messengers asking Bagauddin to return to the village; Magomedov claimed that he needed him in his internal power struggles. Bagauddin took the bait and returned to his village, whereupon he was surrounded and besieged by local police. Because Bagauddin was Shamil's Deputy Chairman in the Congress, Shamil was obliged to defend him.

The Tsumadinskii *rayon* of Dagestan is inland, mountainous, poverty stricken, and of no particular significance. Who would plan an attack on Dagestan to build the caliphate through the village Tando of Tsumadinskii district? Shamil appeared on television twice, appealing to Magomed Ali Magomedov to lift the siege of the village. Then Shamil, Khattab, and about 2,000 fighters went into the neighboring area of Botlikh to draw the Dagestani police and military from Tsumadinskii *rayon*. I don't know the details regarding when or how the Congress intended to "liberate the believers of Dagestan," but when the situation developed with Kebedov, they seized on it. The Congress had intended four operations, each named after one of the historic imams who had led the North Caucasus rebellions in the nineteenth century; this first operation into Botlikh was called "Gazi Magomed."

One had to be deaf, dumb, and blind not to know that the incursions were coming. Kavkaz television was propagandizing it before it happened. There was, for instance, the famous parade in Serzhen Yurt with all the alumni of Khattab's school. They carried black banners with Islamic writing led by Khattab, Shamil, Udugov, and his brother Isa Umarov, all of them in uniform. They had artillery and lots of weapons. The students were well trained and were more impressive than our regular forces, who were just kids, very poor kids, lacking everything. Once the incursions began, they were broadcast on television, including the proclamation of the caliphate and the appointments of Shamil and Khattab. It's notable in this context that there was no attempt to force Kavkaz television off the air. It showed night footage of the column that left Serzhen Yurt to attack Botlikh. They were airing information on how volunteers could join up with the Congress. I noted that Khattab made a televised political speech; until then he had not commented publicly on Chechen internal politics. This was noteworthy for me because it indicated that a very momentous change was occurring.

The Russian border posts, which had been along that frontier for years, were removed before the incursion, making it easy for this column of jeeps full of fighters to enter. This inspired an incredible amount of speculation. I doubt very much that Shamil had entered into an agreement with the Kremlin, nor do I think an explicit agreement was necessary. The Russians didn't need to do anything to make this incursion happen; they just needed to pay attention and make the most of the opportunity that Shamil himself was creating. It took a couple of days for the Russian forces to assemble, but eventually the entire North Caucasus Military District was activated.

The fighters from the Congress went from Serzhen Yurt to Botlikh in one night. The day they arrived in Botlikh they forgot all about Bagauddin and started to put their full political program into operation. They proclaimed a new government with Prime Minister Sirazhuddin Ramazanov of the Islamic Republic of Dagestan, and Shamil Basayev was given the title of "Military Emir" of the Congress of Nations of Dagestan and Ichkeria, and Khattab became his deputy.

I talked to many people who were witnesses to the Botlikh event. Botlikh is among the poorest part of Dagestan, the mountains are all sand, rock, and there is no cover. There was no opportunity for engagement between Russian soldiers and Congress fighters. The invaders were sitting there for about a week getting bombed by Russian aviation. As one participant recounted to me, you could just hear shouting "Rejoice! Our brother has become a martyr!" This welcoming attitude toward death is hardly traditional and for many of us it sounded utterly bizarre.

But there were real battles at the mountain peak *Oslinoe Ukho*. The fighting in Botlikh lasted from August 7–23, and the main events occurred when Khattab blew up a helicopter at the Botlikh airport, killing a colonel and the crew of the helicopter. Apparently, General Kvashnin had disembarked from that helicopter a half hour earlier. I believe they shot down a second helicopter somewhere in the mountains. On August 23, Shamil and his men returned to Chechnya and Shamil appeared on television to let the Russians know that there were no more fighters in Botlikh, which according to Russian television, they were continuing to bomb. Knowing full well that the Congress fighters had returned to Chechnya, Russian aviation continued intensive air strikes and artillery fire for several more days. I think this was deliberate and aimed at stoking the conflict rather than permitting it to die down. The majority of the civilian population of these mountain areas left their homes and went to the flatlands and cities of Khasavyurt and Makhachkala in Dagestan. It was easy for Russian propaganda to use these refugees to stimulate anti-Chechen feelings among the population in Dagestan. They were presented on television as refugees from the "Wahhabi incursions."

The reaction in Chechen society was muted. It was as though the people, the government, and the opposition were each living in different realities. People were inclined to view the fighting in Dagestan as part of the overall chaos, the build up in tension over the border posts. I don't think people were emotionally prepared to view this as the start of a new war; they wanted to ignore it in the hope that it would go away.

There was a government meeting in mid–August that included, the Deputy Prime Ministers Zakayev, Makhashev, Daud Akhmadov, the head of Yunko, and myself. I was new to these meetings so I didn't really understand how they functioned; Maskhadov was visibly in a bad mood, and he didn't say anything. First he let people just talk but after about fifteen minutes, he said he wanted to hear each of us express our own views. Each of us was very careful and hedging. You had to talk about the men who were in Dagestan, and whatever you said could be held against you. For this reason the participants were cautious in how they judged the ones in Dagestan. Those in the meeting reasoned that in the forces that entered Botlikh there are many, if not a preponderance, of Dagestanis, and because both sides of the conflict were predominantly composed of Dagestanis, this was really an internal Dagestani problem. So even though there were some Chechens involved in the fighting, the Chechen government was not to intervene.

When it was my turn, I said, "It's clear that this is a violation of the Khasavyurt agreements. It doesn't matter if the Chechens are a minority of that force; no one will be interested in these fine points. I don't think we have to dig too hard through all the circumstances that led up to this."

I had written an official statement to this effect from the foreign ministry that said the group that had gone into Dagestan did not represent the Chechen government, that the Chechen government condemned the incursion, and that we were calling on the Russians to form a joint commission to investigate this incident. Because the foreign ministry did not have its own press service or website, we relied on Chechenpress, which posted my statements, and were also read on the government's television station, but was only broadcast in Chechnya. Maskhadov approved this statement and made his own statement on television where he called the incursion a provocation.[2]

Chechenpress functioned as a state information agency under the ministry of information and it always posted our official statements. I'm aware that many analysts, particularly those in Russia, deny that we put these statements out but we did. Our statements may not have reached everyone in the West, particularly if people did not know to use Chechenpress as the official website and chose to rely on Kavkaz Center, the mouthpiece of the Congress of Nations of Chechnya and Dagestan. It's understandable if journalists in the West, who had no possibility of traveling to Chechnya, read the wrong website and were misled due to their ignorance of our situation. But the Chechen government did everything in its power to get its message out. We issued press releases and I gave frequent interviews to Russian and European journalists. Moreover, at a rally in Grozny, Maskhadov officially condemned the Dagestan incursions.[3]

I told Maskhadov that I had started speaking to the OSCE assistance group for Chechnya. They had played a very important role in the settlement of the first war, but in 1997 Yandarbiyev had exiled them from Chechnya because they insisted on speaking of Chechnya as part of the Russian Federation. The OSCE assistance group was the only international body whose direct mandate was to facilitate peace building and contact between the sides. This group was now based in Moscow. The chairman of the group was the Norwegian ambassador in Moscow, Odd Gunnar Skagestad. I initiated contact with him through Mayrbek Vyachegayev who had recently been appointed our representative in Moscow, and Skagestad invited me to Moscow to brief the group. Maskhadov was pleased with this and authorized me to go there and to offer the OSCE group security guarantees from us. I arrived in Moscow on September 2, right after the bomb explosion on Moscow's Manezh Square on August 31.

Skagestad and I met at the Norwegian Embassy for the meeting that lasted about six hours. There were representatives from several other countries; I think six or seven, including Bulgaria, Ukraine, Poland, and Moldova. I tried to explain to them that the fighting in Dagestan was the prologue to a new war; that the conflict was escalating and that with each day the potential to avert the war was diminishing. I briefed them on the situation in Chechnya and on the fighting in Dagestan.

My goal was to persuade them that if they couldn't relocate to Chechnya, which we all understood was unlikely, to consider a location in the North Caucasus that would be closer to Chechnya, such as Pyatigorsk. I was making the case that we were on the verge of a new conflict and they should exhibit their desire to avert this conflict. Our conversation revolved almost exclusively around security for their group. They were concerned by a recent burglary at the Red Cross office in Grozny, and, of course, the hostage takings of foreigners. I told them that the Chechen government regarded the return of the OSCE assistance group to Chechnya as a matter of the utmost urgency and would do everything in its power to protect them. I understood that this was not very persuasive. All that Skagestad told me was that he did not have instructions and would remain in contact with me.

Maskhadov tried to do all he could to prevent the escalation of this conflict. In my presence, his Chief of Staff Apti Batalov repeatedly dialled the *hot line to President Yeltsin's office*. The hotline had been installed immediately after the war for the purpose of enabling the Presidents to have direct contact. They tried this line many times but could never reach Yeltsin and within a few days the line went dead.[4]

Maskhadov sent Atgiriyev, who was among his closest and most trusted allies to Dagestan to try to arrange a meeting with Magomed Ali Magomedov. I was present at a meeting soon after Ategeriyev's return to Grozny at which Maskhadov was very upset and disappointed. Magomedov had asked that Maskhadov condemn the incursion publicly, which he had done repeatedly; all that Maskhadov was doing was seeking a meeting. It was very disappointing to him that Magomedov was stalling at such a critical juncture. On the following day Maskhadov tried to drive to Makhachkala but was met around Kizilyurt by a crowd that thwarted his passage. Supposedly this was a spontaneous protest, but we believed it was instigated by the local authorities so Magomedov could save face and avoid a meeting with Maskhadov.

Maskhadov was in touch with President Ruslan Aushev of Ingushetia and with Aleksandr Dzasokhov, President of North Ossetia. Aushev was willing to host a meeting of the North Caucasus Presidents at Magas to take up these matters. Maskhadov went to Magas but no one else came to the meeting. The meeting was publicly announced and it's entirely possible the Kremlin forbid the other Presidents from attending.

During the same days Maskhadov was desperately trying to reach Russian Prime Minister Yevgenii Primakov. I asked him why he had such confidence that Primakov would help and he pointed out several factors. Primakov was the only top-level person in Moscow who understood the Caucasus and would practice caution, and try to bring the conflict into the political rather than the military sphere. Primakov had grown up in Tbilisi and was a long-time friend of Dzasokhov, President of North Ossetia. On a policy level, Primakov was the only member of the Russian Security Council who had abstained from voting for the start of the Chechen War in 1994. When Primakov was Prime Minister in 1998, he had met Maskhadov at the home of Dzasokhov and they made a good impression on each other.[5] Efforts to reach him came to naught; Primakov would not establish contact with Maskhadov.

While we were scrambling to put a political dialogue in place to contain these events and mitigate their effects, Vladimir Putin, newly appointed prime minister paid a visit to Dagestan. He was televised at a meeting with military officers who urged him to propose a toast. He raised his shot glass, and said, "We must drink to the victory; to the victors. We must remember those who perished in this war; to the living soldiers; to the mothers...and to all of this we will drink together after the victory." And with that he put down his shot glass and did not drink it.[6] It was a very symbolic moment: during the days he was in Dagestan the fighting had subsided. As soon as Putin left, the Dagestani interior ministry commenced a punitive operation against Karamakhi-Chabanmakhi, the so-called Kadar zone.

This enclave had proclaimed Islamic law in 1998 and had been given permission by Stepashin a year earlier to live according to its own rules. The Russian Ministry of Justice actually issued a statement that the sharia as practiced in those villages did not contravene the Constitution of the Russian Federation.[7] Putin reversed this decision when he authorized an assault on the villagers.

The Kremlin had a variety of options at this juncture. They could have pursued negotiations with our government, or they could have launched a hot-pursuit raid after Shamil. Instead, they began to pound Karamakhi-Chabanmakhi. However, there was no obvious connection between the Botlikh events and the

Kadar Zone. The two are located in different parts of Dagestan, and the villagers from Karamakhi-Chabanmakhi did not support the incursion into Botlikh.

When the decision to break Stepashin's deal with the Kadar Zone was made, the federal forces gave the local residents no options. They surrounded the villages and bombed them, killing up to 1,000 civilians. It was clear to us that the Russian side was deliberately escalating the conflict. After all, Shamil had returned to Chechnya; why would they start pounding Kadar Zone. The only explanation is that the decision makers in the Kremlin wanted to make absolutely certain that the fighting would escalate. In response to the operation against Kadar Zone Shamil and the Congress's forces again entered Dagestan from Serzhen Yurt to draw the federal forces away from the villages.

This time the fighters went into a very strategic area, beginning with the district Novolaksk and continuing toward Kaspiisk, the Caspian seaport. They took over the Dagestani villages of Novolakskoe, Chapaevo, Shushiya, Akhar, Novoluki, Tukhchar, and Tamiyakh. Russian forces regrouped from the scene of previous fighting and engaged the Congress fighters within five kilometers of Khasavyurt, a stragically significant city. It was along the Rostov-Baku highway, only eighty-two kilometers northwest of the capital of Dagestan Makhachkala, and sixteen kilometers from Kaspiisk, the site of military factories and warehouses. Khasavyurt was not far from Makhachkala, a couple of maneuvers at best. This time the fighters chose an important route that threatened two major cities. Unlike the other battle scenes, this engagement threatened substantial portions of Dagestan.

When entering Novolaksk, which was populated by the minority Lak nation within Dagestan, the leadership of the Congress of Nations of Dagestan and Chechnya probably expected support from Nadirshah Khachilayev and his men. They represented the Laks, had ties to Khattab, and might have staged a revolt. However, there was no uprising of Laks or ethnic Chechens who lived in that part of Dagestan. If they had been successful, Shamil and his men would have taken over an important city and set off a rebellion among ethnic minorities. This did not happen, so when the Russian siege of Karamakhi ended, Shamil, Khattab, and the other fighters returned to their camps in Serzhen Yurt and Urus Martan.

The fact that they were permitted to return, and that there was no pursuit of them into Chechnya, was interpreted by many analysts to mean that they had some kind of safe passage. Their return was also seen as evidence of explicit collusion between the radical opposition in Chechnya and the Kremlin. I think it made perfect sense from the Kremlin's perspective to let them return to Chechnya. If the Kremlin wanted a war, and this was clearly the case, there could be no better *causus belli* against Chechnya than harboring Shamil.

The Congress fighters went back to their bases in Urus Martan and Serzhen Yurt, facing no obstacles in their path, and after a few days Russian aviation started pounding the border villages. On the way to Novolaksk, the fighters had taken over a Russian checkpoint and beheaded one of the Russian border guards. This was filmed and broadcast on Kavkaz television. I saw Maskhadov the day after that broadcast. He was shaking with rage and was saying that everything the Congress did was calculated to leave no other path besides war. This footage was subsequently broadcast thousands of times on Russian television. This beheading became stock footage for any news segment about the Chechen war.

We were so accustomed to living with unresolved political tension that it seemed possible that these incidents might somehow blow over. I'm ashamed to admit it, but I also nurtured the thought that this confrontation might dissipate. This was possible to believe, at least, before the bombings in Russian cities. It was a feeling of vertigo, like we were about to fall down a well, unable to stop our descent, and hardly believing this was all happening to us again.

When the first war started we had many illusions. I remember the New Year's eve assault as something light and easy and in the midst of that battle I didn't realize how bad it was. Only when we took stock and started to dig out bodies from the ruins, did we face the reality. And still, later into January and February 1995 we thought that Yeltsin didn't understand, that he was misinformed, and we thought that once he figured out what was happening he would call it all off. In contrast, in September 1999, there were no illusions.

Within two days of the return of the Congress fighters from Novolaksk, Russian aviation started pounding villages in Chechnya along the entire border, from the segment with Stavropol to the segment with Dagestan. I kept calling the Norwegian ambassador, trying to pry a statement out of the OSCE. All he told me was that he had no instructions on how to proceed.

It was very clear that Russia was on the war path and we had no options. You could see it on television; it was stock footage, the same as was broadcast in 1994. In the state Duma, deputies were demanding war, the men of the North Caucasus Military District were preparing, the build up was very obvious even before bombs exploded in Russian cities. Suddenly there were interviews with army generals saying how they could have won the first war and that it was ended prematurely.

Maskhadov was trapped by the Chechen radicals on one side and the Russians on the other. The international organizations wouldn't do anything; the Russian government wouldn't talk to him, and wouldn't let him initiate any meetings at the regional level. When the bombings began along the border, Maskhadov called a general mobilization. He also had to accommodate those returning from Dagestan. He couldn't react by talking to Russian or Dagestani officials; and he couldn't arrest Shamil and the others because he would need them in the war. This was referred to as Maskhadov's weakness, but it wasn't *his* weakness, it was the circumstances that were unfolding around him.

At the same time as the incursions into Dagestan, there was a series of terrorist acts, explosions in apartment buildings throughout Russia; the first one occurred in Buinaksk on September 4, 1994, then in Moscow and Volgodonsk. The explosion in Buinaksk occurred four days prior to the incursion by Shamil and Khattab. That night a truck packed with explosives that included aluminum powder and ammonia acid was blown up next to a building where families of servicemen from the 136th Motor Rifle Brigade lived. The explosion killed 64 people (including 23 children) and 146 were wounded.

The first explosion in Moscow, at 19 Ulitsa Guryanova on September 8, 1999, killed 100 people and wounded 690 and on September 13, at five in the morning there was an explosion at 6/3 Kashiroskoe Shosse, which killed almost all of the 124 people who were inside. In both cases explosives had been placed in the basements of the buildings. On September 16 in Volgodonsk at 35 Oktyabrskii Shosse there was an explosion attributed to a truck that stood near the building. The explosions killed 19 people and wounded almost 90.

In all of these cases, the Russian government and the "power" ministries immediately started looking for the "Chechen trace." It has been ten years since those bombings and to this day none of them has been fully investigated. There have been several fabricated cases which, even in the context of Russia's rather shaky judicial system, have fallen apart due to insufficient evidence. The Russian government used these explosions to strike fear in Russian society; there was national panic, which permitted the power ministries to begin a new adventure in Chechnya.

The reaction to the explosions in buildings in Russian cities made it absolutely clear that there would be another war against us. It amazes me that people claim that we didn't condemn these bombings. At this point Mayrbek Vyachegayev, our representative in Moscow, made many statements to the press, and Maskhadov and I gave interviews. There were also statements from other members of the government as well as from the parliament. Mayrbek was arrested on October 22, 1999 after speaking to the press in Moscow. After he was handcuffed, the investigators planted a gun inside his suit jacket. This was done in front of witnesses and the policeman said, "Now you'll sit in jail like a typical bandit for weapons possession." Despite the best efforts of Maskhadov's aides to obtain his release, Vyachegayev spent close to a year in prison.

It was very easy to overlook us and ignore what we were saying. Russia was in the grips of hysteria following those bombings and the rage that people felt was very easily directed against Chechens. I don't claim to know who blew up the buildings, but it wasn't the Chechen government. Moreover, during my last brief encounter with Shamil, shortly before I left Grozny, I asked him directly, "I will keep this to myself, but can you tell me who stands behind these explosions?" To which he responded without any hesitation, "Ilyas, I don't know who did it, but I know that they are not human." To my knowledge there is nothing linking any of the Chechen leaders to those explosions.

In Russia there were a whole series of official investigations and trials related to the bombings, including several convictions and reversals of convictions. But among those convicted there were no Chechen names and certainly no names of Chechen political leaders. So far none of these court cases have been finally resolved and there is no clarity. The version that continues to be most discussed in the world press holds that the FSB itself blew up the buildings.[8] This version hinges on a strange incident in Ryazan. The FSB claims that its agents planted a device that resembled a bomb in order to conduct a training exercise for local law enforcement. The tenants of the building, journalists, and human rights activists have argued that the FSB was caught by the local police while planting a real bomb.[9] Whatever the case, the bombings finished off any possibility of Russians opposing this second war; there could no longer be a Russian political opposition to a new war. What was particularly striking was the difference in the attitude of the Russian media. During the first war the Russian press was critical of the government and it reported objectively; during the second war the Russian press was controlled by the government and fanned the hysteria.

The meetings of the Chechen government, now called the State Defense Committee (Gosudarstvenyi Komitet Oboronny, GKO) with about 40 members, were very turbulent. I remember at one meeting we discussed everything from foreign affairs to how to build bases and where and how to involve people in this effort. I made a report about my contact with the OSCE and said that based on the experience of the last war it would be the international organizations that might be more amenable to hearing our side than foreign governments. Shamsudin Batukayev, one of the radical mullahs who sought full sharia law started yelling, "I can't listen to this OSCE, PACE, UN; they're all Satan, the Judeo-Masonic conspiracy! All we have to depend on is our faith." Then Defense Minister Magomed Khanbiev, jumped up and said, "You're Satan, and those like you are the Shaytan! It's you and people like you who brought us to this!" They almost came to blows at a meeting to plan our defenses; and they had to be physically pulled apart. This was tragic to watch. I felt sadness for Maskhadov who was going into the war with such profound rifts among his government and his nation. He just sat quietly and listened to all of this, not speaking at all.

This was another profound change from the first war in 1994 when the Russian bombing campaign solidified the Chechen factions who forgot their differences and lined up behind Dudayev and the war effort. Now we were different; we were profoundly divided. There were two camps: the "moderates" who said that the radicals were responsible for everything that was happening and refused to accept responsibility for their arrogant and ignorant behavior. And there were the "radicals" who said they were sick and tired of hearing about the rest of the world, that there was no one to depend on except ourselves and the Almighty and the use of every means at our disposal.

Another interesting moment occurred at that GKO meeting. Akhmed Kadyrov the mufti of Chechnya was sitting in front of me. I was very surprised that he was sitting there silently, with these discussions raging. Kadyrov was the most passionate speaker, he spoke Chechen well and was usually aggressively anti-Wahhabi and here he was sitting quietly, deep within his own thoughts. I tapped him on the shoulder and said, "Akhmed Khaji, I was recently appointed and I don't have any records, I'm tearing out my hair trying to establish contacts. The muftiate has contacts all over the world, you've traveled extensively. Can you find time to meet with me and give me any advice you may have?" He didn't have much of a neck and he turned his upper body, and looked at me out of the corner of his eye. He brushed me off, and saying, "No, no, I can't help with that." He was rude and I was perplexed that he responded in this way. Several weeks later I learned from a television broadcast that he had gone over to the Russian side.

Kadyrov was a complicated personality. Those who point to him as a KGB agent are over simplifying. It's true that everyone who passed through the religious academies in the Soviet period was vetted by the KGB and if they did not have some measure of trust in a person they would not permit him to become a mullah or a priest or a rabbi in the official muftiate or Orthodox Church or Synagogue. But this sort of approval is different from being an active agent in the employ of the security services.

It's also worth remembering that Akhmad Kadyrov had became the mufti during the first war, when our previous mufti had run away. He spoke very bravely, was active, and gained much respect.

He was not a combatant, but a vocal supporter of the war and proclaimed it a jihad. I don't think you have to be a combatant to be at war; Kadyrov put his life on the line many times. I don't think he was a professional agent; if he had been, he would not have been deep in thought at that GKO meeting. He would have been playing out his role. I believe he really was wrestling with his conscience and making a decision. I'm not trying to make excuses for him; Kadyrov became a traitor and a collaborationist, but I don't think he was a spy. I think that by going over to the Russians at that moment, he committed one of the greatest acts of treason in the history of our nation. I think he had received an offer from the Russian security services to switch alliances and he was quiet because he was weighing his options. The war was pushing a reluctant Maskhadov into a union with the radicals in which there would be no space for Kadyrov, who was very much their foe, so much so that there had been several assassination attempts against him. The Russians were trying to create a new political faction that would be attractive to those who had been in the nationalist camp, and in this respect Kadyrov was an ideal candidate, as he demonstrated repeatedly later in his career.

I said at the GKO meeting that our only option was to appeal to the OSCE, the PACE, and the United Nations, because no matter what their deficiencies were, they were the only organizations that might enter into contact with us. At the same time, I couldn't claim to be obtaining any results. I got the Norwegian ambassador on the phone and asked him whether the OSCE would react to the Russian bombing of civilian targets in Chechnya. I wanted the OSCE to somehow demonstrate that it had a presence and an interest in these events; this was before Putin began his "counterterrorist" operation and the full-scale military assault that ensued. The ambassador responded that he had not received instructions from the OSCE secretariat. I understand that bureaucracies take time to react, but those days before the start of the ground offensive were crucial, and the international organizations we looked to for help did not use their leverage to try to avert the war.

When I was in Moscow I saw some of my former classmates, some had obtained fairly high offices in Russia. They asked, "So what's going on in Dagestan?" And I said "Bedlam!" There had been explosions in Buinaksk and in Manezh, those were seen as part of some criminal enterprise, and they were not interpreted as terrorism. A week later I would not have been able to land at Sheremetevo and go through the VIP lounge and chat casually with Russian officials. From Moscow, the fighting in Dagestan seemed very far away, and people had not realized its potential. There was no response in Moscow to military families getting bombed in some town in Dagestan—Buinaksk— this didn't have much if any political impact.

The explosions in the apartment buildings in Moscow changed everything overnight. It would have been very difficult to persuade the Moscow elite that they had some pressing state interest in the Tsumadinskii district of Dagestan. The explosions in Moscow outraged the nation, Putin's famous phrase, "waste them in the shithouse," is embarrassing for many Russians now, but at the time they were thrilled to hear it.[10] In the days following the explosions, people went to bed frightened that their building would be blown up. Putin's roughness was perceived as strength. His popularity skyrocketed with those explosions.

I don't think that the incursions into Dagestan and the explosions were coordinated. I never found the conspiracy theories to be persuasive. I think the Kremlin or the circle trying to make Putin President was trying to foment a war, I just don't think this requires a conspiracy with Shamil.[11] The Russian Army let fighters from Chechnya enter Botlikh and then leave; they kept bombing Botlikh for five days after Shamil had returned to Grozny. They didn't let the tension dissipate. Instead they started a punitive operation against Karamakhi-Chabanmakhi, to make sure that the conflict wouldn't die down. A more credible version is that the Russians were exerting influence indirectly on Basayev, but it does not make a big difference if the influence came from Islamic radicals or the Russian security services; the result was the same. They were able to exploit Shamil's unrealized political ambitions, win him over, and use him in a way that was enormously destructive to the Chechen nation.

In September, after my return from Moscow and before the incursion began on September 7, our representative to the League of Non-Recognized Nations in the Netherlands, Aslanbek Kadiyev, brought a journalist to Grozny; I think he was a photo correspondent from London. The journalist was desperate to see Shamil and

Aslanbek wanted to keep his promise. I was very reluctant at first because by this time there was tension between Shamil and me, and I didn't even know if he'd be willing to see me. But eventually I relented because I sympathized with this journalist who had come so far and was taking such risk. I wanted to be helpful to a guest.

I had with me an article from a Russian newspaper that contained pictures purportedly of Shamil meeting with Voloshin in Nice on July 4, 1999.[12] I didn't believe this article was based on fact and I didn't think he had actually been in Nice, but I wanted to see his reaction to it. As he was reading it, he started to chuckle and called over to Khattab, "How do you like my legs?" Khattab didn't understand at first, so Shamil had to explain. "This article claims that this is a picture of me meeting in Nice with Voloshin. I'm the one in the shorts." They both laughed. Chechen men, and especially fighters, do not wear shorts. That was all that was said about this article.

I don't take the Nice story seriously. Here are three simple facts explaining why: first, I saw Shamil in Vedeno in June, a few days prior to my June 27 appointment; second, Shamil was a participant in a rally for reconciliation that was held in Grozny on July 3[13]; and third, I don't know of any instance when Shamil left the North Caucasus in the postwar years. On one occasion Shamil was invited to Moscow for the wedding of Tim Guldimann, the former OSCE representative who had played a crucial role in ending the war and signing the Khasavyurt agreement. Shamil had sent me there with an enormous carpet that was adorned with Shamil's face. I had gone to Moscow in his stead because he had not wanted to travel.

In all of this, Maskhadov was a tragic figure; a man who was desperately trying to avert war, who understood fully what horrors war would bring, but in the end was trapped through the circumstances unfolding around him. Under Dudayev none of this would have been possible; you had to be with him or against him. If you were against him you found yourself isolated. Dudayev would not have permitted the various machinations of the opposition, but Maskhadov inherited a different nation. Dudayev used to say, "I can win the war, that's possible. But how am I going to govern the veterans?" He was aware of the postwar governance problem. Maskhadov wasn't a priori weak; the situation made him weak. He was weak because the Russians fulfilled none of their obligations; he was weak because everything was in ruins and there were no jobs; and he was weak because the radicals kept pulling him into their religious disputes where he felt uncomfortable. All of this weakened him and our government couldn't take decisive action on any of the issues facing us.

In late September when the city was already being bombed, I was interviewed by state television. The interviewer asked me, "What level of intensity do you expect from this conflict?" I responded, "If you are not going to be defending the city, my advice is to leave. In the last war the main civilian casualties were victims of the bombardment in Grozny." The following day, when I went to the GKO meeting, someone suggested that we adopt a resolution that families of all the leaders stay in the city. Someone jumped up and accused me of spreading hysteria in my interview. I replied, "I heard exactly the same thing in 1994 and I know for a fact that in 1994 our government did not evacuate even one civilian from this city and now there are tens of thousands of civilians buried under the rubble of buildings. Are you telling me that we are about to begin evacuating civilians? Then I'll take it back. But until then my only advice is for anyone who is not a combatant to get as far away from the main fields of battle as they possibly can." As it turned out, civilians were again the main victims of the bombings—bombings in the city, bombings of convoys of refugees, and bombings of lines of cars at checkpoints.

A few days later, Maskhadov summoned me to a meeting with him and Ruslan Alikhadzhiyev, the speaker of parliament. It was late at night at Alikhadzhiyev's home and both of them were in uniform. The three of us sat down together. Maskhadov said to me, "You understand everything. I don't have specific instructions for you. If diplomats won't talk to you, talk to the parliamentarians. Try to meet with everyone you can, the Parliamentary Assembly of the Council of Europe, parliaments of European states; if you can get to America, have meetings in Congress. Use any forum that you can to say that we have to end this war and that I am willing to take steps to end this."

I had some friends abroad who told me that they could organize meetings for me if I could reach Europe. Maskhadov asked me, "How much money do you need?"

I said to him, "I think my friends in Europe will be in a position to help with my expenses." Maskhadov took out his wallet and gave me $500, which both of us understood would not take me very far, but he did not have very much and they needed money more than I did.

I went home and moved my wife and son to my parents' house, the city was already being bombed. Fighting had erupted in Shelkovskoi and Nadterechnyi rayon and other border districts. I told my parents that I would have to leave immediately and that I understood that I was leaving my family to fate. I asked my father to take everyone out of the city and stay with relatives in the rural areas. I went downstairs to talk to my wife who packed a bag for me; she didn't ask any questions. It was very clear to all of us that I was leaving and why I was leaving. If I knew that night the full magnitude of the separation with my country and with my family, I'm not sure I would have been able to leave. Of the $500 that Maskhadov gave me, I gave $400 to my wife and my father, said goodbye and left.

A car picked me up and took me to a village near the outskirts of town. For several hours I waited at the guide's home. There was a family that was going to make the crossing with me. They were Chechens from Jordan or Saudi Arabia who had returned to Chechnya in the 1990s. The couple was about my age, and the husband's younger brother was about 25 years old. With them were six little children, the oldest was seven or eight. I think that not all the children were theirs; it was common enough in those days for families to take nieces and nephews to get them to safety.

The drive to the Georgian border goes through the highest mountain passes; and in normal conditions it's about a five-hour drive. We arrived at Itum Kale, a spot very high in the mountains, shortly before dawn. Along the side of the road were cars that had been bombed. The Russian air force was systematically bombing any vehicles on that road. A day earlier, they had hit a bus, killing twenty-seven people. The road was very serpentine and narrow. We were in a gully between two sheer slabs of rock face, so I couldn't see the sky. The road was never fully finished and it was getting bombed and patched up. Little bridges were being bombed all the time and just as constantly they were being rebuilt. We were in a medical van and we puffed along as best as we could. Arsanov's men controlled that road and some of his shooters had large caliber machine guns, grenade launchers, and automatic rifles that sometimes were enough to scare off the Russian helicopters.

I kept watching the children, two, three, and four years old. The gorge between the rock walls was so narrow that I couldn't see very much and all I could hear was our engine. If we were bombed, there would be no time to react. In other situations you can see or hear enough to take cover, you might have a couple of minutes warning. I was thinking about my own family all the time and trying to banish the thought that I had abandoned them.

The road ended at the Argun River and from that point we struck out on foot. We had to cross the river, rushing down the mountain in a very fast, turbulent current, and traverse its width of about eight meters. Arsanov's fighters were using an Ural truck to ferry people across. I don't know who they were but I felt enormous gratitude to them. The family had lots of bags in addition to the six children, who were like ducklings following their mother. Our destination, Georgia, lay on the other side of that river, but there was a bend in the river, so you had to cross it twice.

The second crossing consisted of two felled tree trunks lying over the river. If you looked down you'd get dizzy and if you fell in, no one would be able to pull you out. The bark on the trees was slippery and the trees were shaking as we crossed. I said to the family that I would carry all their belongings, if they would carry all the children. I was afraid that I might lose my balance. I begged for their understanding of my caution and I made several trips with the bags. Then the young man crossed and his sister-in-law followed him holding on to his shoulders for balance. Then the two men carried the children across; I could barely bring myself to watch them but they all made it without incident.

On the other side, in Georgia, I was being met by a "Kist," which is what Chechens living in Georgia are called. We approached the border post together in a group. The Georgian border guards seemed embarrassed to see us; their manner was awkward. They asked me the purpose of my visit to Georgia and I said I was a refugee fleeing the war. They permitted me to pass and on the Georgian side I was joined by two more people who had come from Baku. Two cars were waiting for me, so we had enough room to take the family with us to Tbilisi. I spent one night in the Georgian capital and drove to Baku the following day.

Every Chechen family that crossed into Georgia teetered across those treacherous tree trunks. I could not know at the time that a few weeks later, my wife, my mother, and my sister would cross in precisely the same way as I had, holding on to my brother Idris. He would go back across the tree trunks to carry the children across the river. This was the first of many difficult passages that our family took on what turned out to be a much longer journey than we had ever anticipated.

CHAPTER 9

THE CHECHEN RESISTANCE SPLINTERS

The Chechen resistance entered the second war with low morale. We were divided and we harbored no illusions about the extent of the violence that would be unleashed against us. Maskhadov faced far greater challenges than Dudayev, who had just one problem: the Russians. In the first war, the Chechens had united around Dudayev in the face of the Russian invasion. At the start of the second war, Maskhadov faced a more complicated set of challenges. He had to cope with the opposition within his own ranks, the Russians, and the need to appeal to the international community. For me as the Foreign Minister, these divisions created constant problems because the opposition had powerful propaganda that I had to refute at every turn.

There was no unity among the Chechen units and the most battle-ready among them—those with the most experience who had better arms and equipment—were led by people—such as Shamil, the brothers Akhmadov, and Arbi Barayev—who were politically and ideologically opposed to Maskhadov. These forces were by far better armed and trained than the fighters under the Defense Ministry, the Presidential Guards, and the various units formed at the start of the war from the reservists that were composed of younger men who had not fought in the first war. Maskhadov's internal opponents tried to undermine and discredit him, and pursue their own political ambitions, but they all needed each other to fight the Russians, and he felt that he had to demonstrate that he had overall command, even as they did things that he opposed.

Maskhadov's second problem was the Russian invasion. He couldn't hope that the situation of 1996—when the Russian army disintegrated leaving no options other than talks—would repeat itself and Putin was categorically opposed to negotiations. Maskhadov had to prove that he was a strong leader internally and a credible partner for negotiations.

Maskhadov's third problem was the attempt to involve the international community in efforts to bring Russia to the negotiating table. While he was leading the war effort, he also wanted to pursue peace talks through normal channels, and to behave according to the rules of war. The radicals came up with the formula of using terrorism to force the beginning of talks; both the incidents at the Nord Ost theater and the Beslan school were hence attempts to repeat Budennovsk. Terrorism and the active propaganda of terrorism on Chechen websites, which Maskhadov couldn't counteract, was terribly damaging to his efforts.

At the start of the war there was a certain gradualism to the Russian advance. Chechen villages near the Dagestani border were being bombed during the raids into Dagestan in August 1999, then there was the blockade of the borders with Stavropol, Ingushetia, and Dagestan, then there was a ground offensive during which the Russian side said that they would only take possession of the three northern districts, Shelkovskoi, Nadterechnyi, and Naurskii, and refrain from crossing the Terek River. To take the three northern regions up to the Terek River took several weeks compared to the first war when it had taken only a couple of days. This time there was much more resistance. In 1994 those regions had permitted the Russians to roll through but this time there was resistance everywhere. The Russian idea was that they would occupy the portion of Chechnya north of the Terek River and conduct "targeted strikes" into the other parts of Chechnya. There were promises not to repeat the mistakes of the first war; they would not try to storm the city with tank columns. However, by the middle of December they had crossed the Terek and surrounded Grozny. The Russians took greater precautions during the storming of Grozny this time, in 1999, than they had in December 1994, mainly by conducting a more intensive bombardment of the city, which left it as a moonscape. Still they found fierce resistance in the city, which held up the advance for about six weeks until the end of January.

During the early months, Maskhadov tried everything to avert a full-blown war. He attempted to call Yeltsin but was not permitted to talk to him; he attempted to meet with the Presidents of North Caucasus republics; he made appeals to the Presidents of the Azerbaijan, Georgia, and Armenia seeking support, and he appealed to the Russians to make joint efforts to investigate the Dagestan raid. He made numerous declarations and offers of talks to no avail. He did not take repressive actions against the units that had carried out those raids into Dagestan because he feared that Russia would attack as he did so. Russians would only take advantage of infighting among Chechen units. Maskhadov's opposition—Yandarbiyev, Shamil Basayev, and Udugov—was appealing to the nations of the North Caucasus to rise up, and castigated Maskhadov for attempting to engage the Russians in talks. Shamil said that there was no credible negotiating partner in the Kremlin.

In a formal sense, the resistance was subordinated to Maskhadov's overall command with a system similar to that of the first war. Shamil again became responsible for the southeastern front, Khamzat Gelayev for the southwest front, and Aslanbek Ismailov, head of the Grozny garrison. Among the commanders who took part in the defense of Grozny were Khamzat Gelayev, Khunkharpasha Israpilov, Dokka Umarov, Arbi Barayev, Lecha Dudayev, Akhmed Zakayev, Aslanbek Abdulkhadzhiyev, and Issa Astemirov. Shamil, at least in the initial stages of the war, was coordinating with Maskhadov's headquarters whereas many other units such as Barayev's demonstrated their independence from the start.

The first substantial disagreement between Maskhadov and Shamil concerned the battle for Grozny. On one of the tapes that Maskhadov sent me, he expressed disappointment and annoyance that Shamil and Gelayev had pulled out of Grozny earlier than Maskhadov had intended and without Maskhadov's consent. This led to even deeper tensions within the leadership.

Shamil and a small group of men fought their way back into Grozny from the vicinity of Vedeno, passing the main Russian base at Khankala. By this time, the main Chechen commanders

were concentrating their men in Zavodskoi rayon where the
Russian advance was weakest. Commanders met and decided to
leave the city. I don't think it was fair for Maskhadov to blame
the retreat on Shamil and Gelayev; many of the lower-level commanders had already started pulling their men out on a unit-by-
unit basis. Shamil saw that their defenses were broken, many of
the units were disorganized, and the deployment of forces in a
single part of Grozny was dangerously exposing them to a decisive Russian strike. The lack of command and control over the
fighters in the city meant there was no unified defense and left
them vulnerable to complete defeat. He led the main group of
fighters, between 2,000–3,000 men, out of the city, repeating
what he did in 1995, gathering them in Zavodskoi rayon and
breaking through the Russian encirclement, out of the city to
Alkhan-Kala.

The city was surrounded by three encirclements and the men
who left with Shamil had to cross a minefield, where roughly
300 fighters died and a roughly equal number were wounded. I
talked not only to Shamil but also to several other survivors who
described to me how it happened. There was snow covering the
field, they knew it was mined, but they thought that a particular
segment had fewer mines than the rest of it. When they began
their journey the first mine explosions triggered machine-gun
fire and artillery bombardments.

In such situations many armies, including most of the participants in World War II, used to send prisoners to clear minefields by
sending them ahead to be blown up by the mines. The Chechens
had several dozen prisoners (according to some accounts, upto
200) and not one of them lost his legs to mines. Some were shot
by the Russian crossfire as they crossed but they were not used
to clear the field. Volunteers set out in pairs—they knew very
well what the risks were—you can't ask anyone to take this kind
of risk for you. It was night, there was a huge crowd, including
wounded people and prisoners following behind them. Machine-
gun fire was intense; it's hard to imagine the degree of self control and bravery necessary to move ahead looking for mines. We
were not a normal army. We were a Chechen army where the
man next to you was just like you. Men became commanders
for one reason only: the latter had greater charisma which had to

be proved continuously. This is why so many commanders died in that minefield—they went first, ahead of their men. In one night, the Chechen command lost several of their commanders: Aslanbek Ismailov, Khunkharpasha Israpilov, and Lecha Dudayev. Doku Umarov and Shamil were wounded.

In one of our last conversations Shamil recounted to me what had happened that night. He claimed that he cleared twenty mines before the one that got him. One of the guys who picked Shamil up after he stepped on the mine told me that Shamil was yelling he was still alive and that the others shouldn't panic.[1] On the charisma scale Shamil scored the highest; the men around him believed that he was charmed and his first reaction was to maintain the morale of the others. Hundreds died in that minefield and roughly 200–300 were wounded, and they were carried to Alkhan-Kala and other nearby villages. One fighter who lost his leg and was left behind told me that as the fighters were leaving Aslanbek Abdulkhadzhiev who took over command when Ismailov was killed and Shamil was injured calmed the wounded and said, "Don't worry, it will be pro Russian Chechens that take you guys in. You won't get turned over to the Russians." As far as I know that was the only agreement that existed.[2] Instead as some related to me they were taken not to a hospital but to the famous Russian filtration camp, Chernokozovo and beaten and tortured viciously.

Maskhadov perceived the retreat from the city as utter insubordination, even mass desertion, for which Shamil was to be court martialed. He sent me tape recordings about this, full of fury at Shamil. Maskhadov had left a little earlier, in the same way as in the first war, to arrange the headquarters and set up the resistance throughout the countryside. He was furious because he thought that the city was the main theater, the place where the most damage could be inflicted on the Russians, and that the main goal for the resistance was to tie them up there for as long as possible, ideally until the end of the winter. In the first war, we had huge problems after we left the city. We had tactical advantages in the city where we knew the geography extremely well and were able to mount constant attacks against the Russians. The number of casualties we suffered increased dramatically after we left the city.

Maskhadov's was also angry with Gelayev as he felt that Gelayev should have been in charge of the southern district of the city, where there were hills and Maskhadov considered this the best route for a retreat. Maskhadov wanted the fighters to leave later and through a route that would lead them, in his opinion, more directly to the Argun Gorge. Maskhadov blamed Gelayev for abandoning the southern district. By the time Shamil arrived from Serzhen Yurt, he found that the defenses had already crumbled, and many units, including Gelayev's had left on their own.

Shamil also had a logical argument: these fighters had tied up the Russian army for six weeks giving the others an opportunity to arrange bases in the mountains. The fighters in the city were the core of the resistance; it would be a real tragedy to see them destroyed for the sake of holding Grozny just a little longer when we all understood that we would have to give up the city eventually. The Russians had a much larger force and we were in danger of wasting our best fighters without exhausting the Russians. Unlike Maskhadov, Shamil placed greater reliance on diversionary tactics and guerrilla warfare in the mountains. He also placed less of a premium on holding the capital. Shamil did not think we needed to hold the city or territory at all. These two men had very different types of combat in mind.

When I talked to Shamil in March 2000, he was equally bitter at Maskhadov. He complained that Maskhadov would not send him to Vedeno, his hometown, where he could easily arrange his affairs because he was popular among the locals. Shamil's brother, Shirvani, had been sent to undertake an operation in Gudermes, leading untrained men to certain death. Shamil felt that Maskhadov was deliberately reining him in, limiting his options. Shamil sounded exhausted; the fact that he was speaking to me this way over the telephone indicated that he was desperate for conversation; he needed to let off steam and complain to someone. He couldn't speak this way to the other men who were in the trenches with him.

There was also a political dimension to Maskhadov's insistence that the fighters remain in the city. Maskhadov told me that he expected to have a meeting with a high-level Russian official on February 2, 2000.[3] Maskhadov was supposed to board a helicopter that would take him to an initial meeting and he wanted to use this to set up full-fledged talks. For him, it was imperative that our forces control at least part of the city during this meeting—there was no way that anyone in the city could have known this. Tragically, the forces left during the night from January 29 to January 30, 2000 and the meeting on February 2, 2000 was canceled. Maskhadov perceived their early departure as an unwitting act of sabotage against his plans.

After the retreat from Grozny, Shamil became the southeastern front commander because he was from Vedeno, and Gelayev became the Southwestern Front Commander because he was from Komsomolskoe. This repeated the pattern of the first war. It made sense to appoint Front Commanders from their home regions so they could easily establish good relations with the local population.

Maskhadov's next problem was with Gelayev who went to his hometown of Komsomolskoe (Saadi Kotar) in early March. Somehow word got out that he was trying to hold this village and fighters from all over Chechnya started going there. Gelayev was a very talented and experienced commander, and was cautious with the lives of his men. He explained to me that there had been a Russian clean-up operation going on there and he had gone in to chase the federal forces away. He swore to me that he had not appealed for help, but very young fighters, 16–17-year-olds from the countryside had nevertheless appeared and volunteered. From March 5–20 very heavy fighting ensued. The Russians claim 1,000 Chechen fighters died whereas Gelayev told me it was more like 700 or 800. We discussed this when I visited him in the Pankisi Gorge and he disputed the various rumors vehemently.

No Chechen unit had ever sustained this kind of loss. It was a huge blow to our morale, and Maskhadov was furious. He was located in the western part of Chechnya at the time and it was possible that he didn't have all the details about Gelayev's activities, but certainly Maskhadov had not sanctioned anything of this sort. He made a public statement demoting Gelayev. From Gelayev's perspective, the others had really let him down. He had not asked for these volunteers to begin with; he had never intended to hold Komsomolskoe, also, when the other major commanders saw what was happening why didn't anyone help him? Weren't we all on the same side? Did it matter whose fault it was? When Gelayev and his men were being ostracized, they went to Ingushetia and over a period of several weeks they were squeezed out further by Russian paratroopers into Georgia. Gelayev didn't have bases or supplies for the winter. Gelayev's unit made a perilous crossing over snow-covered mountain passes, where there were no roads; his men ate bark to stay alive and get to the Pankisi Gorge. This is how he wound up in Georgia, which immediately posed huge new problems for Maskhadov.

Gelayev crossed into the gorge with several hundred men, and Georgia's army could not do very much to prevent this. The Russians, of course, started denouncing the Georgians. It was a great opportunity for them to intimidate Georgia and wipe out one of the best Chechen units. During the first war the Russians blocked that border from the Georgian side, but this time Georgia denied them permission to do this. For the Georgians this was a real problem. The Russians bombed Georgian territory several times and made repeated threats that they would undertake operations in Pankisi. This situation was an embarrassment for Maskhadov and he made public a statement demoting Gelayev and calling on the men to return immediately or be accused of desertion.

Pankisi became everyone's most convenient argument. The Russians used it to try to get the maximum out of the Georgians; the Americans used it to expand their reach into a strategically significant area and authorize a new degree of military cooperation with the Georgians. After Afghanistan, the Pankisi Gorge became the second front in the global war against terror. The Georgians used it to obtain subsidies from the Americans to modernize their military. The Pankisi Gorge became a convenient problem for everyone to tackle, precisely because it really was not that serious.

In the spring of 2001, when I visited Gelayev and his deputy, Abdul Malik Mezhidov, in the Pankisi Gorge, I wanted to understand their situation because I was often asked questions about them. I explained to them that I did not have any instructions from Maskhadov, but rather had come entirely on my own. We talked all night. The most important thing for me to hear was that they did not intend to remain in Pankisi Gorge but intended to return to Chechnya. There were squabbles between the Chechen refugees and the local Chechens (Kists). Gelayev smoothed out many of these local conflicts; and he kept all the weapons out of sight. The day that I spent there I had many meetings and had an opportunity to look around—everything looked calm to me. I think the Pankisi problem had been exaggerated deliberately by everyone—the Russians, Georgians, and the Americans, to achieve their own objectives. By itself, the Pankisi Gorge, is tiny and not that difficult to control and it was never complicated to find a common language with Gelayev.

Gelayev told me that he received visitors from the Georgian government and was in contact with them. I advised him to follow all of their instructions and not create problems for them with Russia but also avoid getting involved in any of their internal problems. We had to bury the whole topic of Chechens fighting on any side of the disputes over South Ossetia and Abkhazia. The participation of some Chechens, such as Gelayev, on the side of the Abkhaz in 1992 still soured relations between us and the Georgians. I said to him, "What you owe the Georgians is to spend the least amount of time here; you do not owe them anything else." Gelayev agreed with me about this. With regard to Maskhadov, Gelayev spoke candidly, "I know I'm demoted and I understand on what grounds Maskhadov made his decision but he does not have all the information. When I return, I will explain everything to him myself."

In October 2001, Gelayev and his men were involved in a skirmish in the Kodori Gorge, near Abkhazia, which represented an aborted attempt to return to Chechnya. I doubt very much that Georgian President Eduard Shevardnadze wanted them to fight in Abkhazia. He was a subtle politician, and this would have been a provocative stunt. I think the Georgians transported Gelayev and his men from Pankisi to Kodori; where they got into a minor skirmish with the Abkhaz just to dramatize the problem. My interpretation is that the Georgians wanted to raise the issue of the unresolved status of Abkhazia, to bring it to everyone's attention, not to really fight it out. But when this skirmish happened the Russians were alerted and a crossing back to Chechnya could not be undertaken right away.

In the summer of 2002, when I was already in Washington I had two meetings about this with Dr. Zbigniew Brzezinski, who was the Co-Chairman of the American Committee for Peace in Chechnya and the former National Security Advisor. The first time we met he said to me, "Do you think if Gelayev and his men had the option of asylum in a third country they would take it? Would they leave their weapons and move to a third country if provided such an option?"

I told him that I could check into this but my impression was that they would decline. Gelayev had told me that he was waiting to let all his men recover from what they had endured in Komsomolskoe while crossing over the mountains. He also wanted to ensure that he would have bases and provisions when he returned to Chechnya. He couldn't go back without being able to provide for his unit once they were home. The second time that Brzezinski summoned me to talk about this issue, he was much more intense than he had been previously and he asked me if it would be possible to tell Gelayev that the White House asked that every man with a weapon leave Georgia before the middle of September. I relayed this to Maskhadov and to Gelayev through intermediaries.

Gelayev had probably received the same message from several other sources, including Maskhadov and officials of the Georgian government with whom he was in constant contact. News came that he and his men left on September 10. It was clear by that time that the Americans were laying the groundwork for their invasion of Iraq and the Russians were escalating their rhetoric against Georgia. Putin had threatened to begin operations in the Pankisi Gorge in September.

I knew that it would not be easy for Gelayev. He could not return the way that he came because the road would be mined and monitored. My understanding, based on conversations with his former fighters, was that Gelayev had left at the end of August with about 250 fighters and a local guide. They crossed some of the highest mountain peaks of the main Caucasus mountain range, into Ingushetia, and from there into North Ossetia. The others formed smaller groups of up to fifty fighters and traveled along a more direct route to North Ossetia. Gelayev's odyssey lasted over a month, as he and his men zigzagged between Russian posts in the mountains. They climbed impossible peaks with no alpine gear, they lowered their horses and supplies by ropes, and miraculously they all made it. On several occasions they encountered Russian forces and in one case engaged in a real battle near the Osset village of Galashki.

When Gelayev finally rejoined the Chechen resistance, no one helped him and he was continually ostracized. He had never learned politics and he wasn't good at intrigue. Although Maskhadov reinstated him, he remained an outcast. At this time, the resistance was transforming; many began calling themselves mujahhedin but Gelayev was cut from a different cloth. Other commanders wouldn't make room for Gelayev's men, they didn't let them go up to the bases in the mountains. In the end, he tried to return to Pankisi and in the process was killed on February 28, 2005.

Maskhadov made enormous efforts to create a single command on the basis of the general staff, but Shamil, the *dzhaamats,* and various other units had completely different ideas. Every *dzhaamat* commander had his own views and priorities and was autonomous on issues of financing and supplies. Each commander sent out his own emissaries to raise money and they were constantly in competition. For the most part Chechens would go to mosques, make presentations, and collect contributions. Each commander sent his own person without coordinating with others. A few commanders had the support of wealthy Chechens in Russia. But we never had systematic support, and these sums were not as substantial as the Russian media claimed. It was important to know that someone would offer assistance, let you know where others were located, and what else was going on around you; for that there had to be coordination. Coordination would have benefited everyone and only Maskhadov could provide that.

Maskhadov's biggest problem wasn't just that these units would act independently in the field but also that they spoke out in ways that totally contradicted him. To end the war Maskhadov needed the West to put pressure on Russia to come to the negotiating table. To do that he had to prove to both international organizations and the Russians that he exercised control over the resistance.

At the very beginning of the war, the commanders had sworn loyalty to Maskhadov and agreed to submit to his command. But then they went on the website Kavkaz Tsentr and wrote all kinds of things that contradicted him completely.

In my view, Maskhadov's biggest mistake was his equivocation about Kavkaz Tsentr. Sometimes it was our official site, and sometimes it was not. For me, because it was my role to represent us in international settings, this website destroyed our ability to present ourselves as anything other than radicals and terrorists. Maskhadov should have nipped it in the bud but could not do so for reasons that I don't understand. Maybe this failure was rooted in his efforts to avoid breaking relations completely with anyone. Maybe he was just too preoccupied with the daily business of trying to counter the Russian army to appreciate how much harm Kavkaz Tsentr was causing us.

Maskhadov's goal was to end the war and find a political solution through negotiations. He thought it was possible to get the Russians to the negotiating table. To that end, he needed to show that the conflict could go on for a long time, that he was in control of the resistance, that the resistance had transparent and reasonable goals, and that it represented a national struggle for independence. He needed the West to raise these issues, and apply pressure on Russia.

My first trip to the United States was in January 2000, where I had meetings in the Senate and the House of Representatives and made very good contacts right away thanks to the efforts of the American Committee for Peace in Chechnya. My first presentation was at the School for Advanced International Studies at Johns Hopkins University in Washington D.C. I spoke in a room that had standing space only, with probably hundreds of people attending. I gave my presentation and then someone asked me, "How do you view the fact that your government has made an alliance with the Taliban?" I had not heard anything about this. I was totally shocked, but I assumed it was probably true. "I am not aware of this, but if it occurred I assume it was to show moral support to the civilian population. Because the Afghans had suffered a similar fate due to the Soviet invasion they know the situation well and are showing solidarity with victims of abuse." It was very difficult for me to come to terms with the fact that I was Foreign Minister speaking in Washington and knew nothing about Yandarbiyev's mission to form an alliance with the Taliban. I called Maskhadov. I was very excited, but did not mean to offend him. I asked him, "You sent Yandarbiyev to the Taliban behind my back? This is a total mess." He rebuked me, saying, "If you can't address me as the President, at least have respect for my seniority and treat me accordingly." Maskhadov explained that he was dimly aware that Yandarbiyev was making a trip to Afghanistan but he had not asked permission. The Taliban's Foreign Minister made a statement along the same lines as what I had said: the contact was a gesture of sympathy between two nations that had endured a Russian invasion.

Yandarbiyev was a rare symbolic figure, because he stood at the root of Chechen independence but evolved into an ideologist of radicalism. He did not have armed units; he wasn't a commander; he was an ideologist and stood apart from the opposition because of his age. He belonged to an older generation, older than Shamil or Maskhadov, and was relatively independent. Maskhadov made Yanderbiyev an envoy to the Middle East. Maskhadov also removed Udugov from the defense committee, which left him without an official title. He remained close to Shamil who would not permit Maskhadov to neutralize Udugov. After the Dagestan events, Udugov left Chechnya but remained very influential as the dominant propagandist of the radical wing and force behind the Kavkaz Tsentr website.

As far as I'm concerned, only an enemy could do something as provocative as initiating relations with the Taliban. It was clear that the Taliban was the worst possible partner for us. They were recognized by only three countries: Pakistan, the United Arab Emirates, and Saudi Arabia. We had enough of our own baggage: the hostage takings, the raids into Dagestan, and the growing radicalization, without forming an alliance with the Taliban. We could not win this second war, we just needed to stop it and preserve our nation, and for that we needed Western institutions. The survival of the nation hung in the balance, and the radical wing was busy making an ideological point by seeking recognition by the Taliban.

Later, Yandarbiyev, in one of his interviews, denounced me and even talked about turning me over to a sharia court for dishonoring the jihad by failing to support this initiative. In one of his tapes, Maskhadov mentioned that my coolness on the issue of alliance with the Taliban was posing a problem in trying to forge a union of the forces, and that some commanders, for instance Khattab, considered my statements destructive. I understood that Maskhadov had to talk to everyone and try to keep everyone on board. But I was never certain that I understood the full picture. Moreover, I think Maskhadov was trying to keep me clean, to keep me away from things that might compromise me. I know that Shamil thought this way. During that last conversation we had in March 2000, he said to me, "You are establishing yourself well. Just be careful and do not permit anyone to drag you into raising money or procuring weapons. Don't get dragged into the dirt." It was entirely possible that Maskhadov was thinking in similar terms but did not verbalize it this way to me. Regardless, after this incident I never felt confident that I had all the relevant information.

There was another incident similar to this one. I think it was on April 6, 2000 when the Parliamentary Assembly of the Council of Europe (PACE) was considering whether to deprive the Russian delegation of their vote. This was the closest that we had come to a sanction of any type against Russia and it was thanks to me and several Chechen parliamentarians. We had many fruitful meetings, including my two meetings with the chairwoman of the European Parliament, Nicole Fontaigne, once at her apartment and once at the session of the European Parliament. I met with all the fractions of the European Parliament. I was there at the right moment, before the policy was formed and I could have an impact by offering more information. They had only one type of leverage to deprive Russia of its voting rights.

As we were preparing for this session, Shamil took the nine members of the Pskov special OMON police force prisoner and offered to trade them for Colonel Yuri Budanov who had raped and killed a Chechen girl named Elza Kungaeva. Shamil was taunting the Russians. Of course the Russians didn't surrender Budanov and Shamil beheaded the nine OMON officers. Kavkaz Tsentr posted all of this on its website the day before the PACE session. I got a call from the parliamentarians who were preparing to put forth the resolution saying, "What is Maskahdov's view of this beheading?" I got him on the phone immediately and he was very upset but he came up with a statement categorically condemning the beheading. The resolution was introduced and passed; this was one of our real successes.

This sort of thing was Udugov's specialty and I blame him much more than I do Shamil, who was distanced mentally from these issues and acted in a very limited frame of reference. Shamil was not on the Internet checking the news every few hours, and he could not understand the broader context. Udugov, on the other hand, did nothing but watch the news, and had to know that posting photographs of beheaded Russian servicemen on the day before an important vote in the PACE was destructive. It was very hard to represent Chechnya; people didn't always want to learn all the details of our situation, it was hard to get them to this point, and votes could be postponed for months at a time.

Maskhadov's temporary union with the radicals was tactical in nature. I have his private comments on tape where he accused Shamil, and Udugov of starting the war and was in total opposition to them. But Maskhadov's situation was such that he had to oscillate between total opposition; then temporary union, and then something happened like the hostage taking in Nord Ost that discredited us terribly, and Maskhadov had to start all over again. The radical's excesses proved he was right; their ideology would not take us anywhere. But he was discredited anyway, and had to piece things together so he could again try to exert control and assert himself as a credible interlocutor. Then something like the Beslan hostage taking would explode. These unions have to be seen as temporary and tactical: neither side compromised its ideology.

The vote in the PACE depriving the Russians of their voting privileges was the one time that any international organization had exerted anything like sanctions against Russia for its behavior in Chechnya. While they were deprived of the vote, it was possible for them to pass further resolutions. The Russians pretended that being without votes didn't worry them, but it did. Subsequently, they focused their diplomacy on the PACE and got the vote reversed. In my view the PACE should not have hurried to reinstate the Russian delegation.

There were constant misunderstandings between us and the Europeans. We were rarely satisfied with the assessments and reports of different missions on Chechnya from the European Parliament or the United Nations. We wanted them to call things by their proper names. They were less interested in that or in who was right or wrong in any particular situation than in what could be achieved. What benefit was there in annoying the Russians by issuing a critical report when some small benefit could be achieved by making a more modest assessment? There were statements and news stories where diplomats from Western Europe claimed that the situation had improved because an Internet café was functioning in Grozny. I understood my compatriots who were disgusted by such reports. At the same time, many Chechens failed to understand that such small steps represented a different worldview and a different philosophy, a gradualism and rationalism that was different from our psychology. The diplomats settled for a microscopic result rather than any kind of minor conflict. In every meeting I had, the representatives of Western Europe said that if they spoke in the same terms as I, the Russians would simply ignore them. So they reasoned, "We have to find a common language. We have to play a tune that gets some result, even a miniscule result."

Of course, the Russians took advantage of this attitude. The gradualism unfolded in the opposite direction from the one intended. Each year, the Russians offered less and less compliance with European norms, and Europeans still avoided confrontation at any cost. For ordinary Chechens this was very difficult to understand: we were being killed by the thousands, we were desperate and could not wait for a gradual process to evolve. Maskhadov was determined that the only civilized solution was through the corridors of international bureaucracies. There was ultimately no other option.

Our efforts at the PACE had some positive results. Hearings and discussions began in January 2000 and Russia was deprived of its voting rights on April 6, 2000. This might have been only a symbolic act, but for us it represented a breakthrough, the first time that a European institution was imposing some kind of penalty for Russia's war crimes. Of course, the PACE did not recognize us and focused entirely on human rights, but at some point the human rights violations reached a level where they constituted a case for independence; this was clearly the situation with respect to Kosovo. The Russians understood this too and began sending one delegation after another to persuade the PACE that the conflict was essentially within Chechen society.

The Western goal was not so much to end the war but to try and have some influence over Russia, and find ways of affecting Russia's behavior. It was enough to look at the size of the Russian army, the types of weapons and military equipment that was being used, not to mention the extent of civilian casualties, to show that this was a war, not just a counter-terrorist operation.

Russian representatives claimed that they did not care if they were deprived of their voting privileges. They claimed that this simply meant that they would not have to pay their dues to the PACE. Yet, this was manifestly false because they were going through so many efforts to persuade the body to reinstate their membership. Those diplomatic efforts gave birth to the round-table and in tandem produced "Chechenization." The concept was to include the Russian delegation, the Chechen collaborators, and the representatives of the Chechen Republic, Ichkeria, in a discussion with the participation of the PACE representatives to seek paths to resolve the conflict. The obstacle was deciding who would constitute a delegation. It was absurd to present the Chechen collaborationists as a side in the conflict.

Who were the sides to the conflict? There was our side, and there was the Russian side, which could include the pro-Russian Chechens. It would have been fine if the likes of Akhmad Kadyrov, the head of the pro-Russian administration, or Abdul Khakim Sultygov, then President Putin's representative for human rights in Chechnya, participated as representatives of Russia. But it was utterly inappropriate, and a complete distortion of reality to cast the pro-Russian Chechens as a side to the conflict. Russian human rights activists came to a similar conclusion, "It is quite obvious that voluntarily or not, Europe actually agreed to organize a negotiation round with participants of only one side to the conflict, and the work of the PACE on initiating the real political process in Chechnya came to a deadlock without having even started."[4]

Chechenization was actually born in the PACE, which began discussing under Lord Judd, the idea of writing a new constitution for Chechnya. Judd later resigned as Special Rapporteur in protest, because he thought the referendum was being implemented too early. The roundtable that represented different sides would write a compromise constitution, which would of course be in accordance with the Russian Constitution. When the Europeans opened the door to this roundtable, they inadvertently invited in Chechenization.

I told Maskhadov that we should not participate in this roundtable, that only our presence there would give it credibility. My position was that while we could not make claims to membership or voting rights in the PACE, we should at least have equal weight with the Russians in any working group on the problem of Chechnya. We might not be recognized as a state, but we would have to be recognized as a side in the conflict. And there could be only two sides, the Russian side and Ichkeria. Putin's appointees in the pro-Russian Chechen administration could not be a side in this war.

Maskhadov's response was very harsh; he was furious with me. He agreed that pro-Moscow Chechens should not be considered a side in the conflict, and that it was wrong to discuss the possibility of any new constitution that defined Chechnya as a subject of the Russian Federation. But he was very angry because I suggested to freeze temporarily our contacts with the PACE. Maskhadov thought that my suggestion was contrary to our interests and amounted to depriving us of a forum where we actually had some traction. For instance, the PACE delegations were regularly visiting Chechnya and reporting on conditions there. What Maskhadov didn't note was how superficial reports of international observers sometimes were, there was one that claimed improvements because a new *banya* was constructed in Grozny and people were sitting in sidewalk cafés drinking vodka; these were supposed to be indicators of the improvements in Chechnya.

I still can't understand why the Russian delegation hated Judd; he was so useful to them. I'm not accusing him of being pro-Russian; on the contrary, he was utterly European. He thought there were some really delicate notes that he could play and by giving subtle praise he could achieve something with the Russian delegation. Of course, that did not happen; instead the Russians became hardened in their positions. Maskhadov changed his mind after a particularly large and prominent Russian delegation and a pro-Russian Chechen delegation went to the PACE. He could see that the inclusion of the pro-Russian Chechens as a side would falsify the whole process, making it look as if Russia was mediating between two Chechen sides. He called me on the telephone and said to immediately cut off all contact.

In 2004, I saw Lord Judd in Washington at the conference that the American Enterprise Institute hosted to commemorate ten years since the first war. We had a meeting with about four or five people including Anna Politkovskaya, Dr. Brzezinski, and a couple of others, and in the course of the conversation Judd said something along the lines of, "Who had that bright idea of holding elections in the middle of a war?" I responded, "You did. Not you personally, but the PACE, which you represented, came up with the idea of creating a working group that supposedly represented all the sides that would write a draft constitution for Chechnya. If you have a draft constitution, the referendum cannot be far behind." He didn't respond to me, what could he say?

I suspended contact with the PACE working group when they began to falsify the sides of the conflict. After the Zakayev-Kazantsev meeting, I think it was in January 2002, they changed their tune and there was a new flurry of activity. I received a formal letter from the Chairman of the PACE, Peter Schreider. It addressed Maskhadov as "Excellency," and maintained all other matters of protocol and asked that we resume contact. This was what I wanted. They had only casual meetings with us and formal meetings with the Russians. They must have understood that they needed to have our participation to have a genuine process. I forwarded the letter to Maskhadov and discussed it with him. I told Maskhadov that now, in my opinion, we should participate but only on certain conditions. The conditions I suggested were: in the special working group our voice must be equal to the Russians; they must acknowledge publicly through a joint press release that they had formal meetings with us and these were not personal meetings, we represented a side to the conflict, and finally that the pro-Russian Chechens could be included only as part of the Russian delegation.

I did not get to see how the end of this story played out because Maskhadov asked Akhmed Zakayev to attend the PACE meeting. While I did not agree with this decision I had to accept it. I thought I should have been the logical choice but Maskhadov was getting very frustrated with all of his different emissaries competing with each other. So I did not even protest. I sent the conditions to Maskhadov that I thought were necessary; he agreed with them, and told me to brief Zakayev. Zakayev had meetings with the Chairman of the PACE and the General Secretary of the European Parliament. However, I don't think that he followed up on this line with the PACE. In the end, they got us to participate in a series of roundtable discussions that legitimized Chechenization.

Very soon after these events in May 2002, I went to the United States and had no further contact with the PACE.

CHAPTER 10

MY TENURE AS FOREIGN MINISTER

The first Russian-Chechen war was viewed as a post-Soviet conflict, like the war over Nagorno-Karabakh or Abkhazia. Although international actors emphasized Russian territorial integrity, they also condemned Russian human rights abuses and actively sought avenues to end the war. Moreover, the Chechen resistance had a certain romantic public image, because of the relatively unrestricted Russian television and other media coverage from both sides, which gave a reasonably balanced view of events.

During the first phase of the second war, we had several important successes. The two main achievements prior to September 11, 2001 were the suspension of Russia's voting rights in the PACE and the OSCE resolution in Istanbul calling for a political solution to the conflict. These were diplomatic successes that pleased us and indicated that despite the difficulties of our situation we could achieve things in international forums. These decisions gave us hope that such institutions would take greater interest in the war and eventually bring Russia to the negotiating table. Unfortunately, these diplomatic achievements had little actual impact on the events on the ground, and things on the battlefields were changing rapidly.

Things changed dramatically for us after September 11, 2001 when most people in the West, and certainly most governments, started looking at us through the lens of antiterrorism. The pretense that Russia's mass killing of Chechen civilians contributed to the war against terrorism permitted the West to maintain close relations with Russia and absolved its collective conscience of ignoring atrocities. Viewing this war as one of the fronts in the war against global terrorism freed the West from its obligation to uphold standards of human rights and international law in its dealings with Russia. There were several attempts to engage Russia's representatives in negotiations that were promising and important but ultimately unable to overcome the resistance of the Russian government.

The most damaging concession that was made was to accept the Russian line of "Chechenization." Russia pretended that there was an internal conflict among different Chechen groups and posed as the mediator. In fact, one of the Chechen "sides" comprised ethnic Chechens appointed by Russia, who should never have been seen as independent actors. Hence, the Russians pretended that Akhmad Kadyrov or Alu Alkhanov or Ramzan Kadyrov, essentially Russian appointees to be "President," represented a "side" in the conflict and utterly ignored those of us who had taken up arms in the conflict.

Like other representatives of Chechnya abroad, I too was trying to resolve issues of state without access to any of the resources of a state, such as a Foreign Ministry bureaucracy, diplomatic immunity, or basic support. My most elementary need was to be granted visas to enter different states, but every application was a major battle. The logistics were always very complicated, without the added burdens of having no embassies abroad, or staff, or coordination among representatives. Representatives of foreign governments met with us, usually in a personal capacity, and we were permitted to attend international forums, but usually without the right to speak or vote.

I attended the Istanbul summit of the OSCE in November 1999 along with several of our parliamentarians. We could not participate in the work of the summit but it gave us an opportunity to have many side meetings with individuals and country delegations. The resolution adopted at the summit may not have been ideal, but it contained two aspects that were crucial to us: the call for a negotiated political solution, and the reaffirmation of the mandate to OSCE assistance group. The latter had played a crucial role in the Khasavyurt negotiations in 1996 and we were very glad to see that a new group was to be constituted and sent to Chechnya. The Norwegians held the OSCE presidency, and I spoke to them at length about prospects for returning to the field and how their security could be assured. I had constant meetings and it was a good opportunity to brief many diplomats and journalists.

The problem of Chechnya was linked with two related issues on which the summit also passed resolutions: the Conventional Forces in Europe Treaty (CFE), and removal of Russian military bases in Georgia. I don't know what exactly occurred behind the scenes, but U.S. Secretary of State Madeleine Albright, whom I met years later, commented that she had "fought like a dog" for those resolutions. Russia was in violation of the CFE flank limits in the Caucasus, but argued that the excess troops were necessary to fight in Chechnya. There was probably some kind of trade off, permitting Russia to exceed its limits in exchange for agreeing to withdraw all of its military bases from Georgia by 2004. The summit ended on a theatrical note when Yeltsin stormed out of the hall after calling Bill Clinton a "son of a bitch."

Unfortunately, there were real problems in the implementation of the OSCE resolution on reestablishing an OSCE presence in Chechnya. It was two years before a new mission was established, and it was located in the Nadterechnyi rayon, which was traditionally pro-Russian, and far from the actual battle fields. The mission was highly limited in its ability to fulfill its mandate, was sidelined, and in the end the mandate was simply permitted to expire in 2004.

In the United States, the American Committee for Peace in Chechnya had come together in 2000 in an effort to bring high-level attention to the Chechen conflict. The co-chairmen, Dr. Zbigniew Brzezinski, General Alexander Haig, and human rights lawyer Max Kampelman, did a great deal to inform the policy community in Washington, the Congress, and the Presidential administration. With their help I was able to have many meetings in Washington, including with Congress, the Department of Defense, and the Department of State, various think tanks, NGOs and universities, including the Johns Hopkins School for Advanced International Studies, which hosted my first public presentation in the United States. There were other supporters as well, including Senator Jesse Helms who held hearings and sponsored resolutions related to Chechnya.

The meeting that caused the biggest stir was my meeting with the Acting Deputy Assistant Secretary of State for Europe, John Beyrle, which had come about because of pressure from Senator Helms. What made the meeting interesting was not the location, which was a classroom at George Washington University (we had met with State Department officials at Union Station or in hotel bars, so this was not the most exotic location), but the tone. Beyrle informed me that we should exile any and all foreign extremists fighting in Chechnya and break any ties to foreign financing. This was the only dimension of the conflict that he wanted to discuss. He was not interested in discussing the political situation. At one point he asked me, "And who is Mr. Khattab?"

I replied, "You should direct that question to the CIA. Khattab talked about receiving training in U.S. supported camps in Peshawar, and I've asked myself many times the same question that you just asked me, "Who is this Mr. Khattab? We didn't train him and we didn't invite him to Chechnya.""

Beyrle and I didn't touch upon the conflict as such. He didn't ask me what our side wanted. Why we were fighting, and what could make us stop. What could we compromise on? How was the conflict affecting Chechnya, and Russia, and the region more broadly? He kept checking his watch and ended the meeting at precisely fifty-nine minutes, so he could later tell journalists that it lasted less than an hour. The State Department had been forced by Helms to have this meeting, but the department wasn't obliged to make it productive.

From the beginning of the war, the Russian government refused categorically to meet with us, to hold any kind of talks, and the only approach available was a "Track II" process. To this end, there were two meetings organized in tandem by Andrei Mironov, a Russian human rights activist and journalist, who had a long-standing relationship with Moral Rearmament (MRA) and the American Committee for Peace in Chechnya (ACPC). The latter provided coordination and sponsorship in the United States. I attended the first meeting hosted by MRA in Caux, Switzerland, in August 2001 and Akhmed Zakayev attended the second meeting in Liechtenstein in August 2002.

The initial concept was to invite people who did not represent either the Russian or Chechen governments but human rights activists, intellectuals, and influential public figures who had contacts in government and could meet for a couple of days to identify persons and processes that could nudge the sides closer to formal negotiations.

I drafted a report for Maskhadov on the concept for this meeting and identified Chechen participants while Andrei Mironov identified the Russian participants. I liked this approach because all of our attempts at negotiations in 1996–99 had got torpedoed over formalities and protocol. This was by far a more practical way to create a contact group that would maintain dialogue with both sides and exchange information. Andrei was forming a group composed mainly of Duma deputies. At that time, there were a few democratic politicians left in the Russian State Duma and some of them had good contacts within Putin's camp. For instance Andrei wanted to bring on board Vyacheslav Igrunov—who was in Yabloko and was on good terms with Yevgeny Primakov, a former Prime Minister—and General Vorobyev, who was a member of the Duma's defense committee, and several others.

While I was in Baku, I maintained contact with Glen Howard of the ACPC in Washington D.C. and Andrei Mironov in Moscow. In Baku I got a telephone call from Maskhadov; he had heard rumors about our plans from another Chechen who was not directly involved but had informed Maskhadov that this was the initiative of the Russian government and was sanctioned at the very top. Clearly our plans were not exactly secret, because Maskhadov told me over the telephone the names of the potential Russian participants. Maskhadov was very excited and wanted us to form a government delegation to meet them. I didn't want to talk about this on the phone and told him that he would soon have my report on audio tape. After he received my report, I got his response almost immediately; it was a direct military order, he did not give me any opportunities to advise him. A delegation composed of Kozh Akhmed Yarikhanov, Issa Bisayev, Ikhyad Idigov, and Said Khasan Abumuslimov— all ministers or parliamentarians— would be formed and I would accompany them as an advisor, but not as a participant. Maskhadov's approach was very traditionally Chechen. These were elders, ministers, and parliamentarians who had led the post-Budennovsk talks and the Khasavyurt negotiations, and in his eyes they were reliable and experienced. As a younger man, I was to accompany them and assist them, but they would be in charge. I told Maskhadov that I had no need to go at all and that my plan from the beginning was to stand aside. I received a second stern military order to go to the Track II meeting in Caux. So I did. But the members of the delegation failed to show because of logistical problems.

In the meantime, all of this was revealed in the Duma, including the names of the participants, and all of Andrei's delicate work went down the tubes when the Duma deputies backed out of participating. Andrei saved the day by inviting Yuri Shchekochikhin, a Duma Deputy and journalist with *Novaya gazeta* who came at the last minute and largely out of a spirit of contrariness. Andrei literally pulled him out of his *dacha* and took him to the airport, Yuri, who was hearing about all this for the first time, agreed to come because it was dangerous. He thrived on risks; he had been a war reporter in the first war and an investigative journalist for *Novaya gazeta*, and had broken some of the most sensitive corruption cases. For us it was crucial to have at least one Duma Deputy. The Swiss Foreign Ministry insisted on a Russian deputy attending if Guldimann was to attend. Tim's presence was essential because of his experience at Khasavyurt and because he was the Swiss Ambassador to Iran and in this capacity represented U.S. interests there. Another participant from Russia was Abdulkhakim Sultygov who soon after this meeting was appointed Russian President's special representative for human rights in Chechnya.

Caux was a beautiful place, nestled in the Alps, with an impressive history. Jews had been hidden there during the World War II, and very sensitive talks between France and Germany had held there after the World War II. A place where some of the wounds of World War II were healed held out the same promise to us. I arrived in Caux with Lyoma Usmanov, our representative in the United States and saw Tim prior to the meeting. His approach was to hear from us how we perceived the conflict and how we thought a contact group might be formed. That was our whole agenda. Two days of discussion followed, mainly between me and Shchekochikhin. It was really a far-ranging conversation, hardly a negotiation. We drew up a list of potential future participants and

Shchekochikhin was indeed the right man for us; he knew a lot of people not only in the Duma but also in the military. Professor Fred Starr and Tim Guldimann were useful precisely in the same way; they could bring their contacts and experience to bear on this process.[1]

The only member of Maskhadov's official delegation that was able to travel there was Idigov. But he was delayed and arrived on the last day and misread the proceedings completely. We were all sitting around a table. I think Tim was at the head of the table and the rest of us were in no particular order. I was next to Shchekochikhin and Andrei was across from me and next to Lyoma. When Idigov came in, instead of greeting us, he blurted, "So where is the opposing side?" We all looked at each other and Shchekochikhin responded for all of us, "There are no sides here." Idigov's gaffe was a symbolic misunderstanding; it represented two differing worldviews, and it persisted into the second meeting in Liechtenstein, which I did not attend.

Track II was an important effort and maybe under other circumstances it would have been possible to achieve more specific results. The level of repression in Russia was such that the risks were enormous. Shchekochikhin was killed in the summer of 2003 and Andrei Mironov was beaten brutally and sustained a head injury that left him incapacitated for several months. I suspect that Shchekochikhin's murder was related to his journalistic investigations; he had been working on uncovering high-level corruption in the security services but it was also easy to believe that Andrei's beating was very much related to his efforts in this process. At the same time that Russia became increasingly dangerous for our partners, the United States was losing interest in it as well after September 11, 2001. Nevertheless, it was important that the meetings were held and that in principle they could be resumed despite all the difficulties. It is also important to note that the U.S. State Department was present in the background. I have a letter from Ambassador Steven Pifer, Acting Assistant Secretary of State expressing support for the process we had initiated:

In your past meetings with U.S. officials and in the peace proposal put forward by the Chechen side last year, you have said that the Chechens are prepared to begin a dialogue with the Russian government. We are aware that you and other Chechens met with members of the Russian Duma in the hopes of beginning this process. We hope that these efforts were productive and will be sustained.... We remain committed to working for a political settlement, accountability for human rights abuses, and assistance to the civilian population.

The letter was not dated and but it was received by Lyoma Usmanov, our representative in Washington, on September 9, 2001. Two days later everything changed, and Putin understood immediately how he could benefit from Al-Qaeda's attack. He was among the first to call President Bush and express his condolences and say that the Russian public, which itself suffered from terrorism, commiserated with the Americans. Putin drew a parallel between the 9/11 devastation and the bombings of apartment buildings in Russian cities in 1999, and this conversation heralded the Russian-American antiterrorism cooperation. I think this cooperation was very short lived, but had tremendous resonance at the time and profoundly negative consequences for the Chechens.

The U.S. State Department had made several statements saying that among those fighting in Afghanistan were Chechens, but never identified any specific Chechens. The best war reporters covering Chechnya and Afghanistan, (such as Andrei Babitsky, Sophie Chihab, Anne Nivat, Dodge Billingsley, and Carlotta Gall) each of them went looking for Chechens in Afghanistan. Sophie got into the prison camp where Al-Qaeda and Taliban prisoners were being held prior to being shipped to Guantanamo. But none of the journalists ever found any Chechens. In Guantanamo too there were no Chechens. A few people of other North Caucasian nationalities were held there but not one Chechen.

I have asked repeatedly a variety of State Department interlocutors for specific information about Chechens fighting in Afghanistan but have never received any. Anyone watching television had specific information about other nationals who fought in Afghanistan: we know there were Americans, Australians, and Canadians and we know their biographies. Wasn't it strange that Chechens were supposedly fighting there in droves, yet not one actual story has emerged? I can be confident on this topic because this very pernicious piece of propaganda makes no sense at all. If a Chechen wanted to fight, he could do so at home. He did not have to travel half-way around the world to participate in someone else's jihad. Yet if he did he would be the laughing stock at home. Putin was trying to make his war in Chechnya look similar to the U.S. war in Afghanistan. Since Moscow had supplied the Northern Alliance for years, it was not problematic to have them regularly "discover" Chechen fighters in Afghanistan. This was a small thing for the Northern Alliance to do to repay their patron but it had a huge impact. Suddenly we Chechens were viewed as America's enemies.

Similarly, Putin's offer of September 24, 2001 for army General Victor Kazantsev who was the representative of the Russian President in the Southern Federal District, to meet Zakayev, followed closely on Bush's request to the Taliban to hand over Osama bin Laden. Kazantsev offered, as he had in the past, that the leadership of the Chechen resistance could come to the main Russian military base at Khankala and surrender. This was the Russian position; Kremlin spokesman Yastrzhembsky held this line very consistently. In a formal sense Putin had complied with demands made at the PACE and at the Istanbul Summit for Russia to pursue a political resolution of the conflict. He mimicked the offer that the Americans had made to the Taliban. It was important to maintain this parallel: Russians acting like Americans, and Chechens acting like the Taliban.

Maskhadov and Zakayev sought to take advantage of this offer even if it was clearly propagandistic. I thought it was a bad idea to meet, but Zakayev became very active and vocal, and Maskhadov acquiesced since Zakayev had been part of every major negotiation since 1995. The Russians suggested a meeting in Moscow, which we thought would be humiliating for us. I think from the start we weren't worried about the security situation. The Russians would lose in the public perception if something happened to Zakayev. Moscow needed badly to become respectable members of the antiterror coalition.

I was in Baku when I got a call from Seth Winnick at the Department of State who said that they they were watching with a great deal of interest, that the proposed meeting was a positive initiative, and thought that we should take this opportunity to pursue talks. I responded that, indeed, Maskhadov and Zakayev were of that opinion also and that most likely the meeting would take place but we were not sure about the modalities of who would meet whom and where. He offered to discuss the problem of security with the Russians, and I said that we were not worried about security. The Russians would behave correctly in this instance. I related this conversation to Zakayev who suggested that the head of the Liberal Democratic Party of Turkey might accompany him to the meeting. I relayed this suggestion to Seth. The State Department was watching very carefully and was willing to be involved so long as it didn't hurt U.S. relations with Russia. But such occasions were very rare.

The meeting did eventually take place in a VIP lounge at Sheremetevo airport in Moscow on November 18, 2001. Zakayev's companion, Besim Tibuk, the leader of the Turkish Liberal Democratic Party remained on the plane. The meeting itself was very predictable. Kazantsev offered us the opportunity to surrender unconditionally and Zakayev offered him the opportunity to begin peace talks. This was mostly political theater, which showed just how well Putin understood the demands of the moment. Bush had made an offer, of course, it was simply a gesture and Putin could repeat a similar gesture. For Maskhadov it was also advantageous because this was an official meeting at a high level, the first and only such meeting since the start of the war. From Maskhadov's perspective it didn't matter that nothing had been achieved, the precedent was established for further meetings. The Russian leadership recognized the necessity of having contacts with us and this constituted a minimal foundation from which we could build up to a more substantive discussion. The meeting in Sheremetevo solidified in Maskhadov his faith that talks would begin eventually.

The next major event was the killing of Khattab in the spring of 2002. The media image was of the ultimate terrorist, whereas from what I knew of him, the real person was a bit more nuanced. He was very smart and the best description of him was Sergei Kovalev's phrase, "a Muslim Che Guevara." Khattab brought diversionary tactics to us and to my knowledge he sought only military targets. He wasn't a terrorist; he was an exceptionally accomplished guerrilla war fighter and religious emissary.

Khattab, who was of Saudi descent, fought in Afghanistan and brought Afghan methods to us, including public relations: such as videotaping attacks and cruelty in the form of beheadings and cutting off limbs; these were Khattab's contributions. I regard them more as war crimes and gross violations of the Geneva Conventions, than as terrorism. Khattab never acted against the civilian population and his actions were directed against military targets. He was also a symbol of growing religiosity. For instance by 2002, you didn't say "colonel" and "division," you said "muja-hid" and "*dzhaamat*." This was not merely a change in terminol-ogy; there was also a creeping change in the mentality of the Chechen resistance.

According to the dominant interpretation, Khattab was killed by a poison letter. On being opened the glue exuded lethal fumes. I was already in the United States when this happened and I only know what I read on the Internet. But my sense was that this official version was the true one, especially, because the courier who brought the letter was found later in Baku with his throat slit open. This suggests to me that it was indeed, as had been rumored, an inside job. You can also judge from the FSB reaction; for a few days they sat still and said nothing. I had the impres-sion that the FSB didn't want to believe it. Khattab was their best propaganda vehicle. They did not need to do anything to prove Chechen complicity with the Afghans when there was a bearded, long-haired Arab running around Chechnya, cutting off limbs on camera and yelling "Allah Akhbar." What more could the FSB possibly ask for?

For the Russians this was an important loss. For the Chechens, Khattab's death was a real loss too. He was an excellent instructor. Khattab taught a course in diversionary tactics that was critical for building our capacity. It was also a profound loss for Shamil Basayev, who had many people around him, but had a deep and sacred friendship with only two people. The first was Khamzat Khakharov, a Chechen from the Confederation of the Nations of the North Caucasus. He had a romantic vision of the North Caucasus union, the potential for all the nations of the North Caucasus to unite as a state. Shamil and Khakharov had fought together in Abkhazia. Khakharov was killed in one of the early battles against Labazanov in the summer of 1994.

The second was Khattab, a similar figure. From the spring of 1995, when he arrived in Chechnya, Khattab and Shamil became very close. I think Khattab had a tremendous impact on Shamil's worldview. This was not an ordinary friendship: there were many emotions, dreams, ambitions, the common cause, and intense personal friendship, all intertwined. The killing of Khattab must have had a huge impact on Shamil personally. But for the course of the war I don't think there was much of an impact. One of Khattab's men, supposedly Abu Walid, took over his unit. But no one has ever met Abu Walid and there are some who think he was not a real person, just a code name for someone else. When a commander dies, his brother or his cousin, or someone from among his men, becomes the new leader. It is unusual for a unit to join a different commander or to splinter.

There were complicated processes unfolding in the forest during the summer of 2002. I still have the tapes from Maskhadov in which he went off on tangents about how Shamil was Russia's agent. I don't know if Maskhadov really believed this, or was just frustrated with Shamil and was letting off steam. I don't take seriously the notion that Shamil was working for the Russians. I don't find it persuasive, but I know that other people do. Shamil equally strongly believed that Maskhadov's various calls for peace benefited only Russia and that we had to show strength and that by constantly asking for reconciliation we exhibited weakness.

These claims and counter claims were aired all the time and then, very suddenly in the middle of the summer, there was a bombshell: an extraordinary session of the Majalis Shura amended the constitution robbing parliament of authority. The state defense committee, in effect, became the legislative and executive organ. Shamil became the head of the Majalis Shura, in essence something on the order of Commander-in-Chief. Kavkaz Tsentr became our official news agency. Zakayev remained information minister, and Udugov became chief of the information subcommittee of the Information Ministry. Thus, theoretically Zakayev was Udugov's boss, but the two men ran competing websites, Kavkaz Tsentr and Chechenpress.

Maskhadov made an effort to unite all the commanders, and they all swore allegiance to him. For the first time during the war, in July 2002 there was unity. In a superficial way, the picture in 2002 was by far more favorable than at any time since 1999. Shamil even endorsed the concept of a political resolution, albeit he said the negotiations should be held on the basis of the Koran. I, like probably many others, understood that there were too many contradictions for this union to be genuine or lasting. During the period from 1996 to 1999 there were many attempts for everyone to unite, and the failure of each union only compromised Maskhadov. Looking back, I understand that in principle a union between such different things is impossible. Shamil did not really compromise any of his views to join the government, and he did so very superficially.

The hostage taking at the Moscow theater Dubrovka during a performance of the musical, Nord Ost, occurred in October 2002, a few months after all the branches of the Chechen resistance had united into one government under Maskhadov. Movsar Barayev, who was the nephew of the infamous hostage taker, Arbi Barayev, seized the theater during a performance, taking hundreds of ordinary people hostage. There were some novel elements in this hostage taking. First, Movsar Barayev was a very young and unknown figure. Second, there were women dressed in black robes, a declaration that they were martyrs who sought death, and they had given interviews to Al-Jazeera just prior to this exploit. Yandarbiyev and Udugov behaved as advisors and spokesmen for Barayev. The incident ended three days later when the FSB and MVD carried out a siege of the theater. A gas, the nature of which remains a mystery, was introduced by the rescuers through the air-conditioning vents. Rather than temporarily incapacitating everyone inside, it caused at least 129 deaths. Local hospitals were completely unprepared for such an eventuality and no antidote was available.

A few days later, Shamil took responsibility for the Nord Ost hostage taking. This served to discredit Maskhadov, and undermined the efforts of anyone in the West who was trying to help the Chechen cause. I don't believe that Shamil was actually responsible for the planning or execution at Nord Ost. I think it was more likely that he took responsibility for it after it was already over. Shamil thought of himself as a mentor to anyone who was rebelling against Maskhadov. He approved of it in a political sense, but it was so badly executed that it was hard to believe that it could have been Shamil's actual planning and execution. In a technical sense it was unlike Budennovsk, and more like Raduyev's copycat raid into Kyzlyar, which did much more harm than good for us. Barayev did not have a clear line. Whereas if Shamil had been in charge, he would have articulated very specific political demands, and would not have permitted Barayev to deviate from them. Barayev first demanded peace talks, then he demanded that the pro-Russian former mufti, Akhmad Kadyrov, surrender himself in exchange for the hostages. Barayev's goals were never clearly articulated. But regardless of Shamil's exact role in this hostage taking, the fact was that he had taken responsibility for a major act of terrorism while he was nominally loyal to Maskhadov.

It's difficult to reconstruct just what a shock Nord Ost was; it was a new extreme, a new red line that was crossed. It was a watershed for us and it deeply undermined our credibility with international institutions and made it much harder to pursue any kind of political agenda. Of course, immediately after Nord Ost the united resistance broke up again into its former components.

In my estimation, Shamil took responsibility for Nord Ost out of a spirit of contrariness, and seeking attention, even if it was negative. His only consideration was to harm the enemy; it did not matter if it helped or harmed us, as long at it hurt them. In reality, he either didn't have anything to do with it or got involved very late in the game. I think he attached his name to it for political reasons, to spite Maskhadov, but the hostage taking had none of Shamil's hallmarks. This was a tactic he repeatedly employed; Shamil liked to wait and see what everyone else said, and on this basis write his press release. Nord Ost was very unprofessionally carried out in comparison with Budennovsk and Beslan, for which we know Shamil was responsible. None of Shamil's men were there, and Barayev's people did not rake the elementary precautions like closing off the air vents. In Budennovsk, where there was no reconnaissance, Shamil's people had been diverted from their original plan and had taken the hospital spontaneously, they still had sealed off the underground passages and secured all the exits to the building. In Nord Ost the terrorists failed to do basic things like this, even though supposedly there had been elaborate reconnaissance of the theater prior to the raid. Second, Barayev's men did not control the entrances to the theater and people were coming and going. There were hostages who managed to escape and there were people who just wandered inside.

Most important, the hostage takers had no clear statements of their demands; they could not explain coherently who had sent them or what their goals were. Shamil's goals were always political and he was consistent in his actions; Barayev's political message was blurry, he kept contradicting himself. On the tactical level Shamil left his opponent with only two options: accept his demands or accept the consequences. There had been no realistic possibilities of successfully storming the premises in either Buddenovsk or Beslan.

In the theater at Dubrovka two people died at the hands of the hostage takers and neither of them was a hostage, both were people who went into the theater after the takeover. The first was a young woman, who was hysterical and started yelling at them, and was shot. The second was a policeman who was either drunk, or pretending to be drunk, and he also was shot. All the other deaths inside the theater were the result of the FSB-MVD storming the theater; mostly due to the effects of the gas and some due to stray bullets.

Another question that has to be raised is why were all the terrorists killed? There's film footage of how the Russian Special Forces went through the theater and executed all the terrorists, including those who had lost consciousness due to the gas. This is inexplicable from the perspective of wanting to learn as much as possible about the hostage taking in order to prevent further actions of that type. The behavior of the Russian Special Forces in such cases is always the same; it shows total disregard for the lives of the hostages. For this reason the families of the victims of both Nord Ost and Beslan took the Russian government to court. Their suit has reached the European Court of Human Rights in Straasburg, which is holding hearings behind closed doors.

Attempts to repeat Budennovsk were doomed because the situation had changed too much. It's not just that Putin was not Yeltsin, but that what worked in 1995 was not going to work in 2002 after the September 11, 2001 attack in the United States. But even more importantly, the first war had not ended in 1995 after Budennovsk, but in 1996 after we had defeated the Russian army in Grozny in a conventional ground battle.

In the second war, attempts to repeat the "precedent" of Budennovsk were suicidal for us. They pointed to a serious lack of theoretical and ideological basis for our independence movement. Unlike the Ukraine or the Baltic States we did not have a real nationality movement during the Soviet period. Chechens were not ideologically prepared the way that the Balts, or the Poles, or the Ukrainians were. Although most Chechens rejected Soviet ideology and its way of life, these were personal struggles. They weren't formed into movements or organizations, from which institutions could arise more easily. In other countries large segments of the nation were engaged in an underground struggle to bring about their independence. Dudayev and Yandarbiyev saw an opportunity in 1991 and they seized it, and this was an honor and a service to us, but more broadly we were not ideologically prepared for independence. For us independence was a slogan and an ambition, but it had very little shared meaning among ordinary people; everyone interpreted independence differently.

In the Soviet Union we lived with a split consciousness, in two worlds. We knew about the deportations. We knew our history. We knew that we lived by our own rules. We knew that we did not assimilate. But at the same time we joined the Komsomol, as Udugov did and we went into the army and excelled there. Yandaerbiyev became the leader of the Vainakh Democratic Party in 1990 when ethnic leadership was widely popular and sanctioned by the top levels of the Soviet government. But in Chechnya there was no long preparatory work to develop the ideology of nationalism; we didn't spend decades developing our national values through debates, and for this reason something like Budennovsk was torn out of its very specific context and made a symbol of our national success. There were all kinds of unique circumstances. In 1995, people in the West hesitated even to label it terrorism. Now it has been reassessed in a post- 9/11 world. However, by the time of the Nord Ost incident in October 2002, and certainly by the time of Beslan in 2004, these daring attempts were doomed to failure. They were not going to force Putin to negotiate; all they did was to destroy our political legitimacy.

The effect of Nord Ost was to close off the few political avenues that we had been pursuing. It put Maskhadov in a terrible situation. He condemned the hostage taking, he said that there should be an independent investigation leading to an international tribunal, and that he would cooperate, presumably arresting and turning over suspects. Of course this was only declaratory, but it was all that he could do. Many observers criticized him and said that this was just posturing and really he was maneuvering between factions, and that somehow he was responsible. I think this is very unfair. Maskhadov did what he could; he maintained one line during the entire war, until his last breath. He sought a political solution, he sought negotiations, and he thought that Western institutions would help him. I knew him very well and I don't have any reason to suspect that he was in any way involved in Nord Ost or condoned it, or somehow stood to benefit from it. There was simply no logic to that.

In 2002, the resistance was not in such terrible straits, they controlled sizable sections of the republic, in fact most of the south. I think Maskhadov understood very well that terrorism would close off avenues for us to international institutions, which for him were primary. There was still hope in 2002 that the outside world would help us; there were occasional statements, and visits of various commissions, and sometimes even the U.S. State Department criticized Russia's abuses. We had not lost hope in the process of the international system. Maskhadov thought that it was a matter of explaining, informing, persuading, and that eventually the different international institutions would carry out their mandates. He never despaired of the West and always sought this path.

After Nord Ost the resistance split again. Yandarbiyev was offended by Maskhadov's condemnation of Nord Ost. Yandarbiyev had become the ideologist of jihad and his attitude was that he was a representative of jihad; for this he did not need to have an appointed position. He said the Barayevtsy were martyrs, *shahidy*. He was on the phone with Barayev repeatedly. There is a report that, Khanpash Terkibayev, a Chechen thought to be an FSB agent, who was in Nord Ost, connected Barayev and Yandarbiyev on his cell phone. Regardless of precisely how it happened, Yandarbiyev became involved and defended the action as a heroic sacrifice, which Maskhadov was dishonoring through his criticism of it.

Shamil also left the government after Nord Ost. He remained the commander of Riyadus Sallud. As strange as it may seem,

Udugov remained in the government. In the summer of 2002 Udugov became the director for public information and Kavkaz Tsentr remained an official news agency, although of course Zakayev had no influence over what they published. Zakayev as minister of information was responsible for the Chechenpress website and his ostensible subordinate was putting out Kavkaz Tsentr, which was diametrically opposed to Chechenpress. It was very strange, and I don't have an explanation for why Maskhadov didn't separate himself from Udugov, although I suspect that it was due to pressure by Shamil and other commanders. After all it was Kavkaz Tsentr that gave the radical wing not just a voice but a dominant Internet presence through which they propagated radical slogans and terrorist methods. And it was Udugov who had first informed the public that it was Barayev in the theater. It's clear that he had very early information about the hostage taking. The propaganda for terrorism came through Kavkaz Tsentr and it's a mystery to me why it remained an official site.

Nord Ost destroyed the hopes of those in the West who were trying to help us. I was living in the United States and my personal situation was very complicated. I could not travel and I had been told by U.S. officials to keep my public activity to a minimum. I had applied for political asylum in the United States and the Russian government was starting to manufacture a terrorism case against me and was trying to influence the Department of Homeland Security, which was considering my application. This process began in the spring of 2002 and did not end until December 2005 when I was finally granted status and reunited with my family in the United States.

For those of us representing Chechnya, and for those in the West who were trying to help us, Nord Ost was devastating. In our arguments we always relied on Maskhadov's legitimacy and we always said that Chechens were not terrorists and that we were not responsible for the bombings in 1999. These were fundamental facts for us, and Nord Ost ripped the rug out from under our feet. In November 2002, Olivier Dupuis came to see me in Boston; he was a Belgian European Parliament MP from the Transnational Radical Party. He had been very active on Chechnya and was horrified by what had happened in Nord Ost. We talked for a long time about how to revive a political process. Dupuis and I talked about the need for a new initiative and the peace plan came out of that discussion. My assistant Roman Khalilov, who lived in Europe, was also thinking along similar lines. Roman did a great deal to author the plan and Dupuis did a great deal to publicize and advocate for us.

We understood that it would not be adopted, we were not utopian; we had a realistic assessment of the situation. Our most fundamental goal was to put together a set of principles that people could support, that would be a rallying point for Chechens and for our supporters everywhere in the United States, Europe, and Russia. The plan was first of all meant as a statement of what we were trying to achieve.

The fundamental mechanism in the plan was that Chechnya should become a U.N. protectorate.[2] Under the plan, the Chechen government would resign, the Russian military would withdraw, Chechen armed units would dissolve, and an interim government would be formed and administered temporarily by the United Nations. The plan envisaged the temporary presence of U.N. peacekeepers and police forces. Under the plan, Maskhadov would resign and our government would be dissolved. After state structures in Chechnya were sufficiently developed, so that democratic elections could be held, and the overall situation would warrant, Chechnya would be recognized as independent. This approach was modeled loosely on what we saw unfolding in Kosovo, and what we thought would be appropriate for us. We also reasoned that Russia would have a voice on the U.N. Security Council and thereby would be involved in this process and could make corrections as needed. Furthermore, Putin had made a statement that defined Russia's goals in Chechnya as making sure that Russia's southern flank was secure. "Today the question of Chechnya's dependence on or independence from, Russia is of absolutely no fundamental importance. What is of fundamental importance to us is just one issue. We will not allow this territory to be used any longer as a bridgehead for an attack on Russia."[3] If Putin really meant this, if all Russia wanted was a peaceful and stable neighbor, the plan that we wrote and I offered represented the best opportunity to achieve that.

This was a demonstration of our will to compromise, at the highest level, and an attempt to fill up the vacuum created by Nord Ost, and build hope for a compromise. This plan was not popular among my colleagues and everyone commented on my supposed naiveté. But the main point was not whether it was practical, or practical in the short term, the main point was to give us some kind of political argumentation, hope for people at home, and space on which to rebuild our support in the West. We needed an idea around which people could rally. And this aspect of what we were doing was successful.

As for whether it ultimately would have political application: we may still find that the arguments used in 2003, may be relevant in the future. Certainly, the comparisons that we drew with Kosovo remain relevant, and the legal basis for a finding that Chechens have endured crimes that warrant independence. For instance, the decisions in the European Court for Human Rights increase every year and combine to create a sound legal basis for a claim to independence that is bound to reemerge in years to come. The plan is an optimal way of building a state in Chechnya. What has been lacking is the political will to bring it about.

After the plan had been written, André Glucksmann, a prominent French philosopher and writer, and Olivier Dupuis wrote a letter to Maskhadov, which I sent through couriers. The letter said that they understood the resistance was in a terrible situation and that the prospects for a negotiated solution were close to nil, and that given this, Maskhadov needed to show that he understood the mechanisms that were being proposed, and to demonstrate the maximum concessions and compromise that he was willing to make for the sake of peace.

I received Maskhadov's response a couple of weeks later. He explained that he supported this plan, but that I must understand that the mood of the Chechen resistance was increasingly religious and more frustrated with the West and with democracy than it was during the first war. He was saying that people who were suffering would only see cynicism in these frequent mentions of "democracy" as a fundamental mechanism for resolving the conflict. He tried to explain, "You have to understand that what people here see of western democracy are routine statements of concern, empty gestures, which just irritate people. You have to understand that this is all that they have ever seen of those democracies." He commented that it was hard enough for him to keep the factions together, and they did receive some modest funding from the Middle East, and he could not endorse the plan publicly. At the same time, he authorized me to pursue it as my own initiative. I can't blame him for taking this position, it was very understandable and I expected as much.

In March 2003, I presented the peace plan at the National Press Club in Washington D.C. with Olivier Dupuis and Andre Glucksmann, who were the main proponents and locomotives of this plan in Europe. The first thing I said was, "This is my initiative and my peace plan, however Maskhadov is aware of this initiative, does not object to it, and is studying it further." Thus the "Akhmadov plan" was born. The timing coincided with the start of the war in Iraq. The day before the press briefing there was a meeting of Glucksmann and Dupuis with Brzezinski who warned us to keep expectations low, that no one would be interested because there was an expectation that the invasion of Iraq was imminent. Nonetheless, there was standing room only at the press club and there was tremendous interest in the plan. The discussion was interesting: one Russian journalist who attended kept trying to say that Russia "will never accept this." I responded, "Never say never. There was a time when concepts like Finland, Manchuria, and Poland would have brought about the same response in Russia: 'never.' Well, in the right historical circumstances, this 'never' becomes reality."

I still believe that the overall process contained in the peace plan was the optimal way of resolving our relations with Moscow. Russia is the last of the European empires—an anachronism in the twenty-first century—and eventually, if Russia is ever to break the historical cycles of liberalizations and authoritarian restorations to become a normal European state, this will entail decolonization. And the method we outlined was modeled carefully for this process. A U.N. protectorate on the path to eventual independence has been successful many times in other circumstances, and is the most gradual and peaceful way of divesting Russia of the remnants of its imperial possessions.

The main reaction in Chechen society, as usual, was to ignite competition. I think my many detractors mainly did not like that it was called the "Akhmadov plan." I expected the religious factions to criticize the approach that I was taking but many others did too. Other ministers in the Chechen government for the most part did not comment, only one, Khanbiev, the former health minister and Maskhadov's personal representative in Europe, endorsed the plan explicitly and publicly. Among my most vocal detractors was Akhyad Idigov, the former Chairman of the parliamentary foreign relations committee. He wrote voluminous articles saying that I had given up sovereignty, which was proclaimed in 1991 and was undermining the Chechen Constitution. The constitution was not functional in 2003. It had been rewritten many times, the last series of amendments carried out to make it conform to sharia law. It was honored more in the breach than in practice, particularly by my various critics. For his part Shamil said, "I would not quite regard this as treason, rather, I see it as ignorance." In general, I do not respond to criticism, particularly when there is very personal mudslinging among different Chechen public figures that goes on over the Internet. I don't regard myself as a politician; I was a Foreign Minister, and this was not a position from which you should get into personal polemics. In this case, however, I did comment because there was just too much sounding off by people from within our own camp. I made a statement saying that, "I'll accept that citizen Shamil can express his opinion of my plan, but I don't think it's appropriate for parliamentarians and other officials of the Chechen government to contradict a plan that has Maskhadov's support." I don't necessarily mind constructive criticism of the plan, it might be a necessary process to eventually work out a common ideology, but the public squabbling certainly got in the way of the work.

The Transnational Radical Party, and specifically Olivier Dupuis, collected 30,000 signatures from all over the world endorsing the U.N. Interim Administration in Chechnya. Nikolai Khramov, who was an activist of the party in Moscow, collected thousands of signatures in Russia. How brave do you have to be to live in Russia and sign such a petition, particularly after Nord Ost when there was so much popular and official hatred directed at Chechens? Some 145 members of the European Parliament, several former Prime Ministers including Vaclav Havel, as well as different intellectuals and public figures throughout Europe and the United States added their names. This is what mattered to us: to show that if we presented a well-articulated and principled proposal, people would understand our position and would lend support. I can't remember any action like this in Russia and it was hugely impressive that Khramov was able to organize it. And so it was deeply offensive to me to see all the bickering and pettiness on Chechen websites.

When Maskhadov saw what Khramov was able to achieve, he issued a public statement in support of the plan, as reflecting the Chechen government position as a whole.[4] Interestingly, the Russians never officially commented; Yastrzhembsky never said anything. I think it was disadvantageous for them, they wanted to paint us as irreconcilable, but here we were offering to disband our government and our army. It showed that the main obstacle was the will of the Russians. What further compromise could the Chechens offer? The Russians couldn't respond because they wanted these ideas to go away; they wanted no discussion.

Olivier Dupuis, in February 2004, was able to achieve another real feat: the European Parliament resolution recognizing the deportation of Chechens in 1944 as genocide. In a resolution that contained many important thoughts including that the E.U. should study the peace plan I had put forth, there was also a paragraph about the deportations:

> [The European Parliament] Believes that the deportation of the entire Chechen people to Central Asia on 23 February 1944 on the orders of Stalin constitutes an act of genocide within the meaning of the Fourth Hague Convention of 1907 and the Convention for the Prevention and Repression of the Crime of Genocide adopted by the UN General Assembly on 9 December 1948.[5]

This was a very serious and important fact, which held out the hope that eventually Russia's recent two wars in Chechnya would also be viewed as genocide. These were initial steps in what is by nature a long and laborious process of obtaining our independence through legal and peaceful means. The recognition of what the Chechens have suffered under Russian domination, the appalling war crimes committed there, is the basis on which a legal case for independence can be made, as it was made for Kosovo with Western support.

Although we had some successes, we could do little to prevent the implementation of Russia's political conception for Chechnya, that is the referendum on a constitution, Presidential and parliamentary elections, all of which were meant to create the illusion that the war had ended. At same time, the Nord Ost hostage taking heralded an increase in the use of terrorist tactics by the Chechen resistance. It was followed by the explosion in the building of the pro-Russian Administration in Grozny in January 2003 and increasing numbers of suicide bombers; such attacks became a constant drumbeat over the course of 2003 and 2004. The "Chechenization" and the radicalization of the resistance were simultaneous processes and complemented each other.

In March 2003, there was the referendum on the constitution, and in October the election of Akhmad Kadyrov as the pro-Russian President. It was completely obvious that the referendum was illegitimate; the war was continuing, there was not the kind of security environment where a fair referendum could be organized, there were at least 80,000 Russian soldiers who were permitted to vote, there was no discussion of the text of the constitution, in fact it was a secret document. On the face of it the referendum was a farce. It was conducted by an occupying power in a completely controlled environment. No foreign monitoring organization sent observers and Lord Judd resigned his position as rapporteur on Chechnya for the Council of Europe in protest.[6]

It's interesting how Russia tried to create consent in Chechnya for its policies. In September 2003, less than a month before the Presidential election, Isa Timirov who claimed to be the Chairman of parliament after the disappearance of Ruslan Alikhadzhiev, gave a press conference in Moscow announcing that the parliament had initiated an impeachment action against Maskhadov. Yastrzhembsky commented separately, saying that the Russian government did not recognize the Chechen parliament but welcomed this statement as an important step. The three parliamentarians claimed that the full parliament had gathered, but this could not be true since many were already dead and missing and in exile. More importantly, Isa Timirov was one of the fighters who had seized Budennovsk; so, by ordinary logic, he should have been a wanted man in Russia. Maskhadov was not an acceptable inter-locutor for Russia, but Timirov was? Why? Because Maskhadov was the symbol of independence and statehood and the Kremlin had to de-legitimize him, Yastrzhembsky was willing to bring Isa Timirov under his wing. Such desperate attempts show that Maskhadov remained a threat, precisely because of his legitimacy. It was possible to ignore our institutions, which were feeble and barely functioning, but they could not ignore Maskhadov, who was legally and democratically elected.

There were pro-Russian Chechen politicians for instance who put forth candidacies for President, including the business-men, Malik Saidullayev, and Salambek Maigov, Duma Deputy Aslanbek Aslakhanov, and former Supreme Soviet Chairman Ruslan Khasbulatov; all of them having some degree of genu-ine support within Chechen society and at the same totally pre-dictable, reliable, partners for Moscow. But all such figures, who were authentic politicians, were forced to stand down, and in the Presidential election people running against Kadyrov were mem-bers of his own administration. Russia's entire political strategy rested on one person, Akhmad Kadyrov and there was no effort to institute a process or a system, hence Kadyrov ran without meaningful opposition.

The international assessment of the referendum and the subse-quent Presidential and parliamentary elections should have been unequivocally negative; there were no conditions in place for fair elections, there was no possibility of opposition participation of any type; pro-independence candidates couldn't run and even old faithful Ruslan Khasbulatov could not run. The election was obviously fixed from the start for Kadyrov. Instead of categori-cally condemning this exercise, the international community noted "progress." How did this farce connote progress? The elec-tion was a cynical exercise and could only provide ammunition for extremist propaganda.[7]

Kadyrov was killed by an explosion in Grozny's stadium Dynamo on May 9, 2004 and both Maskhadov and I had very subdued reactions. All he said was that "Allah will judge us." All I said was, "This is another casualty of this war." It's inappropri-ate to speak ill of the dead. The other reason we didn't celebrate his death was that it didn't change the situation; we knew that the Kremlin would find another representative. The personality of this person was not of primary importance as it turned out. Simple decency could have so easily been returned when Maskhadov was killed a year later, and I continue to marvel at how badly his memory was treated.

There are different versions of who killed Akhmad Kadyrov. One version holds that the Russian military and Kadyrov could not figure out how to divide proceeds from oil sales. There is a huge mythology about the oil and the oil business, but I don't think this was the motivation for murder. As far as I know, the Russian military had acted independently only once in its history, in 1825 when troops lined up in Senate Square, half of them were drunk and many were peasant soldiers who did not know why they were there. I don't know of a time since the Decembrists uprising when the Russian military acted independently. In fact Putin put the "heroes" of this war in their place. Generals Shamanov and Kvashnin started to seek political status and Putin pretty quickly relegated them to insignificant roles. I don't think Russian Generals would dare kill Kadyrov who was Putin's pet project. Kadyrov was a political figure of greater value than the Generals.

Kadyrov's killing came as a very big surprise for the Kremlin and they quickly had to improvise. The deceased President's son, Ramzan Kadyrov, was summoned to the Kremlin still in his sweat clothes. Today, he is a member of the Academy of Sciences, but then he was an overgrown child in a track pants. He hadn't finished middle school, he couldn't tie two sentences together in either Chechen or Russian and Putin couldn't simply appoint him President, but it was already said that he should continue his father's work. It was immediately clear that Ramzan would be the heir, but there needed to be new elections. Alu Alkhanov was first elected President and Ramzan became the Prime Minister. It seems fairly clear that Alkhanov was willing to play the role of figurehead until Ramzan was old enough to run for office. This seemed to satisfy Alkhanov; he played the role with minimum problems until the very end of his term. The mechanism was that the parliament asked Alkhanov to resign so that Kadyrov could take his place. It was understood by the population that these were sham elections by the occupiers, who were installing their own puppets.

Ramzan Kadyrov, although inexperienced, proved himself through construction projects. As to the elder Kadyrov, I regard him as a traitor, but he was smart and capable. He put the military in their place; they were essentially confined to their barracks. Akhmad Kadyrov was capable of learning, he had good relations with the Kremlin, he was an inspiring speaker who could persuade people, and his authority was growing. I think that though he played a negative role, there's no question that he was an effective leader. The younger one did not have his father's talents or authority; Ramzan's experience in politics was limited to the physical destruction of his enemy. He had only one card to play, and this I surmise was Putin's idea: the reconstruction of Grozny. This was a fundamentally new approach, the Kremlin had money, and it started spending millions of dollars to rebuild the city. Not only did they spend a lot of money, but they actually were able to control the process. But the budget allotment meant for reconstruction actually went into reconstruction.

"Chechenization," the pretense that the conflict was really between Chechen factions and that reconciliation would take place within Chechen society, rested on three key deliverables from Russia: an end to the indiscriminate slaughter of civilians, "amnesty" for certain fighters who would form Kadyrov's police units, and the reconstruction of reasonably comfortable homes and public spaces. Kadyrov's private army, called Kadyrovtsy, is known for brutal treatment of their opponents however, their cruelty was targeted. If the average person hung a portrait of Kadyrov on the wall and avoided politics, his safety was reasonably well assured.

Seeing all of this, how could the Western observers equate Chechenization with normalization or stabilization? The lack of a principled assessment in the West contributed to the radicalization of the Chechen resistance; the West was seen as acquiescing to Russia, leaving only two available paths: submission to Kadyrov or jihad. The radicalization didn't happen in a day and it didn't happen in a vacuum. We never asked for money or weapons, we only asked for an adequate assessment of what was happening and we never got that.

It is easy to conclude that Chechens accepted the Kadyrov regime, but they were exhausted by fourteen years of war and chaos; they were willing to accept any terms that would permit them to survive. The essence of Chechenization is the implicit bargain that the mass-scale bombing raids and cleansing operations would cease and Russia would provide budget resources for reconstruction, some fighters would be amnestied and become Kadyrovtsy. In return, the Chechens would give up their struggle for independence and accept the rule of the pro-Russian administration. People who made a reluctant choice to passively accept a Byzantine regime are being told by external assessments that this bargain is actually a positive good. The West is saying this resolution is not a tragedy. It's either Kadyrov or extermination and that choice is being hailed by the outside world, somehow, as a sign of progress.

I deeply believe this bargain is only temporary. Once physical survival is more or less assured, Chechens will again seek justice, freedom, and independence.

CHAPTER 11

THE KILLING OF MASKHADOV

Our defeat was not on the day that Putin declared military victory, nor on the day that Ramzan Kadyrov was "elected" President, nor on the day Maskhadov was killed; although his death certainly hastened it. The end of our struggle came in October 2007 when Doku Umarov's proclamation of the Caucasus Emirate dissolved the Chechen republic Ichkeria, and ended the Chechen national resistance by submerging it into an abstract transnational jihad. The time period from Shamil Basayev's raid on Nazran in June 2004, to Doku Umarov's proclamation of the Caucasus Emirate in November 2007, saw the deterioration and eventual abrogation of the nationalist cause.

The fledgling Chechen state—the national idea—was vested in the personality of Maskhadov and his legitimacy. Maskhadov was a symbol of the Chechen state and of our aspirations. His legitimacy stemmed from two facts: his legal, free, and fair election in January 1997, and his fundamental decency and moderation. Tragically, when he passed there was no successor devoted to the same vision for Chechnya and the same struggle; instead the ideas that we sought to contain and oppose crept into our official ideology.

I felt a glimmer of the old days on June 22, 2004 when Shamil went into Ingushetia and held Nazran for two days.[1] Several hundred fighters carried out their mission, pinned the military in their barracks, and returned unhampered. It was a show of our martial excellence without cruelty, without terrorism, and without targeting civilians. All the targets were legitimate

military objectives, government buildings, the MVD, and the
FSB. That was how we fought the first war, by demonstrating
our best warrior qualities. Seeing this operation gave me hope;
it made me think that better things were in the offing, that the
new generation of fighters was infused with the spirit of the
first war.

That judgment proved to be premature, because the next major
event was the September 1, 2004 hostage taking of schoolchil-
dren in the town of Beslan in North Ossetia. The hostage takers demanded the withdrawal of Russian military forces from
Chechnya and the start of peace talks; however the possibility of
negotiations was rejected by the Russian side. The standoff ended
on September 3, 2004 when Russian security services stormed
the school, leading to the deaths of 331 hostages, including 186
children. To attack the school they used tanks, grenade launchers,
and flame-throwers. Most of the children who were killed were
burned up in the school gymnasium when the ceiling collapsed.
How that explosion was triggered remains under a great deal of
controversy.

According to the Russian official version of these events the
terrorist had not made any demands and the Russian government
would have been willing to begin negotiations if they had. The
official version also holds that they had to storm the school because
two powerful explosions had occurred inside the school and the
terrorists had started to shoot at the fleeing hostages. In contrast
to the official version there are several independent investigations
conducted by the parliament of North Osettia, the groups Voice
of Beslan and Mothers of Beslan that represent the relatives of
the hostages, and the *Pravda Beslana* (Truth of Beslan) website
that archives the testimony of witnesses, relevant documents, and
articles about the hostage taking.[2] Their findings paint a different
picture: that the explosions originated outside the school building and that many of the hostages were killed by "friendly fire."
The activists documented and eventually were able to force the
Russian government to admit that the Shmel flame-thrower and
T-72 tanks were used against the school.

There were several people who attempted to intervene in Beslan
and they were able to get a few people out. These would-be mediators were punished for their efforts. One such person was Ruslan

Aushev, the former President of Ingushetia, who went into the school and persuaded the hostage takers to release twenty-six hostages. Aushev recalls that he was presented with a list of political demands which included ending the war and removing the Russian army from Chechnya. Aushev says that he gave this list to the representatives of the emergency response center, who should have shared it with their superiors in Moscow.[3] Later Aushev was pressured by Russian security services and brought in for questioning repeatedly. Aushev and the journalist Anna Politkovskaya had contacted Akhmed Zakayev in London in an effort to reach Maskhadov. Politkovskaya was poisoned very mysteriously on an airplane while on her way to Beslan. She had famously attempted to intervene in Nord Ost, and her presence in Beslan was clearly not wanted by Moscow.

Of course Maskhadov's attempts to offer mediation through Zakayev were rejected outright by the Kremlin. Maskhadov stood to benefit if his mediation succeeded because this would enhance his credentials. The Kremlin could not permit anything of the sort. If he negotiated a way out of the Beslan crisis, there would be no excuse not to negotiate with him to end the war against Chechnya.

In the moral realm, the hostage taking in Beslan stands completely outside of any coordinates; the main targets were children, and that takes us into a different plane altogether. It was an attempt to use children to solve our problems and Shamil took responsibility, and this time I believed him. I am convinced that in many terrorist incidents in 2003 Shamil took responsibility for attacks that he did not necessarily plan or execute. I think he wanted the attention and took responsibility whether he was actually involved in the planning or not. In Beslan, however, I think he was involved deeply in the planning and execution of the attack.

It is difficult to reconstruct what set of circumstances led Shamil to Beslan. There is nothing in the timing or the political situation I can think of that explains it, or motivates it, or gives it some kind of context. If we suppose that his motivation was to repeat Budennovsk, to compel the Russian government to negotiate by taking hostages, if he still held the notion that this was possible, I still don't understand why he did it then and there.

I've come up with a version that I consider plausible based on what I know of the situation, but I don't have any specific knowledge to argue that this is indeed what occurred. After the June 2004 raid in Nazran, the ranks of the resistance in Ingushetia must have swelled; we know that most of the fighters in Beslan were Ingush. The school in Beslan had been used to hold Ingush hostages during the brief war between the Ingush and Ossets in 1992 over the disputed Prigorodnyi region. In 1992 the school was a site of violence against Ingush hostages, which included children.[4] It is conceivable that there were local factors of this nature and that Ingush fighters came to Shamil with the concept of this hostage taking and he developed the plan and execution of it. I can't be sure that this is really how it came about; this is merely a hypothesis that makes sense to me. It's also possible that Shamil was not really intending to start negotiations, but to explode the North Caucasus, and took an opportunity to reignite the Osset-Ingush conflict, which has been unresolved since 1992. The conflict is over the disputed Prigorodnyi area, which is now occupied by Ossets, but had been part of Ingushetia prior to the deportation of the Ingush and Chechens in 1944. During the deportation, the Checheno-Ingushetia republic had been dissolved. When it was reconstituted in the 1950s, the new borders did not include Prigorodnyi rayon. The area remains a source of tension for the region.

There are similarities in the execution of Budennovsk and Beslan, and the contrasts between the two and Nord Ost unmistakably point to Shamil's direct involvement in Beslan. As I've described above, he had been diverted from his path and spontaneously wound up in a hospital in Budennovsk. He had not known it would be there and then. Still he secured the premises; several teams of Russian Special Forces tried to storm the hospital and could not. Shamil had made it clear that he would accept nothing less than having his terms fully implemented. There were two options: acceptance of his terms or the death of the hostages. Shamil had also maintained throughout the Budennovsk hostage taking that he was acting independently. He was adamant that no one among the Chechen political leadership knew, and Dudayev said publicly that he would court martial him for it. This is in sharp contrast to the hostage taking of the theater, Nord Ost, where

Barayev first claimed that he respected Maskhadov's wishes and then started taking calls from Zelimkhan Yandarbiyev, a bitter rival of Maskhadov. Moreover, throughout the three days, random people were wandering in and out of the theater. Nothing of the sort had been permitted in Budennovsk or Beslan.

One interesting detail about Beslan is that the terrorists brought gas-sniffing dogs, which was unmistakably a fingerprint of Shamil, and an indication of his caution and careful planning. For Muslims, dogs are outside animals and are not permitted indoors. These men, probably among the more religious radicals, didn't typically take dogs with them on jihad. But Shamil had made sure that they had dogs because he wanted to preclude the possibility of gas being used. He was above all things pragmatic; he was willing to violate any set of rules including religious ones to achieve his objectives.

The contrast in how the hostage crises in Budennovsk and Beslan ended is the difference between Chernomyrdin and Putin; the difference between 1995 and 2004. For Yeltsin and Chernomyrdin it was politically impossible to accept the death of the hostages, there was the sense that the government was accountable to the public for preserving the lives of the hostages. Whereas, in September 2004, I think all of us watching the events through the media, knew that Putin would not negotiate and that the Russians would storm the school. Shamil claimed later that he did not think that Putin would sacrifice the children. He said he thought that was a line that Putin would not cross.[5] But Shamil did everything for the operation to work out precisely as he planned it.

The ultimate responsibility for what happened in Beslan rests with Shamil, but many in Russia, including the victims' families do not believe that the government did enough to save the children. The demand of the hostage takers in Beslan was to withdraw Russian troops from Chechnya and begin peace talks. Why couldn't the Kremlin pretend to comply with their demands? What exactly did Chernomyrdin sacrifice in Budennovsk in 1995? He saved the lives of the hostages; and in exchange he created a commission to administer the cease-fire, which met for a few months before it disbanded having achieved very little. After Budennovsk the war resumed for another year, before the

Chechens defeated the Russian army in a conventional battle in Grozny. The Kremlin on one side and the radicals on the other ascribe to the Budennovsk hostage taking a degree of strategic significance that in point of fact it simply did not have.

Why couldn't Putin do the same in Nord Ost in 2002 or Beslan in 2004 as Chernomyrdin had done in Budennovsk in 1995? One of Russia's most respected liberal voices, Sergei Kovalev put it this way, "[F]or Putin it was more important to try to show the strength of the state than to save the lives of the hostages."[6] In the Soviet Union there were acts of terrorism, but no one heard about them, because everyone involved was killed; the victims and the hostage takers. In Soviet times, the KGB's approach to fighting hostage taking was to destroy everyone involved. In other societies there is a whole science of negotiating with hostage takers, the purpose of which is to persuade them to give up hostages or to trick them into thinking that their terms are being met. In Beslan there were no efforts along these lines and the local population was quite critical of how it was handled. The Osset legislature formed a special commission to study the events, which held hearings and produced an independent report. Similarly, the group of mothers and other relatives who came together in the organization Voice of Beslan, has been repeatedly repressed by the Kremlin for demanding accountability from the state.

After the storming of the school in Beslan, one terrorist was left alive, Nurpasha Kulayev, and the main result of his trial, which was deeply disadvantageous to the Russian government, was to expose the incompetence of the security services. The trial became an opportunity for the families of the victims to pose pointed questions that brought out details of bungling by the security services during the operation. Since the Nord Ost hostage taking in October 2002, one would think that the security services would have improved their procedures. Why were tanks and Shmel flame-throwers employed against the school? Who gave the order to use these weapons? Basic questions like this were being asked and there were no credible answers. In Nord Ost there were people wandering in and out of the theater, and in Beslan, there were armed local men who apparently charged in (and may have been the ones who set off the explosion), but this does not excuse the professionals on the scene, who should have been in total control of the area. The families of the victims of Nord Ost and Beslan have gone as far as the European Court for Human Rights to demand accountability from the Russian government.

For Maskhadov and other representatives of Chechnya, including myself, the horrific deaths in Beslan destroyed our credibility. The questions being asked in Russia about the professionalism and accountability of the security services were not being asked abroad. We were considered responsible for the deliberate killing of children, which is evil in any moral code. Launching into explanations about different factions within the resistance some of which use and propagate terrorism whereas others that try to operate within the Geneva Conventions is not enough of an answer to explain something so terrible and no one was more conscious of that than we ourselves.

There were no opportunities for us after Beslan. The Chechen cause lost all of its supporters overnight. What arguments did any of us have? It was a time of deep despair. Yet, again as after Nord Ost, there were people both in the West and in Chechnya who were thinking along similar lines. Diplomats in the West such as Tim Guldimann, the former OSCE envoy were saying that Maskhadov still had one chance, that he could show that he exercised control over the fighters by calling for a cease-fire. This was communicated to Maskhadov who was told it would send a positive signal to European institutions. When you have fewer men and fewer opportunities to control them, and you know that the other side will only attempt to provoke you, this is a suicidal proposition. Nevertheless, on January 14, 2005 Maskhadov announced a unilateral cease-fire.[7] Interestingly, Shamil stated a few days later that although he considered it unnecessary; he would abide by the cease-fire. The Russian government claimed that the cease-fire was just for show. But the Russian military in Chechnya commented that it was being observed, and Russian human rights activists also commented that it was effective.[8] The cease-fire lasted one month, from January to February 2005 and Maskhadov proved that he was capable of controlling his troops. Representatives of the Russian military commented privately that they were concerned because

Maskhadov had demonstrated control.[9] That cease-fire again gave us hope that not everything was lost.

I continue to respect Maskhadov for maintaining a very consistent line throughout the entire war. I still have the tapes that he sent to me through couriers and it is painful to listen to them. He was a man of conscience, who felt tremendous responsibility for what was happening to his nation. It's humbling to realize that he was sitting in a tent or cave, always in danger, and despite his desperate situation, he gave me very practical and positive instructions. I know that Maskhadov sent many tapes like this to different people; the tapes that I collected paint a portrait of a remarkable man. There was his unwavering belief that there had to be a political solution to the war; there was his faith in international institutions; there was his concern for the suffering of the Chechen people, and his counsel to me.

On March 8, 2005, a few days after the end of the cease-fire, Maskhadov was killed in Tolstoy Yurt. I was surprised by this location; it was a very pro-Russian region, with family ties to Ruslan Khasbulatov, the former speaker of the Supreme Soviet, who had attempted to return to Chechnya in the summer of 1994. In response, Maskhadov had led a raid into Tolstoy Yurt, on Dudayev's orders, and since then Maskhadov was not well liked in this town. It remains a mystery to me how and why Maskhadov was hiding in Tolstoy Yurt. I have made many inquiries and found that apparently he was staying there with a very small group and practically no guards. I think that he may have been staying there because no one would look for him there. The official version of the killing was that he died from the aftershocks of grenade explosions. Then there was the version that his nephew shot him at his request, and the nephew stood trial for this.[10] However, there were also accounts that Maskhadov had returned fire in a shoot-out. Judging by the photos that were published, the bullet hole and small puddle of blood at the back of his head are consistent with reports of having been shot.

Maskhadov's death was a real blow to us, on every level: morally, emotionally, and politically. The abominable treatment of Maskhadov's body was deeply symbolic of how the Kremlin viewed him and, by extension, all of us. They released photos of him lying on the road with his shirt off with some Western-style toilet that was dragged into the street in the background. There were gleeful comments from the Kremlin; in Moscow they relished the moment.[11] The disrespect and mockery of a very decent man, whose death for the vast majority of Chechens was tragic, revealed what the Kremlin thought of him, and what they thought of our grief at his passing. He was not permitted a funeral and they didn't return his body to his family because it was said that he was killed in the course of "the counter terrorist operation." Maskhadov was never involved in terrorism and to apply this law to him was cynical and vindictive.

Approximately two years earlier Maskhadov had sent me a cassette relaying that he understood that he was always on the brink of death, and that he had made provisions for a successor. "Death strikes all people equally, but in my situation I need to make sure that there is a succession in place for the presidency. I have chosen a person who will continue my course, and have given his name to two other people. He will become known to you in the event of my death." When Maskhadov was killed, I called Umar Khanbiev, who from 2003 to 2005 had been Maskhadov's representative and his trusted friend, and Umar confirmed to me that indeed Abdul Khalim Saidullayev was the person that Maskhadov had named.

I did not know Saidullayev, although apparently he had fought during the first war. This was a very sudden and unexpected appointment and it led to many different rumors. First of all, Maskhadov did not have many options; there was not another Maskhadov. He did not have someone else with the same qualifications, someone who had a leadership role during the first war, who had been popularly elected, who was respected and legitimate. There was no one from the old guard that he could choose, all the top people whom Maskhadov had known since the first war were dead, in exile, or had gone over to the pro-Russian administration. Maskhadov did not have a close knit group of top supporters, particularly after the fighting in Grozny, which decimated his men. Shamil, for obvious reasons, was not a candidate and certainly Doku Umarov should not have been. Doku understood very little about politics, which his subsequent actions amply proved.

Maskhadov by necessity chose a successor among younger men, who were not yet well-known. The person he chose was thirty-eight years old, had a religious education, and a secular degree in engineering, and at a fairly young age had been named a sheikh. I don't know what one does to deserve this honor, but certainly there are very few sheikhs in Chechnya, and I would be surprised if there was another one in my lifetime. He wasn't a commander and did not have a military unit behind him; he did not have a warrior's reputation or the pressures of having to take care of the men serving under him. I think this may have made him a kind of compromise figure. People who know him say that Saidullayev was modest and had served Maskhadov faithfully for a long time. If he was chosen two years prior to Maskhadov's death, he was being groomed, and he must have known that others, particularly Shamil, would accept him.

Saidullayev's first statement was moderate; it basically claimed succession from Maskhadov and promised to faithfully follow the same course as first articulated by Dudayev. This had become a mantra for Chechen leaders; everyone claimed continuity with Dudayev even though in reality there was precious little in common between the men or the situations. However, fairly soon Saidullayev diverged drastically from the course that Dudayev and Maskhadov had followed.

It disturbed me deeply when Saidullayev claimed that Maskhadov had been killed because he had sought a political end to the conflict. This was followed by a comment from Shamil, who said, "I warned him not to use his cell phone. This happened because he had spent too much time sending text messages to his emissaries, who were lying to him about these peace plans."[12] It's certainly true that hundreds of people were found and killed because they used their cell phones, but to speak of Maskhadov in such a high-handed manner so soon after his demise indicated disrespect. Of course, reference to emissaries was a dig at Umar Khanbiev, at Zakayev, or at me, or perhaps all of us, and it was totally wrong. Shamil's comments were totally inappropriate.

The radicals and the Kremlin offered similar explanations: Maskhadov was killed because he was tricked by his representatives in the West, or Maskhadov was killed because the Kremlin could not permit the possibility of another dramatic hostage taking. These explanations are based on similar ways of reasoning, both sides reason as though the Russians chose when to kill him. The fundamental point is that the Kremlin could not tolerate a legitimate President of Chechnya and they were always looking for Maskhadov, and it just so happens that they caught up with him on March 8, 2005. If they had found him earlier, they would have killed him earlier. Maskhadov was killed because he had legitimacy in the eyes of the Chechen population and the international community. It did not matter where Maskhadov was—he could be huddling in a cave—but a living Maskhadov was the last barrier to legitimating a pro-Russian government. The killing of Maskhadov was a necessary precursor to the full implementation of the Kremlin's "Chechenization" policy.

Saidullayev was only President for about a year before he was killed in June 2006, and we don't have a great deal of information to evaluate what he intended to do and we don't know how he would have performed once he had obtained more experience. I formed my sense of him and his philosophy on the basis of just five or six statements that he made in the first few months in office. It's clear that he made substantial departures from Dudayev and Maskhadov. He spoke in a more religious style and Islam became more prominent in his public pronouncements. He also belittled the idea of pursuing a political solution, he declared that the only means against Russia was war, and it was never clear what the ultimate goal of that war would be. Would we fight until we could march on Moscow and declare it the capital of the Emirate? Saidullayev said that there would be "fronts" all over Russia: the upper Volga front, the Siberia front, and so forth. This was bizarre; there can be either an underground insurgency or a front. In military terms these two concepts are polar opposites. Apart from the strange terminology, Saidullayev was breaking a fundamental tenet of both Dudayev and Maskhadov with this statement. Our goal was to drive the Russian army out of Chechnya and acquire independence. And that's it. There were no other goals. We had only military targets, and we wanted as much as possible to behave as a conventional military, in pursuit of this one goal. Saidullayev was propogating guerrilla warfare all over Russia against all types of targets as though this was a goal in itself.

In this short period, there were two reorganizations of the government and I think I was the only person actually dismissed from office. I did not mind because I did not like the tendencies I observed in Saidullayev. His comment about me was inappropriate and suggested that he was misinformed. He said that he fired me as Foreign Minister because, "He prefers to pursue some scholarly project at a research institute to working for the benefit of Chechnya." This was silly. I had a Reagan-Fascell Fellowship at the National Endowment for Democracy that gave me an opportunity to speak regularly to the remaining audience of experts, journalists, and politicians—those few who were still interested in seeking peaceful solutions to the problem of Chechnya. It was an important symbol that despite all the terrible publicity that the Chechen cause received, there were still institutions in the United States that were willing to hear our side.

In another bizarre maneuver, Saidullayev appointed Shamil Basayev Prime Minister in one of his government reshuffles. I understood Saidullayev making an error due to his inexperience, but how could Shamil permit this? This was a totally irresponsible step. The Shamil I knew would not have accepted the position, given his reputation after Beslan. To accept a government post was to doom that government to pariah status, and surely he understood this. He continued to claim that he wanted an independent Chechen state, and repeatedly sought to inspire multi-national rebellions against Russia, not as a goal in itself, but rather to establish Chechen statehood. For Shamil, creation of a national state was the main goal. In his way of thinking, other Muslims should support the Chechen struggle for independence from a sense of solidarity. A long interview of Shamil with Andrei Babitsky, contained the following exchange:[13]

> Shamil Basayev: I don't need negotiations, as such. I need an end
> to the genocide of the Chechen people. I need to know that
> our children will not be deported to Siberia as in 1944. That is
> why we need independence. The world recognizes the geno-
> cide of 1944. All right, let's not talk about today's genocide.
> Today the Russians are fighting a colonial war here. It's not
> a war against terrorism, the Russians are the terrorists. From
> our side it's a national liberation struggle. They are trying to
> hang false labels on us.

Andrei Babitsky: You would characterize this as a war for
   national liberation?
Shamil Basayev: How else would you characterize it?
Andrei Babitsky: I think it has religious origins.
Shamil Basayev: In the first place, for me, this is a struggle for
   freedom. Freedom is primary. If I am not free, I can not live
   righteously. That's how I see it. The sharia is secondary.

As Saidullayev developed his ideology, he did not completely renounce what came before him; he did maintain the forms of a national government, a parliament, a government of a Chechen republic. However, after he was killed, Saidullayev was succeeded by Doku Umarov, who on October 27, 2007, in a video that was sent to Radio Liberty, read from a prepared text, which caused tremendous controversy by dissolving the Ichkerian state in favor the Caucasus Emirate.[14] By so doing Doku Umarov substituted the goal of international jihad for the more limited goal of national independence. In response, Maskhadov's ministers and parliamentarians, led by Akhmed Zakayev, had declared that the Chechen Republic would continue in exile, as a parliamentary republic, with Zakayev as Prime Minister until free elections could be held in Chechnya. As a result, the Chechen resistance now has two mutually antagonistic governments: the one in the mountains led by Doku Umarov, which considers itself the headquarters of the Emirate, and a government in exile with Akhmed Zakayev as Prime Minister, which considers itself the continuation of the Chechen Republic of Ichkeria.

Both entities claim Saidullayev's policies as precedents. Saidullayev had maintained some semblance of a Chechen state—he formed a Chechen government, and he spoke of the national liberation struggle. Those who favor the Emirate say that Saidullayev had been laying the groundwork for the declaration of the Emirate, and I think I agree with that assessment. Those who favor the Chechen nation state say that he hadn't proclaimed an Emirate. I think he didn't have enough time to fully implement his ideas. Saidullayev's presidency only lasted about a year because he was killed in July 2006 and Shamil, who was the Prime Minister, would not have permitted the goal of an independent Chechen state to be cast aside. However, from the start of his presidency, Saidullayev had abrogated Maskhadov's approach to international institutions. In August 2005, he had declared:

> If anyone actually believes that the fate of Chechnya is decided in Strasburg, Washington or Moscow, he is deeply mistaken. The last word in the Russian-Chechen war belongs to the Chechen *mujahids* who with weapons in hand defend the freedom and independence of the land from Russian aggression.
>
> All these international organizations that have multiplied in recent years like mushrooms after rain, have not managed to hold one serious event in Europe that could rival even the special operation conducted recently by a small mobile group near the village Rochi Chu.
>
> All of our various special representatives of the government and the parliament, who have in whole groups settled in Western countries have not been able to get the European parliament to pass a resolution regretting the death of the legitimate president of Chechnya and calling on Russia to return his body to his family for a proper burial.[15]

With the presidency of Saidullayev, the Chechen resistance entered into a very unpredictable period. If we don't believe in political processes, if we don't think that the United Nations, OSCE, Council of Europe, and other international institutions are legitimate bodies that we aspire to join, then on what basis are we seeking our independence? After Maskhadov's death, the people who came to power were increasingly isolated and increasingly religious; they narrowed the political field so far that there was no space left for diplomacy at all.

CHAPTER 12

THE NORTH CAUCASUS EMIRATE AND BEYOND

Chechnya is located in Europe. Istanbul is a two-hour flight from Grozny; Sophia is three hours away and Frankfurt is four or five. I drove from Paris to Grozny in three days, making many stops on the way. However, Chechnya might as well be in another universe. It is completely isolated, sealed off, and obscure. This has to do with the peculiar status of Russia in Europe and Russia's ability to cut off access and persistently misrepresent the situation in Chechnya. The conflict has not ended. It regenerates itself from within and mutates, through processes that are difficult to observe from this distance. War has its own rules and algorithms; it is its own cause and effect, what philosophers call "a thing in itself," and this insularity might be its most frightening characteristic.

I was a participant in this conflict and viewed it from various vantage points: I was a combatant during the first war, an ordinary citizen during the interwar period, and Foreign Minister during the second war. I knew all the main Chechen leaders, but even so, there are many things about which I can only speculate, and I don't completely understand. At the same time, there were many situations where the underlying processes, ambitions, and motivations turned out to be simpler and more cynical than they seemed at first. There isn't a logical or predictable process that can be reduced to a set of factors, and what is happening today certainly isn't just a manifestation of international forces and competitions. What makes war so intractable is precisely that it's a process unto itself, where one fact brings to life a new one.

During perestroika, the Supreme Soviet passed a law regarding secession from the Soviet Union. It prescribed a very complicated and lengthy procedure, but in principle it recognized that national and autonomous republics could exercise the right they had under Leninist doctrine and the Soviet Constitution to leave the Soviet Union.[1] In practice, these procedures were overtaken by events during the last years of the Soviet Union. Chechnya, an autonomous republic, wanted to follow the same mechanisms for independence as those implemented by union republics, such as the Baltic States, Georgia, Armenia, and Azerbaijan. Dudayev spoke about adhering to an international democratic charter, and building a national state. We were not all that different from one another in 1991; it was only after they achieved recognition and we did not, that our paths so radically diverged.

One of the crucial differences between us and the Balts was their greater ideological cohesion and organized infrastructure in their underground nationality struggle. They had developed an infrastructure, parties, underground publications, and political debates, which involved broad segments of the population. Each Chechen struggled against Soviet authority; each Chechen believed in God, and rejected Soviet ideology. I do not underestimate the Chechen resistance to assimilation but this is not the same as having a well-developed nationalism. We still lack institutions that could foster a debate about national ideology, which eventually could rise to consistent ideas among broad segments of the population about how we want to organize our polity.

The leaders of the perestroika period, Dudayev and Yandarbiyev were inventing national concepts while in the act of realizing them. There was very little time for this process to take hold before the war forced profound transformations on our consciousness. War requires people to think about mortality, the meaning of life, and justice. It encourages a religious conception of existence. This is natural, but in our particular circumstance greater religious consciousness brought about greater political divisions, which Maskhadov tried desperately to overcome.

I was privileged to know the three men, Dudayev, Maskhadov, and Shamil Basayev who defined this period in Chechnya's history and think of them as heroic and tragic, each in his own way. Dudayev was a charismatic and forceful personality, Maskhadov was a model of personal honor and ethical conduct, and Shamil was an irreconcilable revolutionary. When I listen again to Maskhadov's audiotapes to me, I understand that there had to be a degree of duality; that he had to find a common language with different segments of the resistance.

Dudayev was a forceful personality, and he also was dealing with a different population, whose ideology was much more uniform and secular. Dudayev commanded in politics like a General on the battlefield, he made clear decisions and you were with him or against him. He did not tolerate dissent within his team.

Maskhadov was President of a different Chechnya: he inherited a traumatized population, field commanders who demanded to share political power, and a different level of bitterness and hostility between Russia and Chechnya. Dudayev used religion selectively and instrumentally and he always kept it subordinate to his political goals. Maskhadov had to contend with radicals, who were a minority, but an increasingly active minority. When I received Maskhadov's tapes, I had to be careful how I assessed them and what conclusions I drew. He was walking on a tightrope and so was I, and I knew that the information I received was partial, it was calibrated for a particular purpose.

War is the most difficult test for any society; it requires the mobilization of all the capacities of the nation, and there cannot be confusion at the top about the ultimate priorities and goals of the struggle. Abdul-Khalim Saidullayev and others who came after Maskhadov, sought to focus the Chechen struggle on religion rather than on statehood. They identified religion as the primary issue. Their argument was easy to make, "The West did nothing for us. Maskhadov and his various ministers who exalted western institutions were simply distracting people from the real struggle." It was understandable that this resonated with some Chechens, who were very isolated and have seen so little of the West.

The radicals argued that, Maskhadov's whole approach—to address Western institutions and through them eventually obtain our goals—was wrong. This was attempted and failed because the West itself was not willing to defend the principles on which these institutions are based. There is truth to this perspective, but at the same time, we have to recognize that we contributed to the West's disillusionment through our own inconsistencies and double standards.

For instance, I had a meeting with three State Department officials in February 2002 in New York City, including one who I thought was the most knowledgeable, professional, and competent in matters related to the Russian-Chechen conflict among all diplomats that I have met. This meeting was much friendlier than the meeting with Assistant Secretary Beyrle because this time it was at the State Department's initiative, and we talked for at least five hours. During this meeting I was presented with a list of recommendations on what the Chechen resistance should refrain from doing: reject foreign fighters, reject terrorism, and reject foreign financing.

I responded, "Yes, I accept these recommendations, especially since many are already being fulfilled, but what would the United States be willing to do for us?" And here my interlocutor had only one response, "I do not have the authority to promise anything." The whole problem was that Maskhadov could reject these things but couldn't always enforce this rejection throughout the entire resistance. I can't prove a negative. How can I prove that we were not receiving money from foreign sources? Or that we didn't have any ties to Al-Qaeda? My interlocutor didn't have specific information or wouldn't share it if he did. In the end, we had a good meeting and it was a step in the right direction to explore all these issues together, but we didn't actually achieve very much.

This characterizes all my meetings with representatives of foreign governments. Even when I had the best informed and professional interlocutor, all we could do was to communicate, he had no authority to promise me anything and I could not vouch for the resistance as a whole. All of my meetings essentially boiled down to this: we could transmit information, but that was all that we could do.

The Chechens never asked for money or weapons, not to mention recognition—we asked for much simpler things. Here was the starting point: We wanted the United States and Europe to call things by their proper names. We wanted the war to be called a war and to drop the pretense of a "counter-terrorist operation." We wanted a reassessment of what this conflict was about, the recognition that terrorism was a result of the war, and that the war was the result of important political problems that needed to be addressed. The discussion got nowhere. We went around in circles.[2]

I am recounting this because there are legitimate grounds for Chechens to be frustrated with Western institutions, and I have felt that frustration myself. But with all of their many and varied flaws and limitations, these institutions are a better and more hopeful prospect than war without end and at some point in the not too distant future, the leadership of the armed Chechen resistance must return to this way of thinking.

There were biases built into the whole array of international institutions, which ranged from something relatively simple like applying for political asylum, to the big issues such as the United Nations monitoring refugee camps that testified that somehow conditions were improving (even as camps were being closed and civilians sent back into a war zone), or the roundtables hosted by the PACE, which were never able to go beyond expressing concern about the humanitarian situation and did not dare approach political issues. There were various European resolutions that simply contradicted each other left and right. The biggest disappointment came after Maskhadov's death, when no Western government managed to voice regret about his killing and none dared to say that he deserved a proper burial. It was easy to conclude that the West betrayed its own values, that it will never look at us as anything other than a nuisance at best, or a menace at worst.

Living in the United States, and having gone through a three-and-half-year court case to obtain political asylum, I can see the flaws in Western democracy with greater clarity than many of its various detractors in Chechnya, but I can also acknowledge that Chechens failed to be consistent and failed to adapt to new realities. After September 11, 2001, we entered a new world, where the United States would pursue a new role, and the Chechens failed to integrate themselves into these new realities. We needed to be more flexible, adaptable, and reliable. There were then, and remain today, opportunities to show that we can be transparent and reliable partners. Even for me it was sometimes hard to figure out which way the winds were blowing at home, and I had to calibrate my words carefully. Why would an outsider trust us? Particularly after Nord Ost and Beslan seemed to validate the worst that the Russians had said about us.

Russia has not come to terms with the loss of empire, particularly with the loss of Georgia, Azerbaijan, and Armenia. Russia seeks to maintain control of the Caucasus region by manipulating the local conflicts, which are the results of Stalin's nationality policy. Russia stokes these conflicts; this is their leverage to keep the region dependent on Russia and limit Western influence. In August 2008, in its war against Georgia, Russia showed that it was willing to sacrifice regional stability and violate the most basic norms of international law to maintain control. In various speeches, Putin has made reference to Russia's long-term presence and control of this region and defined Russia's actions in Georgia within long-standing imperial ambitions.[3] In this light, the recognition of Abkhazia and South Ossetia was an assertion that Russia can behave with total arbitrariness. If the recognition of Kosovo was an international precedent that was properly applied to Abkhazia, why shouldn't it be applied to Chechnya? The answer is that the Russia government believes it can do anything it wants to do in this region. This is a terribly dangerous illusion.

The West's reluctance to impose any penalties for Russia's illegal and terribly destabilizing behavior can be misread as license for further misdeeds. The interests of the United States are expanding in this region, in addition to the transit of Caspian oil and gas to European markets, there is the new "northern route," that supplies NATO forces in Afghanistan. The unpredictability of the Russians and the false sense of license suggest that stability will remain elusive.

The politics of the South and North Caucasus are not hermetically sealed off; Russia's impunity in Chechnya encouraged its aggressiveness in Georgia. The recognition of South Ossetia aggravates the existing conflict between Ingushetia and North Ossetia and the recognition of Abkhazia inspires the idealists who dream of North Caucasus unity, the Mountain republic of 1918, which united the nations and gave them a port on the Black Sea as a guarantee of viability. Ambitious young men like Shamil went to fight in Abkhazia in 1992–93 because they dreamed of the North Caucasus Confederation that included Sukhumi. The proclamation of an independent Abkhazia encourages new versions of such projects.

Despite Russian claims to have pacified Chechnya, the armed resistance continues and remains a destabilizing factor in Chechnya; presently it may not be growing, but it is also not declining. The resistance has the potential to exist for a very long time as we can see from constant low intensity fighting in Chechnya itself, and increasing intensity and frequency of fighting throughout the North Caucasus.[4]

In 1999, there was only one problematic republic in the North Caucasus and that was Chechnya. Dagestan was firmly with Russia when the incursions of 1999 occurred; it was safe and calm. Today Dagestan is seething; there are nearly daily special operations, explosions, and high-level assassinations. In Ingushetia, an undeclared war is raging; in Kabardino-Balkaria there are constant special operations. The territory of the North Caucasus is, in effect, a war zone. The Kremlin has three tactics that do not amount to a strategy: offer money, play clans against each other, and send in more Russian troops. They have all been tried since the eighteenth century and are clearly not working. The result has been only a superficial integration.

For the resistance, the long-term prognosis is promising. Russia is in the grips of financial crisis and cannot subsidize local tyrants and Russian military presence forever. The North Caucasus "front" will remain a serious destabilizing force for a long time to come. Today there is an assassination, or explosion, or a shoot out every day. The Kremlin likes to pretend that this is not a problem but the most capable part of the Russian army is tied up there permanently. The more Russia concentrates its military in the North Caucasus, the less real strength Moscow has. Rule through brute strength only perpetuates the absence of political legitimacy. Will Russians always be willing to spend real money to maintain the illusion of control over the North Caucasus?

The North Caucasus today is not home to "separatist" movements. The North Caucasus republics are colonial territories engaged in national liberation struggles. However, over the last few years the insurgencies have become explicitly Islamic. What drove people to this is not Islamic education or emissaries from the Arab world but the state failure, anarchy, violence, and the hopelessness that reigns in the North Caucasus. If one analyzes

why a particular person participated in an uprising in Kabarda
or Dagestan or even Ingushetia you discover that people join
the insurgencies because of very local and personal situations.
It is always about local injustice, arbitrary police violence, clan
rivalries, and the absence of recourse through legal or political
channels. In the 1990s, Chechnya was different. Most people in
Chechnya were motivated by a desire for national independence,
but we were unique in this. The new resistance movements in
the North Caucasus have developed in a different context, where
there is no political space to debate openly, they can't safely pro-
mulgate political platforms, they have not proclaimed independence, and the only apparent common denominator among these
groups seems to be Islam. At the same time we can't judge the
depth of the religiosity. Is it more than a sign of protest? The
dzhaamats, community of believers, are the only alternative to
the prevailing chaos and injustice. The *dzhaamats* offer people stability, social cohesion, and protection from a dysfunctional and
predatory state.

Following the killing of Maskhadov, Saidullayev's brief term in
office was contradictory. He didn't abrogate Maskhadov's policies
nor was he a direct extension of Maskhadov. Doku Umarov, who
became the leader of the resistance after the killing of Saidullayev
in June 2006, said that he was chosen because he was the last
within the resistance who was a commander in the first war.
Umarov had plenty of experience as a fighter. He was always
brave and daring but he had very little experience in politics. He
had briefly been Security Council Secretary between the wars.
He was mostly known for having his own unit that controlled oil
wells and fought in the oil wars. He did not go to Dagestan in
August 1999, and remained aloof from the political alliances and
conflicts that dominated the interwar period.

As President, Doku Umarov initially made a few cautious statements and seemed to be taking a wise course. I thought his silence
was a good sign, internationally we were viewed through the
prism of the war against terrorism, and there was no point in constantly trying to explain ourselves. For the Chechen government
it made by far more sense to wait and let events speak for them.
There were insurgencies all over the North Caucasus. It was, and
is, a gathering storm whose time has not come yet. The Chechens

are exhausted from fighting, while other nations in the North Caucasus are just getting the taste of it. It is to our advantage to simply wait—let the Russians strain their resources putting down rebellions all over the North Caucasus while the Chechen recover demographically from the horrors of the last fifteen years.

In the summer of 2007, suddenly websites were publishing statements from Zakayev, now Foreign Minister, reporting that certain sources were saying an "emirate" would be proclaimed, and that this was an FSB plot. Doku ignored this at first, did not respond publicly, and Kavkaz Center remained silent on the issue. What followed was an intense personal correspondence between Umarov and Zakayev, which found its way onto Chechen websites.

Finally, on October 27, 2007, Doku Umarov made a declaration, in a video that was sent to Radio Liberty, in which he dissolved the Chechen Republic Ichkeria, and proclaimed instead the Caucasus Emirate.[5] Maskhadov's ministers abroad, led by Zakayev, as well as several parliamentarians declared that the Chechen state would continue, as a parliamentary republic, with Zakayev as Prime Minister-in-exile until free elections could be held in Chechnya.

The Chechen resistance now has two competing governments: the one in the mountains led by Doku Umarov, which considers itself the headquarters of the emirate, and a government-in-exile with Akhmed Zakayev as Prime Minister, which considers itself the continuation of the Chechen Republic Ichkeria. This split has generated a whole flurry of statements and recriminations, but I've never seen any other media, apart from Chechenpress and Kavkaz Center, pay any attention to this virtual storm.

Doku Umarov's statement was a watershed event; it is so strange that I don't know where to begin analyzing it. In one fell swoop it abrogated borders and countries and international institutions. In their stead it proclaimed the emirate that is composed of "vilayetes." The vilayetes were administrative units in the Ottoman Empire. By renaming the republics of the North Caucasus "vilayetes" little was achieved. The Chechen Republic Ichkeria was dissolved in favor of the "vilayete" Nokchi Cho. All borders were repudiated and all areas inhabited by Muslims from the Caspian to the Black Sea were automatically appended to the emirate, the contours of which have not been well defined. Occasionally, when Kavkaz Center produces a "map" it consists of the entire Caucasus and a little island, Georgia, presumably left out because it is predominantly Christian (although, I suppose the Muslim parts of Georgia should be ceded to the emirate). It is not entirely clear if Azerbaijan is included and what exactly happens to Armenia. Umarov's decree proclaims that the emirate contains the vilayetes of Dagestan, Nokchi Chu (Ichkeria), Gilgiaoich (Ingushetia), Iriston (Ossetia), vilayet of the Nogai Steppe (Stavropol Krai), the united vilayet of Kabarda, Balkaria, and Karachai.[6] It is obvious that this concept was not well considered and had no coherent ideological foundation.

One of the items that emerged on the Chechen websites was an audio tape of a telephone conversation between Doku Umarov and Udugov, who has been living in the Middle East since the start of the war. On the tape Doku offers this advice, "If a person says the right thing, but does not carry it out himself, I can still accept what he says and apply it to myself. It's possible that you don't live by the concept you have outlined, but you have identified the purpose of his life for a person who wants to follow a righteous path and for this reason we accept it."[7] This suggests that the concept Doku Umarov read was written by Udugov. The reasons behind this declaration are complex, but there are at least three: the resistance found itself at a dead-end after Maskhadov's death; the cowardice and cynicism of the West offered no hope of support; and there was total disillusionment that any negotiated solution was possible. In contrast to of all these disappointments, Udugov's concept was simple and clear.

The "concept" was a foreign innovation being grafted in an artificial way onto the Chechen resistance. There was no internal consistency. For instance, Doku Umarov's only claim to political legitimacy stemmed from Maskhadov's election in 1997 conducted within the borders of the Chechen Republic Ichkeria. It is important to stress that the two wings of the resistance—the radicals in the mountains and the moderates in London—both claim to be the legitimate successors of Dudayev, Maskhadov, and Saidullayev.

The resistance is composed of young men. The new generation that has taken over the leadership has even less experience in politics, and less knowledge of the outside world than we did. Doku Umarov says to his critics in Europe:

> There is a new generation of mujahadin. Today the majority of those who are fighting in the jihad are the Islamic youth.... And they know for a fact that they came out to the jihad to establish the sharia in the North Caucasus.... From the old warriors whom you knew, some were martyred, some joined the traitors to the faith, some left the jihad; there are only a few of them left. The young mujahadin have arrived. They are 19–20 years old and they don't know you and you don't know them.[8]

I can accept that a new generation of fighters can develop the ideology of the resistance, but I don't believe that the concept that Doku Umarov read on that video came from within the ranks of his own men, and I don't see the benefit in promulgating undeveloped views, particularly in such primitive form.

Following Maskhadov's death the resistance made a terrible mistake, by aligning itself with a multi-national jihad and splitting into two rival camps that don't recognize each other. The declaration of the emirate was a crisis point that reordered all the variables around it. It provided space for Ramzan Kadyrov to position himself as the guardian of Chechen tradition. Kadyrov makes possible the postwar reconstruction and recently built a very elaborate mosque in Grozny with Turkish help. He presents himself as the protector of Chechen national tradition and traditional religious practice. When the resistance is divided and behaves in such strange ways, Kadyrov gains legitimacy among broader segments of society. That Kadyrov can occupy this ideological niche is only possible because of the crisis within the resistance. In reality, Kadyrov tramples Chechen values and traditions. There is a degree of subservience to Kadyrov that didn't exist even under Stalin. People are abandoning principles that they held on to even during the deportation. But this betrayal of the Chechen traditions is necessary for survival; ordinary Chechens understand that they are at the edge of extinction and if they continue to resist they will not survive.

I don't think that Kadyrov is anything more than a Russian-appointed puppet; he is totally dependent on Russia. The maximum that Kadyrov can do is to ask for some special favors for himself or members of his government, nothing that is granted to him is institutionalized in any way. Kadyrov is the recipient of favors bestowed by Putin, which can be withdrawn at any time; this cannot be considered independence in any normal sense of the word. Rather the opposite, Kadyrov is totally dependent on support from the Kremlin, military, financial, and personal. Kadyrov is gaining acceptance with a part of the population that has seen nothing but violence and destruction. However, this can not last.

Today Chechens are exhausted and to survive they have to accept Kadyrov's reign, hang his portrait everywhere, and pretend that the conflict is over. They accept the formula that causes them the least amount of physical harm, but under a different set of circumstances the spring will uncoil with greater force. When my generation went to war, we had only the nineteenth century to look back on to find models for ourselves. We lived by the myths and legends of the nineteenth century. The generation growing up today has everything in recent memory: suffering and hope. There is an example in living memory of Russian troops leaving (not even bothering to pack their things—just going) and of a national resistance struggle capable of making them leave, and it will not be long before another generation of Chechens utilizes that example.

The underlying problems have not been resolved and have to reemerge in the future. Doku Umarov is the leader of the armed resistance; the locomotive of the conflict. Zakayev heads a government-in-exile that can maintain the continuity of the nationalist and secular government but cannot influence events at home. Umarov may think that he created a platform for himself, but he did it at the expense of political space. The options for the population are the emirate, which offers them nothing but war, and the Ichekerian national idea, which is now located in London. Everyone needs political space, you can't have war forever and against all—even the emirate will find that it needs the political space; the men with weapons in hand also want to see a political success. The fighters want something more tangible than the feeling of Islamic solidarity, and they will need the experience of those who are in the West. I think that these two wings, sooner or later, maybe under a different set of leaders, will see that they need each other and are likely to reunite in a new form, which will permit them to become more responsible and transparent.

This is the question for the emirate: what happens after the war really stops? They don't even talk about it. What happens after the Russians leave? For the combatants there is only jihad but the society is only interested in what happens after the war. Kadyrov provides a modicum of stability, security, and prosperity. This will only satisfy people for a short period. After basic needs are met, the Chechens will seek to control their own affairs again; they will seek justice, and as many times in their history, they will seek independence. The dream of an independent Chechen state has merely been deferred.

NOTES

1   The War Begins

1. This event is described in Zelimkhan Yandarbiyev, *Chechnya Bitva za Svobodu*, (L'vov: Svoboda Narodov, 1996), pp. 285–286. He described this as an attempted coup d'etat but I don't think it was perceived that way by the participants. They tried to force Dudayev to accept their terms, but they were not willing to attempt any use of force against him. As far as I know, Dudayev simply talked them out of it.

2   Joining Maskhadov's General Staff

1. *Gazavat* is the holy war against tsarist Russia, which in this usage indicates sacrifice or martyrdom.
2. *Zamestitel po politicheskoi chasti*, refers to the political commissar, who was appointed in the Soviet military to ensure compliance with Soviet ideology.

3   Budennovsk: Basayev Forces Peace

1. Dr. Wilhelm Hoynck, "New Challenges on The OSCE Conflict Resolution Agenda," OSCE ODIHR Bulletin, Vol.3 No.2: Winter 1994/1995.
2. Aleksandr Khinshtein, "Yeltsin, Kremlin, the Medical History," *Moskovskii Komsomolets*, August 15, 2006, http://www.mk.ru/178959.html
3. Tomas Goltz made a documentary film, *Return to Samashki*, and published articles and a book about the village. See Tomas Goltz, "Samashki: Belief and Betrayal in Chechen Town at War," *Democratizatsiya* (6:2, Winter 1998) and *Chechnya Diary, A War Correspondent's Story of Surviving the War in Chechnya* (New York: St. Martin's Press, 2003).

4. Sonia Mikich, *Planet Moskau: Geschicheten aus dem neuen Russland* (Koln: Verlag Kiepenheuer und Witsch, 1998) quoted in Tomas Goltz, p. 142.

5. Andrei Blinushov et. al. *With All Available Means: Operation of the MVD of the Russian Federation in the village Samashki, April 5–7, 1995, Memorial Human Rights Center* (Moscow: Memorial Human Rights Society, 1995). Available at http://www. memo.ru/hr/hotpoints/CHECHEN/SAMASHKI/Sam-ru. htm. See also, Andrei Blinushov, "Tragedy of the Village Samashki, Chechnya, April 1995, the Diary of a Human Rights Activist," in *Ichkeria*, a special issue of the journal *Karta*, a publication of the Ryazan branch of the Memorial Human Rights Society.

6. "More Talks Reported," Moscow Russian Television Network in Russian 0008 GMT June 18, 1995 (FBIS-SOV-95-117, June 19, 1995, p. 45) and "Third Talks with Basayev Reported," Moscow Russian Television Network in Russian 1143 G M T 18 Jun 95 (FBIS-SOV-95-117, June 19, 1995) p. 50.

7. Viktor Kurochkin, *Missiya v Chechne* (Moskva: Pomatur, 1997) p. 97.

8. Diane Curran, Fiona Hill, Elena Kostritsyna, *The Search for Peace in Chechnya: A Sourcebook, 1994–1996* (Cambridge, MA: Strengthening Democratic Institutions Project, Harvard University, 1997) pp. 152–173. The July 23 Agreement is in the possession of the author.

4   Maskhadov Is Elected President

1. The way Dudayev was killed remains mysterious and there are many contradictory explanations. The dominant version is that he was killed by a rocket that identified and targeted him from a signal on his satellite phone. A variation on this theory holds that a surveillance aircraft A-50 identified the signal from the satellite phone and sent two fighter jets to strike Dudayev. Both of these versions, because of the nature of the technology involved in the targeting, have been interpreted to suggest that the United States provided technological assistance. Other theories claim that the Russians developed this capability independently in the shortest time. The third, and by far less broadly held version is that Dudayev died due to

an explosion on the ground, and that his car had been mined. This version was being investigated by Basayev who thought that the size of the crater was by far too large for a jet fired rocket. Basayev considered the possibility that someone from Dudayev's close circle could have placed explosives in his car. The Russian official version contained no specific information to clarify this issue.

2. General Lebed's report to the Russian State Duma is quoted in Carlotta Gall and Thomas deWaal, *Chechnya: Calamity in the Caucasus* (New York: New York University Press, 1998) p. 360. Original in *Komsomolskaya pravda*, 16 October, 1996.
3. See testimony of Tim Guldimann in "The Future of Chechnya," Commission on Security and Cooperation in Europe Hearing, March 13, 1997. Transcript available http://www.csce.gov/
4. Op. cit, Helsinki Commission testimony of Tim Guldimann.
5. RFE/RL Newsline, February 3, 1997, http://www.rferl.org/content/article/1141340.html

5   Maskhadov's Impossible Quandary

1. The first act of gross violence against foreigners was the killing of six ICRC nurses in December 1996. Many analysts, including the Chechen procuracy, were inclined to view it as a political crime meant to deter international observers from monitoring the January 1997 elections. The Chechen procuracy accused Adam Deniyev, who had taken refuge in Moscow, and sought his extradition to Chechnya for this crime. The Russian media blamed Khattab. From everything that I have observed about Khattab, he was only interested in jihad; he never got involved in things like this.
2. Berezovsky has confirmed giving the money to Shamil in an interview with IWPR. Tom DeWaal, "Berezvosky Blames Putin for Chechen War," IWPR Caucasus Reporting Service, October 31, 2002. Ivan Rybkin, the secretary of the Security Council at the time has maintained that Berezovsky always behaved in accordance with Russian government policy. See Ivan Rybkin interview on Radio Station Ekho Moskvy August 20, 1997, http://www.echo.msk.ru/programs/beseda/12458/
3. For details concerning the work of the commission, see Ivan Rybkin, *Consent in Chechnya, Consent in Russia* (London: Litton Trading and Investment LTD, 1998) p. 81.

6   The Hostage Trade

1. Alexander Cherkassov, "Hostage Taking in the North Caucasus in the late 1990s: Historical roots," July 3, 1999; website of Human Rigths Center, memo.ru.

2. There are very few credible sources about the hostage trade. In addition to the author's recollections two additional sources were used to cross-reference material in this chapter. One is the articles and interviews with Vyacheslav Izmailov, a *Novaya gazeta* correspondent. The second source is "Confidential Memorandum on Criminality in the North Caucasus, Its Impact on Humanitarian Operations, and Possible Responses in Case of Crisis," which was written in 2000 by the staff of international NGOs operating in Chechnya and contains a detailed chronology of incidents and primary data from the field. Boris Berezovsky said that he participated in the release of hostages in an interview with a Russian newspaper. Aleksandr Prokhanov, "With Berezovksy in London...(a conversation between Prokhanov and Berezovsky)" *Zavtra*, October 1, 2002 (http://www.zavtra.ru/cgi/veil/data/zavtra/02/463/21.html)

3. This can be seen in the very tragic case of a French photographer, Brice Fleutiaux, who was held in captivity for six months, wrote a book about his ordeal, and soon after its publication committed suicide—never having revealed the identity of his abductors. Fleutiaux was abducted at the start of the war while entering Chechnya from Georgia. After his release, Fleutiaux told journalists that his kidnapper had posed as his liberator.

   "The civilian asked me, 'But who kidnapped you?'" recalls Fleutiaux. "I said, 'The big guy.' And he looked at me and said, 'No, it's not possible.' I looked back at him, then said, 'No...I mean...no...I don't remember.' So afterwards, all the time when people asked me, 'Who kidnapped you?' I'd say, 'I don't want to speak about it, I don't remember, it's not my problem, I just want to get released.' "They were saying they had released me from the guy who kidnapped me, but the guy who kidnapped me was there. So I just played the game."

   Anthony Lloyd, "Sleeping with the enemy," *The Times* (London), September 23, 2000 (via Nexis) and Brice Fleutiaux, *Otage en Tchechenie* (Paris: Robert Lafont, 2001).

4. According to the NGO staff report: "There is no indication
   that Khattab and Basayev were ever involved in the kidnapping of foreigners." Op.cit. "Confidential Memorandum..."
5. Tom DeWaal, "Berezvosky Blames Putin for Chechen War,"
   IWPR Caucasus Reporting Service, October 31, 2002.

7   Crisis within Chechen Society

1. A *zykr* is a Sufi ritual of mourning practised by the followers
   of Kunta Khadji of the Kadarski Tariqat.
2. Doku Umarov's decree was published on http:// www.
   chechenpress.info/events/2007/04/30/01.shtml
3. See chapter 5 concerning the departure of Basayev from the
   cabinet in 1997.

8   Incursions into Dagestan: War Resumes

1. Timur Muzayev, "Political Monitoring of the Chechen
   Republic Ichkeria, July 1999," International Institute of
   Humanities and Political Research, http://www.igpi.ru/mo
   nitoring/1047645476/1999/0799/20.html
2. I said the following to a Chechen newspaper, "Regarding the
   events in Dagestan. From the very beginning of the conflict,
   the Chechen Republic Government clearly proclaimed its adherence to the peace treaty with Russia signed on May 12,
   1997. We are strictly complying with this treaty's article on
   noninterference in each other's affairs. On the other hand, we
   dismiss all attempts on the part of Russia's political circles to
   accuse Ichkeria of exporting Islamic fundamentalism to the
   neighboring republic as groundless. They cite the fact that a
   certain number of Chechens, including some of considerable
   prominence, are participating in this conflict. We cannot deprive them of the right to do what they want with their life.
   Each man has a right to his grenade. We are no more responsible for volunteers in Dagestan than Russia is for its own
   who participated in the extermination of first the Bosnians
   and then the Albanians. And, let me point out, in Russia, the
   program of recruiting volunteers for Yugoslavia was widely ad-
   vertised, at the highest official level. Behind such accusations
   are Russia's attempts to pass its problems and responsibility
   for the imperfections of its state system onto our republic."
   "Ilyas Akhmadov: Diplomacy Is an Area Requiring Precision

Work on the Basis of International Law" *Groznenskiy Rabochiy*
August 19, 1999 (FBIS-SOV-1999-0830).

3. There are a number of sources that record such statements. Sophie
Chihab, "Chechnya: An Interview with Aslan Maskhadov,"
Paris Le Monde (Internet version), September 18, 1999 (FBIS-
SOV-1999-0918), "Chechnya Denies Involvement in Moscow
Bombings," Moscow Interfax 1314 GMT September 14, 1999
(FBIS-SOV-1999-0914), "Chechen President warns Moscow
against further raids," Moscow Interfax 0804 GMT September
14, 1999 (FBIS-SOV-1999-0914), "Chechen President Flatly
Denies Dagestan Involvement," Interfax 1703 GMT August
21, 1999 (FBIS-SOV-1999-0821).

4. Aleksandr Voloshin, who was the head of Yeltsin's Presidential
administration met with two senior members of the staff of
the National Endowment for Democracy on October 31, 2006
and in the course of his remarks described how Maskhadov
had called him on the phone during that period and asked to
speak with Yeltsin. Voloshin had refused this request, telling
Maskhadov that to speak to Yeltsin he must first publicly condemn Shamil Basayev.

5. Primakov and Maskhadov met on October 29, 1998 in
Vladikavkaz where Ingushetia's President Ruslan Aushev
and North Ossetia's President Aleksandr Dzasokhov served
as intermediaries. Dzasokhov, whom Primakov characterizes
as an old and loyal friend, was the host. Maskhadov arrived
with Aushev and Akhyad Idigov, the head of the parliamentary international relations committee. The main discussion
between Maskhadov and Primakov took place behind closed
doors. Here is how Primakov describes it in his memoir:

> This is what I learned from that conversation:
>
> Maskhadov and Basayev don't just represent different
> interest within Chechnya such as different *teips*, groups of
> field commanders—they also represent different ideolo-
> gies. In response to my direct question Maskhadov said,
> "I think that independent Chechnya should exist in its
> present boundaries, but Basayev thinks differently. He
> would like to try the Chechen experiment in other bor-
> dering territories, first of all in Dagestan, where he can
> seek access to two seas, the Black Sea and the Caspian."
>
> Shamil's program made him Russia's irreconcilable foe
> whereas Maskhadov showed a willingness to discuss many
> problems connected with 'Chechnya's independence in

the context of a single economic space with Russia, single currency' and so forth.

> Certain Russian circles have close contacts with Maskhadov's opposition. Maskhadov was counting on us to support him with arms, money, and to help restore, not so much Grozny, as four or five main industrial plants—mainly of the petrochemical field. He wanted the reconstruction of these plants to be accomplished by Russian regions bordering Chechnya. We decided (I had [Sergei] Stepashin, MVD Minister and [Ramazan] Abdulatipov, minister for nationalities policies with me) on cooperation between the law-enforcement agencies to combat hostage taking and criminality, the restoration of several enterprises in Chechnya, paying compensation to victims of the deportations of 1944 who live in Chechnya, and the payment of pensions for Chechen retirees from the federal pension plan.

The main result of the meeting was that in return for Moscow's fulfillment of agreements reached at Vladikavkaz and earlier meetings, Maskhadov promised to "begin a public struggle and finish off the terrorists." Yevgenii Primakov, *Vosem Mesyatsev Plus* (Moscow: Vargius, 2001) pp. 101–103.

6. Quoted in *"Vladimir Putin priemnik Yeltsina, syn Chubaisa, khozyain Rossii"* (Vladimir Putin Yeltsin's Heir, Chubais's son, and Russia's ruler,) Vlasti.net, August 10, 2009, http://www.vlasti.net/news/5626.1

7. Izvestia, July 22, 1998 cited in Vakhid Akayev, "Varieties of Wahhabism in the North Caucasus," *Sotsialno-gumanitarnoye i politicheskoye obozreniye,* January 1, 2004, http://www.humanities.edu.ru/db/msg/8219

8. This argument is made in Aleksandr Litvinenko and Yuri Felshtinsky, "FSB Blows Up Russia," *Novaya gazeta Spetzvypusk* (special edition) August 27, 2001 and the longer English version, *Blowing Up Russia: Terror from Within* (NY: SPI Books, 2002).

9. The most authoritative account of the incident, based on independent Russian publications, raises many grave doubts about the veracity of the official version. David Satter, *Darkness at Dawn: The Rise of the Russian Criminal State,* (New Haven and London: Yale University Press, 2003) pp. 24–33.

10. Putin's exact language was: "We will pursue terrorists everywhere. If they are in the airport, then the airport. This means,

I beg your pardon, that if we catch them in the shithouse, we'll waste them in the shithouse. That's it. This question is closed, definitively." September 24, 1999, NTV.

11. The conspiracy theories that came out in the Russian press are discussed in Peter Reddaway and Dmitri Glinski, *The Tragedy of Russia's Reforms: Market Bolshevism against Democracy*, (Washington DC: U.S. Institute of Peace, 2001) pp. 612–614.

12. The photo appeared in several publications including Andrei Batumskii, "Sgovor," *Versiya*, 3 August 1999, which was posted in http://www.compromat.ru/main/voloshin/Basaev.htm

13. Speakers at the rally included Maskhadov, Shamil Basayev, and Gelayev; these men and others called for reconciliation and unity. See Timur Muzayev, "Political Monitoring of the Chechen Republic Ichkeria, July 1999," International Institute of Humanities and Political Research, http://www.igpi.ru/monitoring/1047645476/1999/0799/20.html

9   The Chechen Resistance Splinters

1. The surgeon Khassan Baiev recalls that even on the operating table, in dire need of an amputation, Shamil asked him to take other patients ahead of him. Khassan Baiev with Ruth and Nicholas Daniloff, *The Oath, A Surgeon Under Fire* (New York: Walker Company, 2003), pp. 295–297.

2. I do not give any credence to General Shamanov's famous claim that they had been tricked into going through that field and had purchased a corridor for $100,000. Not only did we simply not have this kind of money, but if for the sake of argument we did, we'd have chosen a simpler route. Certainly no one that I've talked to among the men that left with Shamil gave that version any credence. I also don't find persuasive the rumors that the Russians provided a corridor for Barayev. It's true that he took a different route from the rest, Barayev found an opening through the Chernorechinskii forest, and his men made it out safely. He had fewer men, no wounded, and no prisoners. No one could have taken 2,000 men through that path. It's convenient to argue that he had cover among the Russians and there are many rumors that he worked for the FSB, but I don't know how much truth there is to that. Killing or catching Barayev would have been a fabulous trophy and it's hard to imagine the Russian military deliberately giving up that opportunity.

What I can see clearly is that Barayev was a bandit, and he had a highly experienced, small, and very mobile unit and lots of audacity. It's entirely possible that a combination of agility and luck and independence worked in his favor.

3. Maskhadov's former aide-de-camp Husein Iskhanov confirmed in a telephone conversation with me in April 2009 that Maskhadov had also told him that he expected a meeting with a high-level Russian official on February 2, 2000.

4. "In a Climate of Fear: Political Processes and Parliamentary Elections in Chechnya," a joint publication of the International Helsinki Federation for Human Rights (IHF), International Federation for Human Rights (FIDH), Norwegian Helsinki Committee, Center "Demos," Human Rights Center "Memorial." November 2005, http://www.fidh.org/IMG/pdf/chechnya112005a.pdf. The publication refers to a later period, 2003–04, but my recollection is that this situation arose earlier in the process.

10   My Tenure as Foreign Minister

1. Fred Starr later published an op-ed in which he said that I had conceded a status for Chechnya within the Russian Federation. This was not the case, I had merely been willing to postpone the discussion of Chechnya's status for the purposes of this meeting. The article drew speculation among my own colleagues, such as Idigov, that I was making secret arrangements to give up our claims to independence, which simply was not the case. I was following the format of the meeting and trying to get the practical advantages of participating in a Track II process, and postponing the question of our recognition for a later stage in that process. S. Frederick Starr, "A Solution for Chechnya," *Washington Post*, September 17, 2004.

2. The text of "The Russian-Chechen Tragedy: The Way to Peace and Democracy, Conditional Independence under an International Administration," was published in *Central Asian Survey*, Vol. 22, No. 4, December 2003, pp. 481–509 (29).

3. Press conference with American journalists. Full transcript in Russian is on the Russian Presidential website: http://www.kremlin.ru/appears/2001/06/18/0002_type63376type63380_28569.shtml

4. Maskhadov repeated his position in what became his last appeal to European community prior to his death. See letter

of Aslan Maskhadov to Xavier Solana, February 25, 2005,
http://|feedbackgroup.narod.ru/proetcon/obraschenie.html

5. "European Parliament Recommendation to the Council on
   EU-Russia Relations," February 24, 2004, http://servizi.radi-
   calparty.org/documents/index.php?func=detail&par=3319

6. Thomas de Waal, "Judd: Chechen Dialogue Must Go On,"
   IWPR (CRS No.171, 20-Mar-03), http://www.iwpr.net/
   report-news/judd-chechen-dialogue-must-go

7. A similar view is argued most eloquently in "In a Climate
   of Fear, 'Political Process' and Parliamentary Elections
   in Chechnya," The International Helsinki Federation for
   Human Rights (IHF), Norwegian Helsinki Committee,
   International Federation for Human Rights (FIDH), Center
   "Demos" and Human Rights Center "Memorial," November
   2005, http://www.ihf-hr.org/documents/doc_summary.
   php?sec_id=58&d_id=4161

11   The Killing of Maskhadov

1. Photos of Shamil Basayev during the raid are posted at,
   "FSB Regards Video of Basayev in Ingushetia as Evidence of
   Militant's Raid into Ingushetia," http://www.newsru.com/
   russia/27jul2004/ulika.html

2. The reports of the independent commission under Stanislav
   Kesayev and the work of the Mothers of Beslan, Voice of
   Beslan, as well as other relevant sources are discussed at length
   *The 2002 Dubrovka and 2004 Beslan Hostage Crises: A Critique of
   Russian Counter-Terrorism* by John B. Dunlop, (Soviet and Post
   Soviet Politics and Society: Stuttgard, 2006); there is also an
   update to that monograph, John B. Dunlop, "The September
   2004 Beslan Terrorist Incident: New Findings," Center
   for Democracy Development and Rule of Law, Working
   Papers No. 115, Stanford University, July 2009, http://cddrl.
   stanford.edu/publications/the_september_2004_beslan_
   terrorist_incident_new_findings

3. Op. cit, "The September 2004 Beslan Terrorist Incident: New
   Findings," p. 13 and "Aushev describes the details of his negotiations with the terrorists who seized the school in Beslan,"
   newsru.com, September 29, 2004, http://www.rol.ru/news/
   misc/news/04/09/29_001.htm

4. The website Ingushetia.org maintains an archive of testimo-
   nials about the Osset-Ingush conflict of 1992. This is from

a testimony of an Ingush man, Bashir Magomedovich, who describes being held hostage by Ossets in the gymnasium of Beslan's school #1 from November 1–5, 1992. "Beslan: School No. 1. Gymnasium. Witness testimonies," http://www.ingushetia.org/history/1992/89.html

5. Shamil says this in his interview with Andrei Babitsky, that was aired on July 28, 2005 on ABC's *Nightline*. The aired interview was a small excerpt from an hour-long taped conversation. The transcript of the full conversation, under the headline "Basayev: Today All the Chechens Are at War," was posted at http://www.kavkazcenter.info/russ/content/2005/08/17/36759.shtml

6. Sergei Kovalev had said, "The only thing I can say is that the government, which made the decisions, had a different set of priorities, than we may have expected. Their main priority was not to save the lives of the hostages." "Settling Scores: The Storming of Nord Ost Became an Occasion to Remind the Kremlin of Old Sins," Lenta.ru October 28,2002, available at http://lenta.ru/articles/2002/10/28/teract/

7. Aslan Maskhadov, "My Appeal is Addressed to the President of Russia," *Kommersant*, February 7, 2005, available at http://www.kommersant.ru/doc.aspx?DocsID=545159; Tom Miles, "Chechen Rebel Leader orders Cease-Fire," Reuters, February 3, 2005, available at http://groups.yahoo.com/group/chechnya-sl/message/42772, "Statement of Umar Khanbiev," Kavkaz Tsentr, February 3, 2005, http://groups.yahoo.com/group/chechnya-sl/message/42783, and "Aslan Maskhadov's Last Appeal to Europe," February 25, 2005, http://feedback group.narod.ru/proetcon/obraschenie.html

8. Ruslan Isayev, "Fighters are Observing Temporary Cease-Fire," Prague Watchdog, February 7, 2005, http://www.watchdog.cz/?show=000000-000005-000004-000088&lang=2 "An Open Appeal to the Russian President from Leading Russian Human Rights Activists," February 9, 2005, http://groups.yahoo.com/group/chechnya-sl/message/42950.

9. Jeremy Page, "Putin gets Upper Hand as Chechen Leader is Trapped and Killed," *The Times*, March 9, 2005, http://www.timesonline.co.uk/tol/news/world/article422616.ece

10. See the following: Alina Ivanova, "An Inmate of Chernokogozovo Castle," *Southern Reporter*, March 10, 2006, http://reporter-ufo.ru/1143-uznik-zamka-chernokozovo.html, and Anna Politkovskaya, "The Case of March 8,"

Novaya Gazeta, December 5, 2005, http://www.novayagazeta.
ru/data/2005/91/07.html, and Ilia Barabanov, "The Cook
who Killed Maskhadov got a Jail Term," *Gazeta*, December 1,
2005, http://www.gazeta.ru/2005/12/01/oa_180039.shtml

11. See for instance: "Maskhadov's Body on Display for All to
See," March 9, 2005, http://www.utro.ru/articles/2005/03/09/
415374.shtml, or Natalia Vinogradskaya, "Yesterday's Hero:
Experts Give Contradictory Assessments of the Implications
of Maskhadov's Death," *WPS*, March 15, 2005, http://www.
wps.ru/ru/pp/tv-review/2005/03/15.html.

12. "Basayev Described How the Russians Found Maskhadov,"
Kavkaz Tsentr, March 15, 2005, http://www.kavkazcenter.
com/russ/content/2005/03/18/32308.shtml

13. Op.cit. "Basayev: Today All the Chechens Are at War."

14. For the video of Doku Umarov proclaiming the Emirate
see http://video.google.com/videoplay?docid=-394920843
4693962870&hl=en For the English see http://caucasus.
wordpress.com/2007/12/02/the-statement-by-amir-dokka-
umarov-about-the-declaration-of-the-caucasus-emirate-
07102007/, and in Russian, http://www.kavkazcenter.com/
russ/content/2007/11/21/54480.shtml

15. "Appeal of the President of CHRI A. Kh. Saidullayev to the
People of Chechnya," *Kavkaz Tsentr*, August 19, 2005, http://
www.kavkazcenter.com/russ/content/2005/08/19/36843.
shtml

12   The North Caucasus Emirate and Beyond

1. "On the Process of Deciding Questions Related to the
Separation of a Union Republic from the USSR" Supreme
Soviet USSR, April 3, 1990 No.1409-I (BBCC 90–15)
*Vedomosti S'ezda Narodnykh Deputatov SSSR i Verkhovnovo
Soveta SSSR*, M., 1990, No.15 pp. 303–308.

2. For a detailed discussion of US foreign policy positions
and their evolution over the two wars see, "Chechnya," by
Catherine Osgood, in David P. Forsythe Ed. *Encyclopedia
of Human Rights* (Oxford: Oxford University Press, 2009),
pp. 290–299.

3. "Vladimir Putin: Russia Will Not Leave the Caucasus," ANN
News, December 4, 2008, http://www.annews.ru/news/
detail.php?ID=174029. Putin explained the Russian invasion of Georgia as follows: "The fact of the matter is that for

centuries Russia has been playing a positive, stabilizing role in the Caucasus, as a whole. It was a guarantor of security, cooperation and progress in this region and nobody should doubt it." "Putin: South Ossetia Move Blow to its Statehood," *Civil Georgia*, August 9, 2008, http://www.civil.ge/eng/article.php?id=19000&search=

4. An empirical study that tracked violence in the North Caucasus found 1,100 violent incidents resulting in 900 fatalities in 2009 in the North Caucasus. The figures for 2008 were 795 incidents and 586 fatalities. Sarah E. Mendelson, "Violence in the North Caucasus, 2009, a Bloody Year," Center for Strategic and International Studies, January 14, 2010, http://csis.org/files/publication/100114_Violence_NorthCaucasus_2009optmize.pdf

5. For the video of Doku Umarov proclaiming the emirate see: http://video.google.com/videoplay?docid=-3949208434693962870&hl=en For the English see: http://caucasus.wordpress.com/2007/12/02/the-statement-by-amir-dokka-umarov-about-the-declaration-of-the-caucasus-emirate-07102007/ and in Russian: http://www.kavkazcenter.com/russ/content/2007/11/21/54480.shtml

6. Official News Agency of the Emirate of the Caucasus, "Decree of the Emir of the Caucasus," December 12, 2007, http://generalvekalat.org/content/view/9/30/

7. Poslanie Dokki Umarova Movladi Udugovu, Chechenews, March 24, 2008, http://www.youtube.com/watch?v=hpboeNdGYsg&feature

8. "The Response of Amir Umarov to the Opponents of the Declared Emirate of the North Caucasus, Parts One and Two," http://www.kavkazcenter.com//russ/content/2007/12/30/55392.shtml

INDEX